CALEDONIAN
and Beyond

The story of
Caledonian Omnibus Company
and its successor, Western SMT,
in the Dumfries and Galloway Region

Garry Ward

An Autobus Review Publication

ISBN 0 907834 30 2

To Mum and Dad for all their support and encouragement.

In memory of Jim Calder who epitomised so much that is good in the industry

The brass nameplate carried over the enquiry office at Whitesands, Dumfries was an early casualty of the Western takeover. Thankfully, it was rescued from the scrap heap by Willie McGrath and has now been donated to Michael Hayton of Dumfries who has had it fully restored for his planned commercial vehicle museum.   (Garry Ward)

Cover paintings by J.McLellan

Designed & Typeset by Autobus Studios

Autobus Review Publications Ltd.,
42 Coniston Avenue, Queensbury,
Bradford BD13 2JD

CONTENTS

FOREWORD

I have had a lifetime fascination in buses, in particular those of Western S.M.T. (to give them their "traditional" name) and their predecessors, as well the larger companies they acquired. That's how I came to start the writing of this book.

However, that is only part of the story. Neil MacDonald wrote the book on Western S.M.T. which is likely to remain the standard work on that company for years to come; this book represents my contribution to the story of one of the Companies "Western" acquired, the Caledonian Omnibus Company Ltd. of Dumfries. At the same time, it is designed to bring the story up to date, covering more than forty years of "Western" operation in the Dumfries and Galloway region.

Two people in particular encouraged me to write this book; Jim Calder and Hugh McCreadie. Jim Calder joined Harpers of Peebles in 1925 and moved to Caledonian on the former's acquisition. He spent a lifetime in the bus industry, ultimately becoming District Traffic Superintendent for the Dumfries and Galloway region of Western S.M.T. He had always been keen to see the history of Caledonian in print and was able to help me with much of the early work. It is to my deep regret that he did not live to see the "finished product"; I hope he would have approved of it. Hugh has been a long time enthusiast of Caledonian and "Western" in the region and he has helped in much of the detective work to track down others who have been able to help with information, as well as provide help from his own records.

I started the work with some fundamental problems. Caledonian ceased to exist before I was even born and I have had to rely on the many valuable pieces of information gathered from books and people who worked for or remembered them. Though various ledgers relating to Caledonian survived, the text has had to be written without the help of Minute Books which have not turned up, despite a comprehensive search. Ironically, the pace of change since 1983 and especially since de-regulation of bus services in 1986, has been even more difficult to accurately document than the early history. Photographs (especially those which have not been used before in publications) have been extremely hard to find. Where possible, I have used views which have not appeared before, but inevitably a large percentage of the small number in existence have and I hope readers will forgive this unavoidable repeat of photographs seen before.

Despite these handicaps, I have been able to unearth a considerable amount of missing information. Comprehensive data has been obtained on the large amount of rebuilding which took place during the war. Some gaps in information on the fleet like bodywork, withdrawal dates and sales have been uncovered, whilst information on the variety of properties used has been articulated. The build up in the service network, details of the disputes with S.M.T., their pre-war review of potential for expansion and some insight into Caledonian's post-war plans for development are given.

More recent developments under "Western", especially the

massive number of service changes and plans for the area (some successful, some unsuccessful) are recorded.

Errors in a work of this nature are inevitable, especially given the passage of time and the lack of much "official" information; every effort has been made to check the facts and keep these errors to a minimum, but much depends on people's memories. Where discrepancies are found I would ask readers to advise me of any corrections, in the hope that I can include these in some later edition, or at least through the medium of the "Western Enthusiasts Club" newsheets. Readers anxious to keep up to date with developments with "Western" are recommended to join this club; those with broader tastes are commended to the main national societies, The Omnibus Society and The PSV Circle.

Despite the trials and tribulations involved in producing this work, much pleasure has been derived as well; if readers gain as much enjoyment from reading this book as I have had in compiling it I will be delighted.

PREFACE

The establishment and existence of the Caledonian Omnibus Company was far from "plain sailing" over its 22 year life. Established in 1927, the company was a relative latecomer to the field of road passenger carrying and had to carve out a profitable operation amongst established operators, some of them, like South of Scotland Motor Company, being quite large.

The resignation of two of the directors within a year of start up, who had originated with the operators purchased to get Caledonian "off the ground", hardly got the new company off to a good start. Though the option of buying out competitors was followed, as was the process of agreeing joint operation on a couple of routes, skirmishes with SMT and its associated company Midland Bus Service undoubtedly cost them financially in the early days.

Development was always going to be limited within the "wedge" which is South - West Scotland. The physical limitations of the Solway Firth to the south and the tentacles of routes of the associated companies of the large S.M.T. combine to the north and east, together with the largely rural nature of the area was always going to make growth and profitability difficult to attain and maintain.

The phenomenal growth experienced during the war set new challenges, both on the traffic and vehicle side and post-war developments were not all smooth. That the company handled the sometimes rapid changes and managed to trade profitably and successfully is a tribute to all involved in it.

Their successor Western S.M.T. has had to battle with much reduced patronage and has had to "cut its cloth" accordingly over the last forty years or so. Smaller more cost effective outfits have sprung up to challenge for what traffic there is, but all has not been doom and gloom. Development of express services linking with the ferry traffic and considerable private hire has helped somewhat. The company has proved recently that they have maintained the tradition of coping with rapid change, with the demise of Dicksons of Dumfries and the need to cover their operations at the twelfth hour.

A poignant recent reminder of the changes which have taken place in the bus industry has been the virtual withdrawal of "Western" from Carlisle during 1992, some sixty five years after their predecessor Caledonian first entered the city.

ACKNOWLEDGEMENTS

Many people have helped to turn an idea into the reality of the book which you are reading now. I have listed below many of the individuals who have helped me over the years with information and photographs on Caledonian and Western S.M.T. in Dumfries and Galloway region, but I regret that some names will have been missed. I apologise in advance to any in the latter category; so many have given their time voluntarily that it is impossible to record everyone. Whether they are named or not, I hope they will all know that I am deeply indebted to them for their all their help.

Grateful thanks are given to the following; The PSV Circle for permission to quote from their comprehensive records, Alan Wilson Managing Director of Western Scottish Omnibuses Ltd. and his management team, especially Mrs Dorothy Bradley Financial Director, who have been a great help in "opening doors" to much information which might otherwise have been lost for ever and tolerating patiently many hundreds of questions for more data, as well as employees of the company, past and present, Ray Scott of Wigtown, Willie Love of Renfrew, Mrs E.Huxtable of Port William, Mrs M.Bark of Stranraer, Bill McGowan of Dumfries, the late Jim Calder and the late Mrs Calder of Dumfries and their son Jim Calder (Junior), Chris Taylor of Cardiff, James Solley of Castle Douglas, the late Sid Young of Annan, Angus Currie of Gretna, W.Shankland of Castle Douglas, Douglas Harper of Peebles who provided much of the Harper's family history, Keith A. Jenkinson of Queensbury, Bradford, Roy Marshall of Burnley, Arnold Richardson of Kendal, John C.Gillham of London, Ian MacLean of Bishopton, G.E.Bell of Lockerbie, Jim Little of Lockerbie, Walter Sturgeon of Dumfries (a particular thanks to Walter for carrying out considerable detective work for me as well as providing much information himself), Mrs Lauder of Dumfries, A.Bryden of Lochmaben, Campbell Jackson of Annan, T.Geddes of Carlisle, Stan Parker of Carlisle, Miss Margaret Ward of Carlisle, A Bell of Carlisle, Jack Scott of Carlisle, Tom Dalton of Carlisle, Mr Whalley of Carlisle, Robert Ross of Carlisle, Mrs M.Clanachan of Kirkton, J.M.Clark of Dumfries, M.Hayton of Dumfries, Hugh McCreadie of Dumfries, Mr Carson of Auldgirth, Miss T.Paul of Dumfries, Doctor J.G.Roberts of Dumfries, J.Templeton of Carlisle, D.L.G.Hunter of Linlithgow, Steve Warburton of Darlington, Peter Betts of Carlisle, David Mitchell of Barrhead, Tom MacFarlane of Ayr, Alan Cross of Solihull, Ritchie Smith (my boss) who was both very tolerant of the time I devoted to this Project and also provided me with technical guidance, Dr. John Sinclair of Milngavie, the many local newspapers in the district (too numerous to mention) who printed my appeals for help, Gordon Bain of Greenock, Douglas Blades Manager of A1 Bus Service for access to their comprehensive collection of Notices and Proceedings, Robert Grieves for seeking out photographs from his collection and giving permission for their reproduction, as well as kindly checking this draft, George Waugh for originals from his postcard collection and permission to reproduce them, D.Lambie of Biggar Museum Trust, Denise Livett for translating the text onto 'PC', Eddie Shirras of Winchester, Jim Paterson of Castle Douglas and finally John McLellan of London who produced the paintings for the covers of the book.

IN THE BEGINNING

The Caledonian Omnibus Company Ltd. was in existence for the relatively short period of 22 years. Yet it left its distinctive mark on what is now the Dumfries and Galloway region of south west Scotland which it served and evidence of the company's existence remains to this day, over forty years after its disappearance.

The story of road passenger transport in the area into which Caledonian established itself goes back to the mid to late 19th century with the coming of the railways. Tourism increased in the largely agricultural area and hotels established their own transport to connect with the railheads and provide both transport to and from their establishments and local tours for their patrons. Further developments, prompted no doubt by the need to keep their vehicles busy in the winter months, involved regular services being established between surrounding towns. Many of these focused on Dumfries, with others connecting smaller towns. The hotels switched to motorised transport as this became more available and more reliable, many offering repair and maintenance services as well. Into this scene came Caledonian and, as will be seen, a number of early acquisitions involved operators based at these hotel garages.

As a relative latecomer, Caledonian had little choice but to buy out existing established operators to give itself an operational base. The company was registered on 9th April 1927 by the British Automobile Traction Co Ltd. with an authorised capital of £60,000, of which 38,840 £1 shares were issued. The British Automobile Traction had been formed as the bus operating arm of the large British Electric Traction Group, who had been operators of many of the company owned tramways throughout Britain. BET did control some bus operations directly, sometimes setting up a holding company to operate both tramways and buses, as was the case with Scottish General Transport, one of Caledonian's neighbours to the north.

Caledonian took over five diversely spread companies who operated across the three counties of Wigtown, Kirkcudbrightshire and Dumfries in south west Scotland. At the western extremity, the business of H.Brook and Co. Ltd of Stranraer was acquired. The background to Harry Brook's involvement in road passenger transport is complex but worth recounting here. He hailed from West Hartlepool and became involved in road passenger transport when he acquired the business of Border Buses with a base in the Selkirk area. A Yarrow man, Mr. Adam Scott had founded Border Buses before the first world war and services were developed to Peebles, Innerleithen, and Galashiels. On Scott's death, the business was acquired by Harry Brook who was by then based in Galashiels, where he had been involved in the catering business. Shortly afterwards, he took on a partner called Jimmy Amos who came from a Borders farming family. Thus, Brook and Amos of Galashiels was formed. Harry Brooks moved on to Stranraer in 1924 taking with him some of the men who had worked in his Galashiels based operation, the business of Brook and Amos being acquired in April 1926 by the large S.M.T. empire. Brook's partner, James Amos moved to S.M.T. and ultimately became chairman of the Scottish Bus Group. Harry Brooks established his first service in the area in June 1924 when he started a service of red and white liveried vehicles from Stranraer to Portpatrick via Lochans running five times per day, with an extra early run on Sundays and Fridays and an extra late run on Thursdays and Saturdays which waited until the "Kinema" turned out. Vehicles operated under the fleetname of "Pilot". The service was timed to take ten minutes to Lochans and forty more minutes to Portpatrick and the first vehicle operated is believed to have been a 20 seat Thornycroft. His base was the garage at the rear of the Kings Arms Hotel in Charlotte Street, the hotel having been his accommodation since moving to Stranraer. The mechanic for the hotel cars was an A.P.McGhie and Harry Brook asked him to manage the Stranraer operation. A.P.McGhie's daughter recalls counting the days takings and preparing the tickets for the conductors for the next day in their front room in King Street before they moved to more purpose built premises!

Mr A.J.McDonald also kept a bus in the garage of the Kings Arms, running a service from Stranraer northwards to the village of Kirkcolm and this service was acquired. In 1925, the operation had been further expanded with the start of a long service from Stranraer via the coast road to Isle of Whithorn via Glenluce, Port William, Glasserton and Whithorn. Despite the name, Isle of Whithorn was not an island by this time, being simply a small coastal village at the tip of Wigtownshire; buses ran down to the harbour, reversing outside McWilliams Store. The terminus in Whithorn was the Grapes Hotel and garaging space was made available at the rear of this property. A connection was made here with Brook's other service from Whithorn to Newton Stewart via Wigtown, which ran in competition with the railway service between these two points and is believed to have been operated by Berliets and an AEC "chara".

Further expansion came with the takeover of a McCulloch of Glenluce with a service from that village to Stranraer and Brook completed the triangle by extending the service eastwards to Newton Stewart. Operations also extended over the water to Northern Ireland with services being initiated in the Armagh area. Vehicles were regularly shipped (at high tide long before the days of the current car ferries), between Stranraer and Larne. The Irish operation also operated under the fleetname of "Pilot". On acquisition, Harry Brook was appointed a director of the newly

An early H.Brook & Co. Ltd. vehicle photographed at the rear of the The Kings Arms Hotel in Charlotte Street, Stranraer. Driver Willie McDowall pictured on the steps drove the first bus between Stranraer and the Isle of Whithorn. A number of Brook's vehicles carried the trading name 'The Pilot", as can be seen on the rear of the bus parked behind.

formed Caledonian, although he only served in this capacity for a very short period of time, resigning after the first year of operation. For the record, his Irish operations were sold to the Belfast Ominibus Company Ltd. around the same time as Caledonian acquired the Stranraer based operation.

The second of the five operators acquired was Brooks Motor Company of Kirkcudbright. This company operated from the appropriately named Harbour Garage in Kirkcudbright, the property being adjacent to the harbour. The garage, which was owned by Brooks, passed to Caledonian with the business, but the land on which it was built was owned by Kirkcudbright Town Council, requiring Caledonian to negotiate a new lease. The company quickly set about rebuilding the garage, adding waiting rooms and an enquiry office. Brook's brown and white liveried vehicles operated routes eastwards to Dalbeattie via Dundrennan, Auchencairn and Palnackie and also by the direct route to Castle Douglas and Dumfries.

The substantial business of J. & J. Scott of Dumfries was the third acquisition. This company were based at the Kings Arms Garage in Dumfries, adjoining the hotel of the same name. The firm was fairly large for its day operating buses, haulage vehicles, taxis and car hire, as well as maintaining garage premises and dairy shops and having interests in farming. Services were established from Dumfries north eastwards to Lockerbie, operating every two hours, south westwards to New Abbey, Southwick and Douglas Hall. (Scott had a contract for carriage of mail on this route and are remembered for the operation of a 20 seater Albion regularly on this service) and northwards on the 26 mile route to the coal mining village of Sanquhar. Connections were made with the Ayr and District Motor Services vehicles, who operated from Ayr and Cumnock southwards to Sanquhar. Vehicles were painted in quite an elaborate livery for the period of blue lower half, grey top half and

white roof, with a gold or red waistband. Though their vehicles were acquired, the garage remained in Scott's ownership.

The remaining two operators purchased to establish Caledonian were Annandale Motor Company of Lockerbie and G.P.Bell of Ashgrove, Ecclefechan. Annandale Motor Company was the trading name of a Mr. Botterill who operated from the Kings Arms Garage in Lockerbie. One service was provided northwards from Lockerbie to Moffat with a more minor service operated between Lockerbie and the village of Boreland to the north east. Gideon Bell operated a daily service between Lockerbie and Carlisle and the acquisition gave Caledonian their first important link "over the border". Bell had kept one vehicle at Lockerbie and the other in Carlisle (he only lived at Ecclefechan, no buses being kept there) and the importance of this route is reflected in the fact that Caledonian allocated their new ADCs (referred to later) to this service on their delivery.

Some of the original agreements drawn up to acquire these operators have survived. In an agreement dated 12th July 1927 between Walter Edward Bennet and the British Automobile Traction, the following businesses were transferred;

From an agreement dated 3 March 1927 between W.E.Bennet and J.J. and D.Scott eleven buses, four charabancs, spares and services for the sum of £9,000.

From an agreement dated 15th March 1927 between Bennet and J.H.Brook and Company Ltd. six buses, eight charabancs, a garage and petrol pump and use of Kings Arms Garage and services for the sum of £7,500 of which £5640 was paid in the form of shares in the newly formed Caledonian Company.

From an agreement dated 15th March 1927 between Bennet and Harry Brook and John Hodge and Walter Bryson for five Dennis buses and one Morris saloon car and two Dennis charabancs plus let of ground at Kirkcudbright for £8,610.

Other agreements related to the purchase of part of Annandale Motor Company and non competition agreements with Annandale, J. & J. Scott, Brooks Motor Company and H.Brook and Company.

The most interesting agreement was the purchase by Bennet of two Albions at £1200 then their transfer to Caledonian in time for the incorporation on 31st March 1927. Readers will note from the fleet history appendix that the numbers quoted in the agreements do not tally with those recorded; unfortunately, despite research, the discrepancies remain. Similarly, the identity of the two Albions remains a mystery despite research of the Albion records held by the Biggar Museum Trust. It is possible, however, that these might have been PJ26s with Penman of Dumfries bodywork as three such chassis were delivered to Penmans at this time.

By June 1927 the various timetables had been sorted out and Caledonian got under way. The County town of Dumfries was selected for the company's head office. Land was purchased at Eastfield Road about a mile east of the town centre where a garage and office premises were built during 1927, the office premises being designed by Crosville Motor Services. Whilst the garage was being built, space was rented from J. & J. Scott until June 1928. The registered office was established at 1, 2, 4 and 7 Loreburn Chambers in King Street, Dumfries and a enquiry office was leased at 17 High Street. Premises were also rented at 25 Whitesands, opposite the "country" bus departure points.

The company also quickly set about establishing additional premises in their first year to cover the territory acquired with the above operators. In the extreme west of this operating area, a garage with offices and house was acquired in Trade Street, Stranraer with the business of Thomas Young, the premises having originally been a coal yard. Young operated one return journey from St. Andrews Street in Stranraer on the seventeen mile service to Scotland's most southerly village of Drummore. An agreement was made that Thomas Young would occupy the house attached to the Trade Street premises apart from two rooms. The two rooms were converted into offices and the premises were in use by October 1927. A store and garage were located at the back of the house and Thomas Young became a stance inspector. As an aside, Young was not the first operator of buses to Drummore; the Portpatrick and Wigtownshire Joint Railways tried their hand at operating two steam road cars as early as May 1907, the service lasting until November 1908 when the vehicles unreliability and lack of profitability caused the service's demise. Despite the acquisition of Trade Street the garage at the rear of the Kings Arms Hotel was retained and all services originating from Stranraer operated from there. Later, services were moved to a departure point at Port Rodie which was slightly less central but convenient for any ferry traffic. Thomas Young later moved, allowing Caledonian to take over the whole house, establishing a new counter, switchboard, ticket room, stationary store, lost property area, kitchen, coal house, lavatory, typists room and managers office. A.P.McGhie transferred to Caledonian on the acquisition of Brooks and became the manager of the Wigtownshire and Galloway district as far as Gatehouse. A well liked man, he even inspired a local Stranraer poet to write a poem on his retirement!

The service acquired with Thomas Young's business was to be a useful bargaining tool for Caledonian in negotiation with an established operator in the Stranraer area R Murray & Sons. Murray was planning to introduce a service from Stranraer to Kirkcolm in competition with "Caley's" newly acquired service which extended infrequently to Ardwell Shop. An agreement was reached resulting in Caledonian withdrawing from the Stranraer to Drummore service leaving the road clear to Murray, who also operated on this route with Murray in turn cancelling the introduction of a service to Kirkcolm. Caledonian's successor Western S.M.T. finally reached Drummore again with the acquisition of the Murray business some forty years later in 1966! As well as the services acquired, a route was also opened northwards between Stranraer, Ballantrae and Colmonell which formed the basis of later extensions, first to Girvan and then to Glasgow.

To the south east garage premises were established at 22 Glasserton Street Whithorn, on the south side of this small town, to serve the Machars area around Whithorn, Isle of Whithorn, Wigtown and Newton Stewart, extending west towards Stranraer. A corrugated iron and wooden structure was erected, set back off the road and surrounded by "But and Ben" cottages. The garage was capable of holding five vehicles, three at the back and had sliding doors, a petrol pump on the left hand side and a small office on the right.

To the north east of Dumfries, land was purchased at Mains Meadow, Netherplace in the town of Lockerbie in preperation for the building of a garage, this being established to service the Lockerbie to Dumfries, Carlisle, Moffat and Boreland routes. Gideon Bell, whose service to Carlisle had been acquired as part of "Caley's" start up, was put in charge as Depot Superintendent. As at Dumfries, garage space was rented from the operator they acquired, Annandale Motor Company; by October 1927, four buses were being garaged there until the new garage was ready for occupation in June 1928. Services departed from the Annadale's Kings Arms garage until the opening of the new premises while Bells operated from the main street. At the Carlisle end, arrangements were made for a bus to be garaged at the premises of the Lonsdale Garage Company in Lonsdale Street in the centre of the city from May 1927. In October 1928 they moved to the County Garage on the north side of Carlisle near the River Eden, where a "lock up" was rented. This could barely hold one bus, the vehicle actually being pushed in the last few inches with the engine shut off in case the starter handle touched the wall! The "lock-up" continued to be used until the larger garage premises of Farrer and Faulder were inherited in 1931. Other arrangements were made for the garaging of buses throughout Caledonian's operating territory, particularly at outposts of a route, where it was impractical or uneconomic for them to establish their own garage. Motor Engineers premises were the natural choice, especially where arrangements could be made for the fuelling of buses (cleaning and sweeping out was the responsibility of the driver in those early days). Thus, as soon as their services were initiated, arrangements were made with Penmans, a well known Dumfries coachbuilder, to garage a bus at their Castle Douglas premises, as well as at outposts at Sanquhar, where arrangements were made with Peter Turnbull and Sons, motor engineers and bus operators themselves, and Murchie and Picken of Newton Stewart, again motor engineers, who had a further claim to fame of producing at least one car as well Moffat,

One of the first new vehicle deliveries to Caledonian were three ADCs with bodies by Strachan and Brown of Acton, London. First of the batch was number 43 (SW 2543), photographed at the Coachbuilders prior to delivery.

Four normal control Dennis vehicles, also with Strachan and Brown bodies, were delivered in 1927 and numbered 39-42 (SW 2546-9).

which the infrequent Lockerbie - Moffat and Dumfries - Moffat services terminated. Later, vehicles were garaged with McKeand of the same town. In Dalbeattie, buses were garaged with Thomas Johnstone and Sons, another motor engineer and small bus proprietor. These arrangements became long established, the Sanquhar and Dalbeattie garage space being rented until Caledonian's demise. The Newton Stewart premises were similarly long established. The company spread even further south with the acquisition of the Business of T.G.Wood of Cumwhinton (a village south east of Carlisle) in April 1928, one of two small businesses acquired by Caledonian in the Carlisle area in their first year of operation. Wood operated three services from Carlisle to Cumwhinton village, from Carlisle to Cotehill and from Carlisle to High Hesket village on the A6 near Penrith. Wood's former garage premises (a corrugated metal shed which, incidentally, still exists today) were also put to use, the services and premises being the most southerly point which Caledonian reached. This extension was to prove very short-lived however, with Wood's services and premises being sold to a local independent, Armstrong and Siddle of Penrith for £425 on the 18th December 1928.

The other operator acquired is believed to have been Bert Everard who operated from the city centre over the River Eden to Stanwix Bank, the route covering the same roads within Carlisle as the much longer Caledonian route to Lockerbie. Accounts for the first full year of operation to 31st March 1928 presented in July at the Station Hotel in Dumfries reported that the revenue had been adversely affected by exceptionally bad weather! Traffic receipts of £35,160 were reported, private hires being £974 and parcel traffic already recording £814, emphasising the importance of this source of revenue. A figure of £1625 was written off as losses on sales of "obsolete rolling stock". A revenue balance of £543 was reported of which £367 was proposed for setting aside for "preliminary and formation expenses", with the remaining £176 to be transferred to reserves.

The directors had originally been C.D.Stanley (Chairman), Thomas Wolsey, Walter Bryson, J.Hodge and Harry Brook. However, J.Hodge, formerly of Brooks Motor, and Harry Brook, from H.Brook & Co resigned. Both were to be responsible for local management and development of the company. The loss of two directors familiar with the local terrritory must have been a blow to the fledgling company; to partially fill the gap J.H.Martin was brought in as General Manager, coming from the associated BAT owned Gravesend Tramway Company.

One interesting early example of the bigger company bowing to local preference was the "Caley" giving up the Dumfries - New Abbey - Southwick - Douglas Hall service inherited from J. & J. Scott of Dumfries. Passengers showed loyalty to their local operator J.Carruthers of New Abbey who competed on the same route. Indeed, its only very recently that the wheel has turned full circle again with Caledonian's successors, "Western" operating some of the journeys over the New Abbey road. Four other services which were abandoned early on, amongst which was the Lockerbie - Moffat service acquired with the Annandale business which ceased and was taken over by Hunter and Gardner of the Crown Garage, Lockerbie. The infrequent Dumfries - Moffat service was given up in favour of the major operator to this day, Gibson of Moffat, the abandonment of these two routes resulting in the closure of the Moffat out-station. Similarly, the Lockerbie - Boreland service was abandoned, operation being by Rae of Boreland for many years. Finally, the Dumfries - Kirkton via Locharbriggs service was abandoned being covered by the existing Sanquahar service. This consolidation no doubt removed some of the less promising routes and allowed Caledonian to concentrate on services with greater potential. One early move was the linking of the two arms of the operation by extending services westwards from Kirkcudbright over the unserved section through Gatehouse of Fleet to Newton Stewart, the services then being extended to Stranraer over the existing route between these two points.

Caledonian's 1928 deliveries comprised of Leyland Lions only. These sturdy vehicles continued to be the standard choice in 1929 and later (in LT2 and LT5 form) until 1932. Two Lions are seen at Annan terminus, including number 61 (SM 6967), delivered in 1928. (Robert Grieves Collection)

Turning to the Caledonian fleet, the company started with a mixed bag of vehicles from companies acquired. From H.Brook and Company came Fords, Berliets, AECs, Daimler and a Fiat all new in the early to mid 'twenties. Brook's Motor Company donated eight normal control Dennis vehicles, the majority being bought new in 1926. J.& J.Scott of Dumfries supplied nine Leylands, seven Albions and a Morris ranging in age from 1921 to 1927. Annandale Motor Company deposited two Vulcans dating from the mid 'twenties and G.P.Bell supplied a Gotfriedson and a Thornycroft, again dating from the mid 'twenties. The normal control Dennis machines of Brooks' Motor Company and the younger Albions, Leylands and the solitary Morris of J.& J.Scott of Dumfries were to remain in "Caley's' fleet well into the 'thirties, but the other acquisitions were quickly disposed of. In order to replace some of the diverse fleet the company acquired three ADCs (numbered 43-5, SW2543-5), four Dennis' (SW2546-9 costing £2435 excluding delivery) all being bodied by Strachan and Brown of London, two Leyland Lion PLSCs (numbered 46/7, SW2551/0) with Leyland bodies and two Albions. The Dennis' were later re-seated from 28 to 32 seats whilst the ADCs were allegedly up-seated from 32 to an incredible (for those days) 40 seats. The Albions remain a mystery as indicated earlier; official correspondence confirms their existence though not, unfortunately, their identity. To supplement the fleet an ADC was hired from the makers at the rate of £20 per month between 12th April 1927 and 2nd October 1927.

It is known that two buses from the operators acquired by Caledonian were traded in to Leyland in part exchange for the Lions, although unfortunately records have not survived of which machines they were. The hardy Leyland Lion continued to be specified for the twelve 1928 deliveries at a price complete with body of £1275 (numbers 48-50/3-61, SM6741-3 and SM6918-20/48/63-7) and were to be the standard choice (in LT2 form from 1930) for new vehicles until 1932. A number were converted in later years to parcel vans and some lasted as PSVs until the takeover by Western S.M.T. in 1949. Further second hand vehicles were inherited with the business of T.G.Wood of Cumwhinton in 1928, a Bean and a Morris being acquired.

A livery of red and cream was selected for the vehicles, the red apparently being similar in shade to that used by United Automobile Services in pre NBC days. Vehicles were painted with a cream roof and window surrounds and red below the waist, separated by a deeper red band between the two colours. The large "Caledonian" fleetname, applied in shaded gold and underlined and a simple fleet numbering process was chosen, vehicles being numbered from one upwards, no numbers being used more than once. The Bell-Punch ticket system was selected. New "punches" were hired and a batch were also purchased secondhand. Two secondhand Thornycrofts registered CC1743 and CC3164 were purchased for £75, having originated as a charabancs with the Llandudno Coach and Carriage Company. It is thought these vehicles might have later been used to inaugurate the haulage operations in 1934.

In May 1928 the parent British Automobile Traction Co. Ltd. became Tilling and British Automobile Traction Co. Ltd. Tilling was another organisation with interests in a large number of bus companies and had held stakes in various British Automobile Traction Companies. This reconstitution resulted in a more sensible formalization of the relationship between Tilling and BET and the influences of the two organisations were to be witnessed through the lifetime of Caledonian.

EXPANSION, CO-OPERATION .. AND CONFLICT

In their second year of operation revenue was again reported to be adversely affected, this time by competition from another operator on the Dumfries to Lockerbie route, J.Robertson from the latter town. Robertson began operation on the route in competition with J. & J. Scott, who had initiated the service. Originally, a charabanc had been operated for hires and he then bought a "saloon" and operated this in a white livery on the route. When Scott was acquired by Caledonian, the competition continued with this new adversary for the available passengers and the two operators engaged in a battle to reduce their fares to "rock bottom", the lowest fare reaching Caledonian's 6d return for the twenty eight mile round trip! Caledonian finally won the battle when Robertson's vehicles started to break down, money no doubt not being available with this level of competition to maintain them properly. One of Robertson's vehicles, a 20 seat Guy with bodywork by Massey Bros. of Wigan was acquired in June 1928. By February 1929, Caledonian had extended their Stranraer to Colmonell service northwards to Girvan and around this same time a new one-person-operated route was also inaugurated from Wigtown to Portwilliam. For this, a couple of small 20-seat vehicles, a Guy and an Albion, were garaged in Loves builders yard in Wigtown.

The directors reported a profit of £446-17-11 and were able to advise that the garage and repair facilities at Eastfield Road, Dumfries and the garage at Netherplace, Lockerbie had been completed and were in use. A further 3000 £1 shares were issued at face value. However, whilst road competition on the Lockerbie Road was removed, the heavy cutting of rail fares in the area

Robertson of Lockerbie operated this Albion, amongst other vehicles, on the Lockerbie - Dumfries service in fierce competition with Caledonian, before finally succumbing to "Caley" in June 1928. (Robert Grieves Collection)

caused some concern. Railways in the area at the time of Caledonian's start up comprised the line from Carlisle which branched off the main Glasgow line to Dumfries. From there, passenger services radiated westwards through Castle Douglas, Gatehouse and Newton Stewart to Stranraer, with a branch to Kirkcudbright. North-eastwards from Dumfries, one line extended to Lockerbie, gaining the main Glasgow line there and another line headed north up the Nith Valley to Sanquhar, Cumnock and Kilmarnock, whilst a light railway branched off to serve Moniaive (of which more later). In the west, a line branched from Newton Stewart to serve Wigtown and Whithorn, with a branch to Garlieston, the latter having been a very early casualty in losing its passenger service. From Stranraer, one line headed south to Portpatrick whilst another line turned north for Girvan and Ayr. In June 1929 the Stranraer to Girvan route was further extended to Glasgow, a distance of 86 miles, when a joint service was inaugurated with the BET controlled Scottish General Transport Company, by then based in Kilmarnock, who operated under the fleet name of Scottish Transport. The agreement for operating this service provides an insight into the complexities of joint running arrangements. The dividing line of the companies areas was the coastal resort of Girvan, Scottish Transport being responsible for all mileage and the revenue north of the town with "Caley" (as the company quickly became locally known) being responsible for all mileage and revenue south of that town. Any mileage imbalance was chargeable at 8d (3.5p) per bus mile , but could be "run off" i.e. the company with the shortfall in miles could make this up in mileage rather than remunerating the other. Through tickets were available, each company's conductors carrying a batch of the other's tickets and waybills. Two waybills required to be filled in over the route to record the sale of each companies' tickets. "Caley" cashed in the Scottish Transport's takings at the British Linen Bank at Stranraer , whilst Scottish Transport was to cash "Caley" takings at the Commercial Bank of Scotland branch in Paisley, suggesting that Scottish Transport's Paisley garage was responsible for operation of the Glasgow-Stranraer service. The Bank slips were then forwarded to each company. Through tickets were advised and cash adjustments made monthly. No local passengers could be carried between Turnberry and Girvan, although it appears that this was irrelevant, as the route did not operate between these two points, the agreement originally drawn up perhaps referring to a previously proposed route. The joint route south of Ayr was via Crosshill and Dailly to Girvan (for one return journey), the remainder operating direct from Maybole to Girvan. In October 1929 all journies were routed via Crosshill and Dailly. South of Girvan the main service operated direct through Lendalfoot, whilst a connecting bus served Pinmore and Colmonell villages before connecting with the through service back on the main road at Ballantrae. Advance booking of tickets was possible at locations where extra buses could be provided if required, namely Stranraer (Caledonian), Ayr, Kilmarnock and Glasgow (all Scottish General Transport). Midland Bus service also operated five through journeys between Glasgow and Stranraer with "extras" to Girvan in competition with Scottish Transport and Caledonian. This service had actually been inaugurated two months before the joint service although this operated at different times and followed a different route over certain sections south of Ayr, travelling via Maidens and Turnberry to Girvan, then direct on the A77 over Kennedy's Pass through Lendalfoot to Ballantrae. The original proposed route of Caledonian and Scottish Transport may have been changed as a result of Midland establishing their service over the same route. Relationships with Scottish Transport were obviously quite cordial from the start, as Caledonian arranged for the repair and overhaul of a couple of vehicles in their first year of operation (Leyland SM4681 and TC5273), as well as regularly purchasing "stores" until Scottish Transport's formation into Western S.M.T. in 1932.

The road traffic act of 1930 resulted in Caledonian having to apply in common with all operators to the newly formed Traffic Commissioners to operate the routes they were running. The days of uncontrolled running over competitors routes ceased, although competition still existed over routes which had more than one licensed operator. As a result, takeovers were increasingly used by Caledonian as a means of obtaining a monopoly on routes, as will be seen as the company's history unfolds.

During 1930, the High Street premises in Dumfries were vacated in favour of the Whitesands premises which by that time consisted of a house, hall and offices which were converted for use

CALEDONIAN & SCOTTISH TRANSPORT
Omnibus Company Ltd
GLASGOW—PORTPATRICK SERVICE
Time Table—1st October, 1929, until further notice.
DAILY, INCLUDING SUNDAYS.

GLASGOW TO PORTPATRICK.

		a.m.	a.m.	p.m.	p.m.	p.m.
GLASGOW	dep	—				
KILMARNOCK	dep	—	9.0	12.30	4.0	6.30
AYR			9.55	1.25	4.55	7.25
MAYBOLE		7.30	10.30	2.0	5.30	8.0
CROSSHILL		8.0	11.0	2.30	6.0	8.30
DAILLY		8.8	11.8	2.38	6.8	8.38
GIRVAN		8.22	11.22	2.52	6.22	8.52
COLMONELL		8.45	11.45	3.15	6.22	8.38
BALLANTRAE		9.15	12.15	3.15	6.45	8.52
STRANRAER		9.30	12.30	3.45	6.45	9.15
PORTPATRICK	arr	10.15	1.15	4.0	7.15	9.45
		10.50	1.45	4.45	8.15	10.0
			2.45	5.30	8.45 S.O.	10.45

PORTPATRICK TO GLASGOW.

		a.m.	a.m.	p.m.	p.m.	p.m.
PORTPATRICK	dep					
STRANRAER	dep		11.0	1.15		6.0
BALLANTRAE		7.45	11.30	1.45		6.0
COLMONELL		8.30	12.15	2.30	5.15	6.30
GIRVAN		8.45	12.30	2.45	5.15	7.15
DAILLY		9.15	1.0	3.15	5.30	7.30
CROSSHILL		9.38	1.23	3.38	5.0	8.0
MAYBOLE		9.52	1.37	3.52	5.23	8.23
AYR		10.0	1.45	4.0	5.37	8.37
KILMARNOCK		11.5	2.15	4.30	5.45	8.45
GLASGOW	arr	12.0	2.50	5.5	6.15	9.15
			3.45	6.0	6.50	9.50
					7.45	10.45

Italics denote departure times of connection.   S.O. Saturdays only.

FARES

Fares to intermediate places at proportionate rates.
Children's Fares approximately half above rates.
Anywhere Tickets not available on this Service.
Return Tickets are available on either Company's 'Buses. Connections all over AYRSHIRE, RENFREWSHIRE, WIGTOWNSHIRE, KIRKCUDBRIGHTSHIRE, and DUMFRIESSHIRE.

A timetable was produced in June 1929 for the Stranraer - Girvan - Glasgow route, introduced jointly with Scottish General Transport. The Glasgow terminal point was George Square but had moved by 1931 to North Frederick Street.

Although the timetable implied a through service, in practice vehicles had a layover at Stranraer before continuing to Portpatrick. 'Anywhere' tickets were an early form of unlimited travel ticket, valid in specified areas.

as an enquiry and parcels office and staff canteen. Initially rented, the buildings were purchased in 1932. The attractive location had one particular disadvantage in that the River Nith, which flowed behind the stances could, on occasion, flood the bus stance area. Jim Calder never remembers the flood waters reaching the Whitesands office but there were occasions when the buses had to be moved up the "Sands" due to flooding of the bus parking area. In the west, Port Rodie enquiry office and staff room was established in Stranraer in March 1930 around the corner from the main departure points.

The accounts up to March 1930 showed a healthier upturn in profit to £1,530, allowing a dividend of 3% to be recommended by the Directors. However, comment was made that the revenue was being depleted by competition from an associated S.M.T. company from April 1929 over 57 miles of their operating territory. This referred to competition from John Sword's Midland Bus Service over the Girvan - Stranraer section of Caledonian's Glasgow route and over the whole of the Sanquhar to Dumfries route. Competition over these routes was to influence events later in Caledonian's life, of which more later. A further development was the purchase of James Clark of Lockerbie in June 1930 for £761. He ran a service between Lockerbie and Annan using two vehicles, a 26 seat Thornycroft and a 20 seat Bean in maroon and cream livery, both of which were taken into stock with the purchase. Arrangements were made with the L.M.S. railway to rent standing space at the forecourt of

to Newton Stewart via Twynholm, Gatehouse of Fleet and Creetown four times a day. Although this service was acquired, together with two Albions for £1200 (the family business being keen users of this chassis), they retained their other service from Castle Douglas to Carsphairn via Dalry and New Galloway. Known as the "Mail Run" as mail was carried on the service, the service operated over the same route which Midland Bus Service covered on their longer Ayr to Castle Douglas service. A considerable amount of traffic was generated on this route from the building of dams for Hydro Electric generation, of which there were a number being built in the 'thirties at Clatteringshaws, Loch Ken and New Galloway. Local passengers on this rural route had an interesting method of hailing their bus; for those whose properties were just off the main road, yellow flags were handed out by Solleys. On seeing a flag displayed the driver would stop his vehicle, give a hoot on the horn and await the appearance of the intending passenger; many a potential soaking from waiting for buses in exposed spots must have been avoided by this novel idea. Unfortunately for Solleys, just as Caledonian had competed heavily with them on the Newton Stewart route, so did Sword's Midland Bus Service, which put on a bus in front of and behind theirs and lowered their fares as well. Solleys carried provisions from the local Co-operative shop free; passengers were known to send their provisions via Solleys and travel themselves on the Midland bus, much to the annoyance of the former!. As well as this route, Solleys also continued to conduct hire and day tour work

The business of James Clark of Lockerbie was acquired in in June 1930, together with this Thornycroft, a Bean and a service between Lockerbie and Annan, on which this bus is seen. The use of paper stickers to give points en-route and destinations was commonplace.   (Robert Grieves Collection)

Dalbeattie Station in July 1930. Services to Dalbeattie terminated here and services through Dalbeattie passed the Station. Again, this was to become a long established feature, Western continuing to use this point long after the station had closed. Also, a short term arrangement was entered into with the L.M.S. at Wigtown station for the garaging of two buses from August 1930. The vehicles (Leylands) were used on a contract to carry workers to Cairnsmore between Creetown and Newton Stewart where construction of a new water supply to Wigtown was being undertaken. Another form of collaboration with the LMS Railway was the introduction of combined road/rail tickets between Newton Stewart and Whithorn. A further joint service was inaugurated with the large S.M.T. organisation in 1931 between Dumfries and Edinburgh (Chambers Street) via Moffat, Broughton and Penicuick. When the service was inaugurated, Caledonian operated the one departure in each direction on Mondays, Wednesdays and Fridays, with S.M.T. operating on Tuesdays, Thursdays and Sundays. On Saturdays two departures were operated in each direction with both companies providing a return journey allowing the buses to return to their home base. Leyland Lions 53 and 54 (SM6918/9) were initially used on the route.

Accounts up to March 1931 reflected a much improved profit of £7499, allowing an increase in dividend to 5%. In May of that year, the main service of S.Solley and Sons of Castle Douglas was acquired. "Solleys Yellow Buses" as they were called, operated from a garage at the rear of the Imperial Hotel King Street, which they also owned. Their main service operated from Castle Douglas

in the area as well as being an early operator of a tour to Blackpool. After acquisition of the Newton Stewart service and vehicles, Caledonian began to garage vehicles in Solleys garage and continued to do so until March 1943 when the requirement to garage vehicles in the town ceased. When Solleys gave up the remainder of their operations in the mid 'thirties, Midland started to garage their vehicles on the Ayr - Castle Douglas route at Solleys premises.

The following services were operated in October 1931 : Dumfries - Lockerbie (operated daily); Lockerbie - Annan via Ecclefechan, Eaglesfield, Kirtlebridge Station and Brydekirk (operated daily); Lockerbie - Annan via Bankshill, Failford, Waterbeck, Eaglesfield, Brecon Beds and Creca Crossroads (operated Thursday - Saturday); Dumfries - Sanquhar via Kirkton and Thornhill (operated daily); Lockerbie - Carlisle (with all journies being advertised as travelling via the famous Blacksmith's Shop at Gretna Green). The main service diverted to Eaglesfield from Kirtlebridge Station then returned to Kirtlebridge but a few journies went direct from Eaglesfield to Wyseby Lodge (operated daily); Dumfries - Stranraer via Castle Douglas, Twynholm, Gatehouse of Fleet, Newton Stewart and Kirkcowan (six through journies operated on weekdays taking 3 hours and 35 minutes. The service followed the main A75, except when diverting to serve the villages of Tywnholm and Kirkcowan - operated daily); Dumfries - Stranraer operated by the same route except it diverted between Dumfries and Castle Douglas to serve Dalbeattie, adding 30 minutes to the journey time (operated daily); Dumfries - Kirkcudbright via

Dalbeattie, Haugh of Urr and CastleDouglas (in practice, this appears to have operated as part of the Dumfries - Stranraer service for the first four journeys out of seven from Dumfries and five out of the eight journeys from Kirkcudbright. For the remainder, a change of bus was required at Castle Douglas. The first departure from Dumfries operated via Hardhills instead of Haugh of Urr with a teatime journey making the same diversion in the opposite direction. Similarly, beyond Castle Douglas these journeys operated via Gelston village for school children. On Saturdays and school holidays these journeys took the most direct route by the A75 and A711 to Bridge of Dee and Tongland, most other journeys running further along the A75 to Ringford before turning onto the A762 for Kirkcudbright); Dumfries - Kippford via Dalbeattie (operated daily); Dalbeattie - Kirkcudbright via Auchencairn and Dundrennan, with connections to and from Dumfries; Kirkcudbright - Stranraer via Twynholm, Gatehouse of Fleet, Newton Stewart and Kirkcowan (this appears to have operated as Kirkcudbright - Twynholm connecting into the main Dumfries - Stranraer service at Twynholm. Kirkcudbright was connected direct with Stranraer from 1934); Newton Stewart - Isle of Whithorn; Newton Stewart - Portwilliam; Stranraer - Portpatrick via Lochans; Stranraer - Ardwell Shop via Kirkcolm; Stranraer - Glenluce; Stranraer - Isle of Whithorn; Stranraer - Glasgow via Ballantrae, Girvan, Ayr and Kilmarnock (five through journeys were operated daily, the first departure to Stranraer being from Ayr, with a Saturday only short-working between Stranraer and Ballantrae).

Further expansion arose from a complex reorganisation in the Carlisle area in October when services to the north of Carlisle operated by Richard Percival Limited of 97 Lowther Street, Carlisle were inherited. The Percival undertaking was quite substantial with two operating bases in Carlisle and Dumfries, the latter operating under the name of South of Scotland Motor Company Limited. The Carlisle operation had been started in 1922 by Richard Percival, a

well known figure in the border city, who had a coal merchant and haulage contracting business. The Richard Percival operation had become part of the Balfour Beatty Group which also owned the Carlisle tramway undertaking. Percival operated his grey liveried vehicles on the following services; Carlisle - Annan - Dumfries by the direct route to Gretna through Todhills (started c.1925); Carlisle - Longtown - Gretna - Eastriggs - Annan (started c.1922); Carlisle - Longtown - Canonbie - Langholm; Carlisle - Warwick Bridge - Brampton and Carlisle - Crosby - Irthington - Brampton plus a city service to Blackhall. Carlisle Corporation applied to operate buses to replace the ageing tramway network and also applied for licences to run services to Langholm, Gretna and Dumfries. However, the newly formed Traffic Commissioners (Northern Area) rejected the application, one reason being that the Corporation was not an established operator and requested, instead, that the four Tilling and BAT companies of Ribble, United Automobile Services, Cumberland Motor Services and Caledonian Omnibus Company, Carlisle Corporation and the twelve (!) independent operators in the area submit a scheme for operation of co-ordinated services. The final agreement resulted in the tramways being replaced by the buses of Ribble Motor Services in November 1931, together with the acquisition of Richard Percival Ltd. (but NOT the Dumfries associated operation, of which more later) and seven of the independent operators, including the substantial business of Carlisle and District Motor Services Ltd. For the record, the other independents acquired were; White Star Motors Ltd., George Bristow, Frederick Waugh, Henry Hayton and Raymond Wicken.

The acquisition at last gave Caledonian a second route south into Carlisle. The rural services were split geographically amongst the major companies, those to the north operated by Percival being acquired by Caledonian but with the town service passing to Ribble Motor Services and the Brampton services to the north east passing to United Automobile Services, together with any services of the

independents acquired operating to the east. Percival's offices at 97 Lowther Street were also inherited. Ribble took the services to the south and Cumberland Motor Services took those to the west. Six Daimler CF6s from Carlisle and District were purchased by Caledonian for £3,500 as part of the agreement. This operator (originally called Carlisle, Dalston and District) had themselves acquired a number of local operators. Rumour had it that Ribble had been behind many of the acquisitions they had made. "Caley's" experience of Daimler chassis was limited, one being acquired with Harry Brook's Stranraer based business, although three ADCs were amongst their first new purchases. The complexity of the final settlement resulted in a Carlisle Joint Transaction record being maintained in the company accounts for a number of years.

Another take-over was accomplished in December when the business of Farrer and Faulder of Carlisle was acquired for £8400. They operated between Carlisle, Gretna, Annan and Dumfries via both the High Road through Carrutherstown and the more frequent Low Road via Cummertrees, this operating on the hour, Percivals having run on the half hour. Other routes operated were between Dumfries and Annan via Carrutherstown, Carlisle and Gretna via Longtown, Gretna and Longtown via Smithfield, Gretna and Evertown, Annan to Chapelknowe via Kirkpatrick Fleming, Annan to Creca via Hollee and Irlington and Carlisle and Rockliffe via Cargo. Farrer and Faulder also operated a Gretna - Longtown - Smithfield - Newtown - Brampton service operating along the A6071 and this also passed to Caledonian. Two journeys operated daily Monday to Saturday, with further shortworkings between Gretna and Longtown. The service was hardly likely to have ever been profitable, cutting west to east across hamlets which were served by services operating in the more popular southward direction to Carlisle. The Gretna - Longtown section was already well served and the section beyond must have relied heavily on locals wanting to travel to the

market town of Brampton. Caledonian persevered with the route for eight months before abandoning it in August 1932. Farrer & Faulder also operated a Carlisle - Newcastle service which had, for a time, been advertised as a through Dumfries - Carlisle - Newcastle route. The latter section of this, eastwards from Carlisle passed to United Automobile Services, however, along with three Maudslay buses. Timings of the Carlisle - Dumfries service were modified in conjunction with the South of Scotland Motor services (the last competitor over the total route) after the acquisition. Farrer and Faulder traded under the name of "Farraulder", running dark blue liveried machines operating from a garage in South Henry Street at the foot of Botchergate, backing onto Union Street. The Garage was used by Caledonian (who ceased renting the inadequate "Lock-up" from the County Garage), until they built their own Bus Station and Garage in Lonsdale Street in 1936. Access was extremely difficult until the Council demolished the slums in Union Street and built new Flats, renaming the street Rydal Street. This provided an opportunity for opening up the back of the premises and eased the access problems. Lack of space, however, continued to be a problem and buses had to be parked out in the Street. The price paid (£11070), reflected the size and importance of this acquisition. Farrer and Faulder donated a "mixed bag" of thirteen vehicles, including six Maudslays and Joseph Farrer was put in charge of the Carlisle office on acquisition of the business.

Another business acquired in that year was J.Bell of Penpont. Bell operated services between Thornhill Station and Moniaive Cross via Thornhill, Penpont and Tynron, a Penpont to Thornhill station short working, a Saturday only working between Thornhill Cross and Penpont via Burnhead and a Penpont to Dumfries service via Kier Mill and Barjarg, joining the main A76 south of Auldgirth before progressing directly to Dumfries. A 20-seat Morris was also acquired with this rural operation. Bell had acquired the services from Carsons of Penpont who operated a haulage, taxi, bus and coach hire business from a garage south of Penpont Cross. Carsons vehicles were named, a Star charabanc 26seater being the best remembered called "Vale of Scaur", all vehicles being fitted with an ornate 'stag's head' radiator cap. Caledonian rented space at the garage until they arranged the building of their own garage a few hundred yards further down the road. The service between

Another important acquisition was the business of Farrer and Faulder of Carlisle in December 1931. A Maudslay ML2 (HH 3345) and a Lancia to its left (probably 14 seater HH 2901) await their passengers at Whitesands, Dumfries. The purchase of Farrer and Faulder gave Caledonian a further share in the Dumfries to Carlisle traffic. (Garry Ward Collection)

A line up of Farrer and Faulder vehicles wait to leave on a private hire, headed by a Commer Invader (HH 5595), followed by two Maudslays (HH 5596 and 5180 respectively). All three vehicles identified passed to Caledonian for further use. The bill in the window of the Commer reads "Farraulder", the company's trading name, whilst the next two carry route boards for the important Carlisle - Dumfries route. (Robert Grieves Collection)

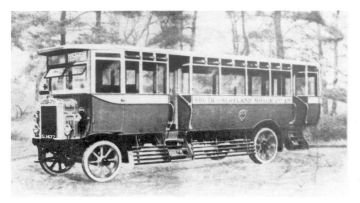

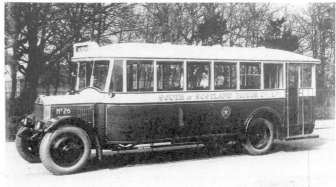

An early delivery for Percivals associated South of Scotland fleet at Dumfries was this dual-entrance Leyland - probably an SG-type. (Robert Grieves Collection)

A number of Albions were also operated by South of Scotland including number 26 which was probably their 1930 PKA26 model, registered SM8565, which carried NCME bodywork and passed to Caledonian in whose fleet it was numbered 113. (Robert Grieves Collection)

South of Scotland was a keen Leyland user like Caledonian, though this Lion PLSC1 did not survive long enough to pass into the fleet. The star within the fleetname garter was common on vehicles in the fleet.

Thornhill and Moniaive had much older origins, being operated together with a route from Stranraer to Drummore by the Glasgow and South Western Railway with Milnes Daimlers during 1906/7. Like the Drummond route, the service was abandoned as unprofitable.

The most important take-over of the year, however, came later in December when Percival's associated South of Scotland Motor Company Ltd. of Dumfries came into Caledonian ownership, the price paid being the very substantial sum of £32,400. Caledonian's efforts to further expand in and around Dumfries had been frustrated by the presence of this company who had introduced local bus

services in Dumfries in 1923 and developed a comprehensive network to cover all portions of the town, as well as running an equally extensive range of "Country" services. Twenty one vehicles, chiefly Leylands, came with South of Scotland Motor Company. The background to this company and its development is an interesting story. Prior to the introduction of buses in Dumfries, there had been talk of operating electric trams between Gasstown on the Annan road east of Dumfries across town to the west, terminating at Maxwelltown on the Dalbeattie road. A William Irving of Dumfries Motor Company brought a saloon from Carlisle and ran it around Dumfries for 2 weeks. It is not known if fares were charged or what

One of the last deliveries to South of Scotland was this Leyland bodied Tiger TS1 (SM 8910) which arrived in 1931. It survived long enough to pass into Western SMT ownership in 1949, albeit with a different (secondhand) body.

the locals reaction was. No further developments appear to have taken place from this trial run until the morning of October 24th 1923, when Richard Percival introduced two Guy single deckers running across town from Brasswell (a little further east along the Annan road than the proposed starting point of the trams) to Dalbeattie road at the junction of Park road (later generally termed Janefield and again near the proposed western terminus of the tram service). The operation was under the control of a Mr.Cook who had served with the Carlisle Tramway company. Though he was officially an inspector his job appeared to be "jack of all trades", his duties not finishing until the last run of 10pm. The service ran on a half hour frequency until 11am, then every fifteen minutes, the Guy single deckers quickly being augmented by further Guys and Leylands to support the service. Initially, vehicles operated with Percivals fleetname, having been drafted in from the main fleet but the company was known as Scottish Southern Motor Services and, apparently, most of the local population had sampled the delights of omnibus travel by the end of the first week of operation. No doubt, many took their first journeys for the novelty value, but support for the new service was sufficiently encouraging for new routes to be operated between the odd sounding suburb of Stoop to the north end of Dumfries and the Crichton Royal Infirmary in the south and between the Cresswell housing scheme and Heathhall, where the car factory of Arrol Johnston generated a considerable amount of traffic. Arrol Johnston had moved to Dumfries in 1911 to be nearer the English markets. Despite its popularity, or perhaps because of it, some people questioned why "locals" had not set up a bus company, rather than allow an "outsider" to reap the rewards. Percival reacted quickly to quell these rumblings by floating a public company called South of Scotland Motor Company Limited (was the original title too close to Scottish Motor Traction for comfort?), which ran in a blue and cream livery. A report in the Dumfries and Galloway Standard in January 1924 stated that the new company's Directors consisted of a majority of Dumfries men with Richard Percival as Managing Director. A total of £15,000 of the capital of £25,000 was issued in £1 shares to the public. The new company acquired ground in Hood's Loaning off English Street and near the centre of Dumfries and built a bus garage with workshops. Surplus ground was sold off in later years to the owners of the Regal Cinema to build a theatre. Late theatre buses were provided for the three flourishing 'Picture Houses' after 10-30pm. With the development of the Locharbriggs housing scheme, the Cresswell to Heathhall service was extended and revised to operate via Moffat Road or Edinburgh Road. Also, the building of the St. Michaels Bridge in 1927 allowed new routes to be added in the Maxwelltown area, Maxwelltown being joined to Dumfries in 1929 by Act of Parliament.

Licences for the following Dumfries town services were acquired with the business : Locharbriggs - Queensberry Square : Crichton - Stoop; Troqueer - Cresswell; Janefield - Brasswell; and High Street - Victoria Avenue (this service operated on Saturdays and other days when football matches were being played at the Queen of the South ground at Palmerston Park. The licence allowed the operation of buses every ten minutes to the ground between 1.30pm and the start of the game and then until 5.15pm from the finish). The out of town services were : Dumfries - Castle Douglas (King Street) via Crocketford and Springholm; Dumfries - Castle Douglas (King Street) via Crocketford and Springholm and Kirkpatrick Durham; Dumfries - Moniaive via Newbridge, Dunscore and Crossford; Moniaive - Glencairn Church; Dumfries - Annan via Collin and Carrutherstown; Dumfries - Carlisle via Mouswald, Clarencefield, Cummertrees and Annan; Dumfries - Dalton via Carrutherstown; Annan - Langholm via Kirkpatrick Fleming and Canonbie; and Annan - Dumfries via Cummertrees, Clarencefield and Mouswald.

The garage premises did not pass to Caledonian, however as Eastfield Road was capable of absorbing the increased vehicle requirements.

No new vehicles appeared in 1929 but four Leyland bodied Leyland Lion LT2s (numbered 64-7, SM8315-8) were delivered in 1930 (costing £4753.19.0) followed by a further four in 1931 (70-3, SM8851-4). The delivery of the 1930 signalled a slight simplification of the livery with the abandonment of the deep red waist band. Side destination boards were fitted above the windows, a practice which ceased in the early 'thirties with the movement of vehicles around the area.

The most important (and most contentious) purchase, however, took place on 18th January 1932 when the substantial business of Andrew Harper of Peebles was acquired for £14521. Andrew Harper had been in operation as a "Carrier" in Broxburn, some 10 miles west of Edinburgh, since 1894. He was joined by his sons in the business early in this century and the business developed profitably. Four working horses and their drivers, one two horse lorry, two vans plus a horse and gig for family transport, collected and delivered anything from a small parcel to a bank safe. Furniture removals and emptying ashpits (before the days of refuse collection by the local councils) were typical work, but the major source of business was the contract for delivery of all goods from Holygate Goods Station, owned by the then North British Railway.

After the 1914-18 War, ex War Department lorries were bought and the business expanded further with carrier work from Edinburgh, especially from Leith Docks collecting and delivering basic goods like sugar and flour to merchants in Broxburn, Pumpherston and Bathgate districts. The Broxburn business was probably at its peak around 1920, with the "fleet" including a 4 ton "Sentinal" chain-driven lorry on the Edinburgh/Leith runs and a 2.5 ton Austin Lorry. However, the shale miners and railwaymans strike of 1921 signalled the end of Broxburn as a thriving town, many families moving away and some even emigrating to find work. It also caused Harper's to look around for alternative locations to serve; Andrew Harper's wife suggested that a carrier service should be tried between Leith, Edinburgh, Peebles, Innerleithen and Walkerburn. The Peebles business was started in Spring 1922 with one ex.W.D. 4-ton Dennis solid tyred lorry (SX1469), stabled at Alexander's Garage in Station Road (renamed Dean Park when the former LNER Station was demolished to make way for road developments). Collections were made in the Leith and Edinburgh districts on weekdays (except Wednesdays) with deliveries being made the same evening in Peebles. On Wednesdays and Saturdays deliveries were made in Innerleithen and Walkerburn and "empties" were collected for return to the warehouses on Thursday and Mondays when business was quieter. Some of the carrying was to "accommodation addresses" and could easily have been "poached" salmon but no questions were asked! For the record, charges were around 25/- per ton for sundry goods, with higher rates for carrying spirits and other high-risk goods. The operation expanded, a second Dennis lorry frequently being pulled from Broxburn to pick up complete loads and to help out generally. A reputation for first class service was quickly built up and carefully maintained.

As the Station Road Garage could not accommodate two lorries, to avoid the risk of pilfering, bigger premises were found in what was later Dovecot Road. A corrugated iron shed was rented from Peebles Town Council which had previously been used by them for garaging road rollers, trucks etc. These premises were to continue in use, much enlarged and altered, by both Harper's and, after the take-over, by Caledonian. The Shed is still in use today by Tweeddale District Council (the successor to Peebles Town Council) for a similar purpose as in 1922! By early 1923, three lorries were in use in Peebles and as the Broxburn business was rapidly declining, a decision was made by the family to diversify into the operation of bus services in the Peebles area. Andrew Harper and one of his sons, H.G.Harper set off from Edinburgh by overnight train to London with £700 in their pockets to buy their first bus from a Mr. J.W.Roberts of Shepherds Bush. The bus was a 20-seat Daimler registered XN3932, the chassis being ex.War Department, the body having being built by Roberts. A second hand Dennis was also acquired which had last operated for the War Department but originated with Walter Alexander (MS4054) to start operations. In April 1923, the first service commenced with the newly acquired Daimler, driven by Andrew Harper's other son Joe Harper. The initial route was between Peebles, Innerliethen and Walkerburn. Having obtained permission for picking up and setting down passengers at recognised points, as well as the terminus at Peebles end of the journey from the Peebles and Innerliethen town councils, the terminus at Walkerburn was selected. Walkerburn had no such authority so the terminus was chosen in Hall Street which was not ideal, being a steep hill. The High Street terminus which they would have preferred was foregone, due to objections from the proprietor of the George Hotel, who did not want buses standing outside his premises, sometimes for long periods. Competition on this service became fierce, as other operators worked the same two mile stretch between Innerliethen and Walkerburn. One of these competitors acquired a 14-seat Chevrolet which ran in front of the Harpers bus;

The six bay body on the South of Scotland Tiger TS1 makes an interesting comparison with Caledonian's Leyland Lion LT2 SM 8315 delivered in the previous year, with a five bay Leyland body of similar design. Both companies vehicles carried route boards, the Caledonian vehicle illustrating the one used for the Stranraer service.

Harper's first bus was this 20-seat Daimler with a body fitted by J.W.Roberts of Shepherds Bush. Purchased in 1923 it is photographed, as were a number of vehicles, in the yard of the Dovecot Road premises in Peebles.   (Douglas Harper Collection)

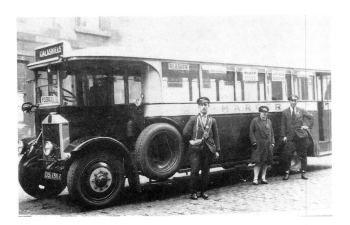

A rare view of a Harpers vehicle in Cunningham Street, Glasgow, the western extremity of the long route from Walkerburn which took some 3 hours and 20 minutes to complete. The destination blind on this Albion PM28 (DS1362) shows Galashiels, although Harpers route did not extend beyond Walkerburn where a connection could be made with SMT vehicles. Despite their dislike for each other, SMT and Harpers obviously saw the commercial advantages in lonking their services. The small lamp above the windscreen is probably the blue lamp which incurred the wrath of the Lanarkshire police, this form of identification being reserved for royalty at that time.

they in turn retaliated by running one in front of the Chevrolet! The purchase of small fast vehicles, often on hire purchase, to combat competition was common practice in those days. Harpers then purchased their own fast little vehicle, a 14-seat Reo (registered DS1024), fitted with pneumatic tyres in early 1925. They triumphed, the public supporting the operator who ran seven days a week and who were considered to be better maintained and, very importantly, reliable and punctual; the competitor gave up. However, other competition existed on the route with Brook and Amos (Mr.Brook moving to Stranraer to set up H.Brook and Company as mentioned earlier) and Galashiels Transport Company, who both operated between Galashiels and Innerliethen, the latter using 32-seat Caledons.

During 1924, the family planned to fill a perceived gap in the existing services to Edinburgh, using the "High Road to Linton". Harpers felt that public demand existed from the residents of Silverburn, Nine-mile-Burn and Carlops, who wanted to get to Edinburgh or West Linton or Biggar, there being no railway service between these villages. The nearest stations were at Penicuick or Broomlee (the latter being the station for West Linton, about a mile south of the village). Passengers for Edinburgh then had to change at Leadburn Station which was on the Edinburgh (Waverley) - Peebles North British line. Harpers decided to make their southerly terminus at Biggar, because no direct rail link existing between there and the city. Operated at first at weekends only, the service soon became daily. Having initiated the new service, they broke their final links with Broxburn, selling their garage and house to West Lothian County Council. With development being focused on road passenger transport, they realised that they could not finance the haulage side as well, the two Dennis lorries being sold to their two regular drivers who set up as the partnership "Plenderleith and

Stevenson". An adventurous long route was initiated between Walkerburn via Innerleithen, Peebles, Biggar, Lanark, Carluke, Wishaw, Motherwell, Hamilton and Uddingston Glasgow via Peebles in 1926, the first journey being driven by Jim Calder. A novel idea was introduced to allow intending passengers to identify Harper's blue and yellow liveried vehicles at night. A blue coloured light bulb was affixed adjacent to the destination blind box, until Lanarkshire police stopped the practice. They pointed out to Harpers that blue lamps on the front of vehicles were reserved for royalty!

The Edinburgh - Dumfries service of Dickson of Kirkpatrick Durham, near Dumfries was taken over in 1929, together with two dark red Guys SW1861 and SM4387. This service had operated as a type of "tour cum service" to Edinburgh from Dumfries via Thornhill, Dalveen Pass and Biggar, returning via Broughton, The Devils Beef Tub and Moffat. After acquisition the service was formed into an Edinburgh - Dumfries service via Carlops, West Linton, Biggar, Culter, Abington, Crawford, Dalveen Pass, Durisdeer and Thornhill and a Peebles - Broughton - Moffat - Dumfries service. Harpers had also instigated extended tours to the Highlands, for the more adventurous! Timetables were issued and a Motor Services and Tours Handbook, entitled "Through the Romantic Borderlands", published in 1931 listed the bus services, as well as the Motor Coach Day tours and "forenoon and Evening Coach Tours" operated.

Harpers' Northgate enquiry office in Peebles with Number 17 (DS 1402) Thornycroft A6, carrying Hall Lewis canvas top coachwork, popular in the late twenties. The bus did not survive to pass to Caledonian, being burnt out in 1930. (Douglas Harper Collection)

As well as the garage in Dovecot Road, Peebles which could hold 8 buses, an enquiry and parcels office had been established at 24A Northgate, Peebles adjacent to the Cross Keys Hotel. Garage space for 1 bus was rented at Biggar for the Edinburgh route from J.Stephen and Sons of Central Garage. The Glasgow bus was garaged at the premises of Grant, Melrose and Tennant, who were motor engineers based on the New City Road. Edinburgh based vehicles had originally been kept at the premises of the Peebles Motor Company in Russel Road in the Roseburn district of the city. The Edinburgh terminus was agreed with the Council at Castle Terrace, to the west end of Princess Street and, whilst this was some way from the terminus of the mighty S.M.T. operation in St Andrews Square, Harpers were more than satisfied with its location, being close to Edinburgh's west end. An enquiry and parcels office was established at number 5, rented from an R.Mackintosh in an elegant Georgian terraced row, opposite the stance. This served as a general and enquiry office which also dealt in parcels and doubled as a wages office, with a room for the depot superintendent. All the premises used were inherited by Caledonian; however, they quickly moved the enquiry and parcels office at Peebles into premises in the High Street. Castle Terrace continued to be used as the terminus for all but the joint S.M.T. service from Dumfries via Moffat which continued to use Chambers Street. S.M.T. Sales and Service (the S.M.T's car side of the operation) had taken over Peebles Motor Company and, with it, the Roseburn Garage in Russell Road which had been rented by Harpers. Increasing difficulty had been found in accommodating all the vehicles required at the garage and, as a result, Harpers rented additional space and progressively took over the whole space available at a newly built garage in Gorgie Road called Hayfield. When Caledonian took over, they appear to have taken a lease on a portion of the Roseburn garage whilst continuing to rent space at Hayfield.

Twenty six vehicles passed with the Harper business to Caledonian. Sixteen Thornycrofts, five Albions, three Leylands, one AEC Regal and a Commer Invader were inherited and all saw

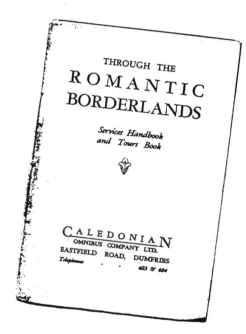

The tours handbook published in 1931 which also included details of Caledonian's regular bus services.

Thornycrofts were popular with Harpers, twenty being purchased between 1925 and their acquisition by Caledonian in 1932, with a further two on order at the time of takeover being delivered direct to "Caley". The Thornycroft A1 carried 24 seater bodywork by Northern Counties and illustrates the Edinburgh licence number 295, its Harpers fleet number being 13 (DS 1209). (Robert Grieves Collection)

Leyland Lion LT5 DS1477 was purchased new in 1929 and survived long enough to pass to SMT via Western SMT in 1949 with the Edinburgh allocation of vehicles. A youthful Douglas Harper, grandson of the founder, is dwarfed by the new bus.
(Douglas Harper Collection)

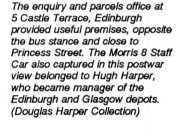

The enquiry and parcels office at 5 Castle Terrace, Edinburgh provided useful premises, opposite the bus stance and close to Princess Street. The Morris 8 Staff Car also captured in this postwar view belonged to Hugh Harper, who became manager of the Edinburgh and Glasgow depots.
(Douglas Harper Collection)

A very rare view of former Harpers vehicles in Caledonian livery in Peebles circa 1932 outside the High Street enquiry office. Left to right are DS 1498, the only Commer Invader, an unidentified Albion and Thornycroft and OU 8821, a Thornycroft BC.
(Garry Ward Collection)

further service with "Caley", a Leyland Lion surviving to be inherited, but not operated, by Western S.M.T. in 1949. Andrew Harper retired when the business was sold and Hugh Harper became the manager for the Edinburgh and Glasgow operations, moving to Edinburgh. Joe Harper moved to Dumfries to take up the job of Traffic Manager, later becoming traffic manager of Western S.M.T. at Kilmarnock after the take-over of Caledonian while Jim Calder moved to Dumfries to become Senior Inspector. The purchase of Harpers by Caledonian and the independent entry to Edinburgh by a second route from Dumfries which the acquisition gave them has always been quoted as the major reason for a "cooling" in the relationship between S.M.T. and Caledonian, but the reason was more deep-seated. S.M.T. had tried in vain to buy Harpers on a number of occasions but the company had firmly rejected all overtures by S.M.T., relations between Thomson (Chairman and founder of S.M.T.) and Andrew Harper being decidedly "icy", to say the least. For Harpers to succumb so easily (at least on the face of it) to a bid by a company whose main operating base was well outside the Edinburgh area was particularly annoying. Indeed, Harpers had been offered for sale before. In a letter to C.D.Stanley, the Chairman, dated May 1929, Harpers was offered for £30,000. Also offered was the three vehicle business of Fairbairn of Kelso which was available for the value of the vehicles plus £100, the latter operating in the Hawick - Selkirk - Galashiels area. The cost of Harpers was felt to be excessive, but Caledonian were further constrained by the interest which the LNER were taking in S.M.T., these acquisitions possibly prejudicing the negotiations. Concern was expressed that if the Midland Bus Service, an associate company of S.M.T. by this date, was being allowed to attack and, potentially, destroy one of the Tilling Companies, then this process could be repeated indefinitely throughout the country. In the event, Fairbairns business was acquired by S.M.T. in July 1929. Stanley's reaction is unknown: what is known is that the strained relationship with S.M.T. was to continue for 18 months, before a new agreement "cleared the air", of which more later. A more minor development was the renting of a timber garage at Dunreggan, Moniaive from Thomas Little from March 1932, to provide accommodation for vehicles outstationed on the Dumfries-Moniaive service. To finance their expansion Caledonian increased its issued capital in March 1932 from £41,844 to £125000. The accounts to March 1932 reported profits of £3275 and recommended a dividend of 5% again. Thomas Wolsey retired as a director, his position being filled by S.Kennedy.

Early adverts of the 'thirties cleverly extolled the advantages of travelling with Caledonian with slogans like "C.O.C. Confidence, Obliging, Careful" and "Travel C.O.C. and save £.s.d." The company was also being more heavily promoted to a steadily growing tourist trade, publicising the virtues of travelling, using adverts like; "Travel by Caledonian - The Route with the view".

Thornycroft Cygnet 149 (SM 9325) with Harrington body photographed before being licensed was one of two ordered by Harpers, but delivered to Caledonian in 1932.

Apart from the Thornycroft Cygnets, Caledonian took delivery of four Leyland Lion LT5s in 1932, the first vehicles to be bodied by Eastern Counties and the prelude to a fairly regular supply of bodies from Eastern Counties and its successor, Eastern Coach Works.

Caledonian were sufficiently impressed with the Thornycrofts inherited from Harpers to make regular purchases for their small vehicle requirements. Complete with a cream coach side flash was the second of two Brush-bodied 20 seaters delivered in 1936 (188/9 ; BSM834/5).   (Roy Marshall Collection)

Also, up to date saloon coaches were advertised for hire. A regular form of advertising used from 1932 was in the Cinema advertisement.

Caledonian received two Thornycroft Cygnets in 1932 costing £1502 each, which had been ordered by Harper's (numbers 149/50,

The 1933 deliveries included the only AEC Regals purchased new; 163 being the first of the batch numbered 163-5 (SM9977-9) with coach bodies by Eastern Counties. Their regular allocation when new was the Dumfries - Thornhill - Edinburgh service for which a connection could be made from Dumfries to Carlisle as the destination boards illustrate.

SM9335 and 9484) with bodies by Harrington of Hove which included roof mounted luggage racks, as well as receiving four more Leyland Lions, differing from previous batches in being LT5s (costing £706) and the first to be bodied by Eastern Counties of Lowestoft (numbered 151-4, SM9501-4). Eastern Counties and its successor, Eastern Coach Works, were to figure in subsequent Caledonian vehicle orders as we shall see, being a popular choice amongst Tilling and BAT companies. However, they were equally at home in BET companies. C.D.Stanley, Caledonian's chairman at the time, was a member of the British Electric Federation and these bodies were to the "Federation" design. Included in their specification and another "first" for "Caley" was the use of a large

The considerable comfort offered by these vehicles must have been equally appreciated on touring work as well as on the longer distance routes such as the Dumfries - Stranraer service on which 173 (BSM173) is seen near Creetown. Although other road traffic was scarce, obstacles like the stray cow were evrey day occurences.

BEF style destination indicator at the front. Later deliveries on Lancets bodied by Brush, Weymann and ECW continued this trend. These vehicles were allocated to the Dumfries - Stranraer service, a common practice being to allocate the newest vehicles to long routes such as this or the Dumfries to Edinburgh service. They were later to be converted from outward opening to inward opening doors due to the incidence of accidents with passengers.

The Thornycroft continued to be chosen by "Caley" for its small vehicle requirements being favoured for its "good chassis" until 1939 and the chassis was also chosen for a small batch of "big" buses in 1933. A Bean was inherited when Williamson and Proudfoot of Annan was acquired in December 1932. This vehicle was operated from Kirkcudbright for a time and is remembered for having a battery underneath the driver's seat. One day, smoke appeared from this area and the driver, who was blissfully unaware, had his attention drawn to the fact that his bus was on fire, caused by a short at one of the terminals! Services were operated between Annan and Lockerbie via Brydekirk and Eaglesfield, an Annan circular via Stapleton, Hollee, Kirkpatrick, Merkland, Kirtlebridge and North Bretton and between Annan and the Engineering Works at Newbie. No vehicles appear to have been taken over when J.Dunlop of Holm Street in Moffat was absorbed also in December 1932. He operated a service between Moffat and Annan via Lochmaben. Further expansion had been planned with another rural route from Moffat to Selkirk in 1931, but the application for a licence failed. Also acquired in the same month were Huntington Brothers of 24 Annan Street, Gretna for £3000, who operated between Carlisle and Gretna. The brothers Millward, Harold and David, had their buses garaged and serviced from James Currie's Garage in Annan Road, Gretna. Using a black livery, one of their charabancs was named "Lady Betty", named after their sister and a local has memories of regularly having to push this vehicle down Central Avenue in the village. Their Uncle had operated bus services from Carlisle, selling out to Percivals. A Guy and a Lancia passed to Caledonian with the business. This helped to consolidate "Caley's" position between Carlisle and Dumfries, although a further seven years were to pass before they effectively had the road to themselves.

Three chassis makes were represented amongst the twelve vehicles delivered in 1933; six Dennis Lancet 32-seat buses costing £3282 (numbered 157-62 ; SM9971-6), three AEC Regal 28-seat coaches (the chassis costing £2194 and the only AECs purchased new, numbered 163-5 ; SM9977-9) and three Thornycroft Cygnet 28-seat coaches (numbered 166-8 ; SM9930-2), all carrying Eastern Counties body work, the Regals and Thornycrofts providing the "up to date saloon coaches" promoted in company literature. The Cygnets had roof mounted luggage racks, whilst the Regals were particularly luxurious with comfortable seats, heaters, window curtains, outward opening coach doors and roof luggage racks. They persisted with the side destination boards, carrying one for Carlisle - Dumfries - Broughton - Edinburgh. The Lancets were to become the standard choice for service bus purchases until 1938, taking over the position from the Leyland Lion. During the same year, a number of vehicles had their seating capacity altered - Thornycroft 126 (DS1438) was reduced from 24 to 20-seats while in reverse, Leyland LT2s 64-7 (SM8315-8) and 70-3 (SM8851-4) were upseated to carry 32 instead of 28 passengers.

The three Regals were based at Edinburgh when new for the Dumfries - Edinburgh services and, indeed, appeared in advertisements of the period by AEC on this route. Jim Calder discovered that these were only travelling as far south as Abington where an unscheduled changeover with the bus originating from Dumfries was being made; vehicles were scheduled to run through. He challenged this practice at Abington one day and the Edinburgh driver replied that the buses were needed back at their home base for private hire work. Much argument followed, but Jim Calder insisted that the vehicles ran through to Edinburgh, his belief being that Edinburgh garage wished purely to hold on to their best vehicles. The unscheduled practice stopped, as a result!

An attempt was made to introduce a third route to Glasgow, by applying in May 1933 for a service starting from Moffat and operating north via Crawford and Abington (where connections could have been made with the Dumfries to Edinburgh via Thornhill and Biggar service which crossed over), Lanark, Carluke, Motherwell, Hamilton and Uddingston, a further potential connection being possible at points west from Lanark with the ex.Harpers Walkerburn to Glasgow service. Two return journeys were proposed daily, with an additional journey during the period June to September and a Saturday only short working between Moffat and Crawford. If the application had succeeded, the Moffat to Crawford section of the route from Edinburgh would have been withdrawn. Unfortunately, the licence was refused and no further attempts were made to initiate a service, no doubt due to the negotiations which were taking place. Those negotiations finally healed the rift with S.M.T. in an agreement made in October 1933, under which Caledonian sold their services in the Peebles area for £5250 including the garage at Dovecot Road which passed to S.M.T. on the 1st of October. Though Caledonian were only "residents" in Peebles for a short period, enough time had been found to continue the Harpers practice of producing a "Services and Tours" handbook, still entitled "Through the Romantic Borderlands". Licences for the Walkerburn/Innerliethen to Glasgow (Carlton Place) service were transferred to the S.M.T. associated company Central S.M.T. whilst the Peebles - Walkerburn via Kaikzie, Cardrona, Traquair and Innerleithen service passed to S.M.T. Caledonian gave up their share of the Glasgow (North Frederick Street) - Stranraer service operated originally with Scottish General Transport, although by this date the service was run in partnership with the newly formed Western S.M.T. Both Central and Western S.M.T. actually applied for the licences in August of that year. In return S.M.T. ceased to operate the services between Carlisle - Longtown - Langholm and Carlisle - Penton acquired with the business of G.Hudson & Sons of Carlisle in November 1931. Not documented previously as part of the agreement was the introduction of protective fares on the Glasgow to Dumfries service instigated by Midland Bus Service in April 1929. Caledonian and Midland had been in severe competition on this route over the section between Dumfries and Sanquhar and this had long been a thorn in the company's side. A formal agreement was actually made between Caledonian and S.M.T. agreeing not to compete with each other.

The history of the long running battle over the Dumfries - Sanquhar road is worth recounting. Caledonian had originally planned to operate joint services with Scottish General Transport between Glasgow and Stranraer and Glasgow and Dumfries. In the

AEC did not miss the opportunity to advertise the Caledonian purchases which introduced large destination boxes to the fleet. Two of the batch pose at the meeting point at Abington; the outward-opening coach door and early petrol pump are noteworthy.

event, a joint service between Glasgow and Dumfries was not initiated. Nevertheless, competition was experienced between Sanquhar and Dumfries (and also Girvan to Stranraer as indicted earlier), with Midland, who were operating through services from Glasgow. Caledonian had reported revenue being seriously impacted by this competition in their annual report of March 1930, as already stated. It appears that Midland applied for licences for services which would have competed with Caledonian over a further 91 miles according to a submission made by them to the traffic commissioners. The LMS Railway, on hearing of Midland's proposals called a meeting between S.M.T. (Midland's parent company by then), Caledonian and themselves in July 1929, LMS being anxious to avoid wasteful competition. The railway companies had bought into a large number of bus companies in 1929 as a means of protection against the increased effects of competition of the bus on the railways and, though Caledonian had no railway involvement, other Tilling and BAT companies did have a degree of railway ownership as did the S.M.T. Group (and therefore its

subsidiary Midland) by this date. An agreement was made that, until more permanent arrangements could be made, "no one of the three parties would in the area of South West Scotland either buy any business or extended its existing services without previous consultation with the other two parties". The meeting was referred to in future correspondence by virtue of its location, as the Euston Agreement. On the strength of this agreement, Caledonian made efforts to reduce what they viewed as wasteful competition, without success it would appear, because in November 1930 Midland applied to the Dumfries magistrates to double the frequency of their Glasgow to Dumfries service. By then, Midland had become a subsidiary of the S.M.T. as stated above and much correspondence flowed between the latter company and Caledonian during November. In spite of the seeming support of S.M.T. that additional journies would be "undesirable", Midland obtained licences for three additional return journies per day in December 1930 and in March 1931 two of these journies were introduced; a March 1931 timetable shows nine journies were in operation in either direction. Caledonian viewed this as breaking the "Euston Agreement". In May a conference was held in Edinburgh between Caledonian, S.M.T. and Midland Bus Service in an attempt to resolve the issues but there was deadlock with S.M.T. indicating that the additional journies had been put on to combat the threat of competition from an "outsider" between Auchinleck and Glasgow. The "outsider" was Liddell Brothers of Auchineck who failed to gain a route to Glasgow and were soon to be acquired by Western S.M.T. Caledonian, who claimed that their profitable route was now losing money took their case to the newly formed traffic commissioners and proposed that : Midland's service would not pick up or set down passengers between Sanquhar and Dumfries effectively making this portion an express service, with "Caley" providing connection at Sanquhar with the Midland service for local traffic between Sanquhar and Dumfries : that the number of Midland journies per day should be reduced : and that the timetables between the companies be properly co-ordinated (Caley had "submitted" a proposed integrated timetable). It would appear, however, that Caledonian lost this case and, in September 1932, a more aggressive approach was tried when application was made for a Dumfries to Ayr service to operate

This poor quality photograph is the only one available of the old Salisbury Street storage and haulage premises in Glasgow opened in 1936. An Albion lorry peers out of the garage in this view taken just after the war.   (Douglas Harper Collection)

Lined up on the south side of Whitesands bus stance, Dumfries for a British Legion trip to the Solway coast on which staggered departure times were necessary, are eighteen Caledonian vehicles. The ex.Carlisle & District Daimlers feature furthest away from the camera together with a selection of Albions, probably from Harpers and the South of Scotland fleet, at least one Leyland Lion and a Thornycroft in this early-mid 'thirties view.   (Jim Calder)

The garage in Penpont in the days when Carsons operated services around Thornhill, prior to takeover by Bell of Penpont. Caledonian rented space in this garage until their own was built some 200 yards down the road.

three times daily, extending beyond Sanquhar via Kirkconnel, New Cumnock and Cumnock. Not surprisingly, the application was opposed by "Western", who countered with their own application for a two hourly service over the same route. Both applications were refused and some twenty years were to elapse before a through service between Dumfries and Ayr was introduced and another year elapsed until agreement was reached over the Sanquhar to Dumfries section.

Some interesting service developments by October 1933 are worth noting : Special return fares were advertised between Carlisle and Langholm on Thursdays and Saturdays and Public Holidays of 2/6d (12.5p) being charged (normal Fare being 3/- (15p). Also, between Dumfries and Moniaive. Special return fares were advertised for Wednesdays and Saturdays; 2/2d (11P) compared with a standard return fare of 2/6d (12.5p). This route had some unusual competition in the shape of the Cairn Valley Light Railway who ran three times daily between Dumfries and Moniaive, with two extras on Saturdays and four times daily from Moniaive, again with extras on Saturdays. The rail journey took 55 minutes compared with a bus journey time of five minutes less, which operated six time daily with extras on Tuesdays and Saturdays. In addition a Sundays only service operated for the benefit of church goers between Moniaive and Glencairn Church. Three services were acquired with the business of J.Bell, Penpont : Dumfries and Penpont (Garage) running on Wednesdays and Saturdays only; Thornhill Station and Moniaive Cross; and Penpont Hotel and Thornhill Station whilst other services were Annan and Lockerbie via Hoddam Cross; Annan and Langholm with some short workings to Kirkpatrick Railway Bridge via Kirtlebridge and West Bretton (ex.South of Scotland Motor Company) and in Annan and Creca district, two journeys on Saturdays only operated between Annan and the local communities*; Annan circular via Kirkpatrick, Kirtlebridge and West Bretton*; Annan and Moffat via Lochmaben+; Annan and Newbie

and Kirkcudbright - Ringford via Tongland. (* ex.Williamson & Proudfoot, Annan; + ex.J.Dunlop, Moffat). The Dumfries - Stranraer via Dalbeattie, Haugh of Urr, Castle Douglas etc. had ceased with the Dumfries - Stranraer service which operated direct to Castle Douglas, thence through Gatehouse etc replacing it. Basic garage premises were opened at Canberra Road, Gretna where a dormy shed capable of housing four buses was used from February 1933. "Caley" opened an office at 109 Lowther Street in Carlisle by October 1933, replacing the premises at 97 Lowther Street inherited from Percivals.

The Directors report for Caledonian's financial year to the end of March 1934 referred to the building of offices adjacent to the workshops at Eastfield Road, allowing the registered office to be moved from Loreburn Chambers in the town. Also reported was the purchase of the Hayfield Garage in Gorgie Road, Edinburgh from its owner P.McConnell.

No new vehicles were purchased in 1934; no doubt, the transfer of the Harper's routes to S.M.T. already detailed above without the loss of any vehicles allowed the company to consolidate the fleet. A further second hand vehicle was acquired when a Morris Viceroy in the orange and brown livery of Frank Bisset and Son of Kirkmahoe was taken over in June 1934, together with their business and services between Dalswinton Lodge, Kirkton and Dumfries and Kirkton and Duncow and an excursions and tours licence from Whitesands, Dumfries. This effectively removed the last competition on the Dumfries-Auldgirth "back road", (Midland followed the main road through Hollywood on their Dumfries to Glasgow route). The Morris, incidentally, provided a handy day tour and private hire vehicle with its folding roof. Also in 1934, the following service changes were made : Annan - Langholm service revised to operate via Kirkpatrick Bridge, Chapelknowe, Milltown, Evertown and Canonbie replacing the Annan circular service inherited from Williamson and Proudfoot; Dumfries - Stranraer

Vehicle purchasing policy was still settling down in 1935, with four Leyland Tigers (the only Tigers bought new) arriving, fitted with Weymann 28 seat coach bodies. The first of the batch, 170 (BSM 170) illustrates the interesting mix of small aperture front destination box and large side indicator display. Matching registration numbers and fleet numbers were obtained for the only time (170-3; BSM 170-3).

Caledonian turned back to Dennis for the Lancet II model in 1936; 177 (BSM 823) was one of the seven bus seated batch. Gardner 5-cylinder diesel engines were specified for this batch and all subsequent Lancets delivered. The bus was waiting at the Town Hall in Carlisle, terminus for Caledonian vehicles until that year when the new Bus Garage/Station was built and opened in Lonsdale Street. (C.F.Klapper Collection)

service was diverted to operate via Kirkcudbright whilst that from Kirkcudbright to Ringford was extended to Castle Douglas, with one journey via Gelston, instead of Tongland and Ringford.

Continuing the company's policy of establishing outstations at the extremities of their routes, land was purchased and a small wooden Garage built at Penpont in May 1934 to replace the rented premises which had belonged to Carsons. At Langholm, garaging space was rented from Jeffrey Brothers of Townfoot Garage for the accommodation of the Carlisle bus. The Church of Scotland was paid £150 for a disused Church in Station Road, Annan. Rebuilding of the premises amounted to clearing out the interior and rebuilding the frontage with a large entrance, facing towards town. The character of the Church building was nevertheless retained as photographs of the depot after the 1939 fire illustrate. Vehicles had been originally garaged at the South of Scotland Motor Company premises and also on open land at the Merse, whilst Caledonian had rented garage premises in Port Street for a period. A recreation hall was also opened in 1934, fronting Eastfield Road and containing a large dance hall, billiard room, kitchen and toilets. The building was further extended soon afterwards to hold a carpet bowl area. A social committee was formed and, for a year, a magazine called the Caledonian Gazette was issued. The other business acquired in 1934 was that of James Bell (haulage contractor) of Dunragit near Stranraer. His business, complete with three lorries and garage premises at Dunragit and a small garage at Edinburgh Road in Stranraer was taken over. Haulage had been introduced during that year, initiated by the conversion of an (unknown) bus, which incidentally caused the finance people considerable confusion in how to reflect the vehicles in the accounts for the year ended March 1935.

The accounts for the year up to March 1935 reported profits of £7,700 and the company reported that the improvement in business was due partly to the agreement reached with S.M.T. Four further small businesses of Dobie, Alexander Love, T.Y.Varrie and Carslaws were acquired in 1935. Dobie of Thornhill had one small bus which was acquired with the business, probably being a 19-seat Morris registered SM7209, although he is also known to have run an Albion 14-seat SM1988 at one point. Varrie had a small parcels delivery service operating from his base at College Street in Dumfries and his vehicle passed to Caledonian; Varrie became a bench foreman at the company's Eastfield Road garage. Alexander Love was a haulage contractor with a garage situated in North Back Street, Wigtown. His main haulage work was a daily run from Wigtown to Glasgow and back. Groceries, fresh fruit and bread were carried south daily from Glasgow, the bread being delivered to the Glasgow base at 2am. Provisions were deposited from Barrhill southwards; being very early in the morning the practice was to leave these on the door steps of the shops. To get a full load for the northbound journey was more difficult, the main produce carried being cheese from the creameries, plus eggs and potatoes. The Wigtown garage which was acquired with the business had room for two lorries inside, plus a wooden loading and unloading platform. The Glasgow truck was unloaded and a smaller vehicle used to deliver provisions in the area. With the acquisition of the business, Caledonian was able to move the garaging of their bus from Love's

builders yard in Wigtown. Originally, a Morris Commercial, believed to have been SM5609 acquired with the business of South of Scotland Motor Company, had been garaged here. The bus side of the business was built up in the Wigtown area with the gaining of school contracts as well as the development of services and, though the garage was small, buses could be parked inside at night whilst the large lorry was away in Glasgow. The remaining vehicles were kept on waste ground on the north side of the garage, facing the entrance, with space for one more vehicle on the other side of the garage. Regrettably, nothing is known of Carslaws, although it is suspected they may have been a small haulage contractor in the Edinburgh or Glasgow area.

The 1935 purchases were in the shape of four coach seated oil engined Leyland Tiger TS7s with Weymann 28-seat bodywork (numbered 170-3 ; BSM170-3). The supposition was that these were for the Edinburgh routes, but it is more likely that they were purchased with a view to development of the private hire and touring work, which continued to be heavily promoted. They carried an interesting mixture of destination boxes, a small aperture being fitted at the front in a style typical of those carried by coaches, but with a

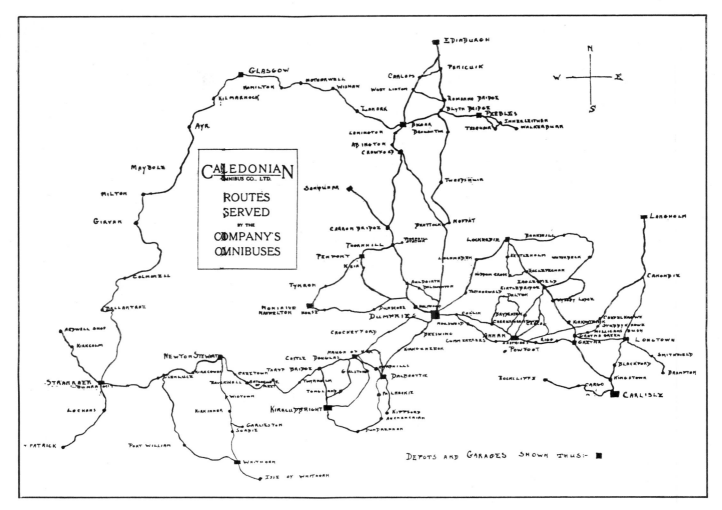

large "BET Federation" style box towards the rear nearside. Again, the bodywork was to high specification with roof mounted luggage rack, sliding roof, window curtains and heaters.

The 1935 timetable gave places of interest served by the company's routes with adverts like "Private Hire with Private Luxury" appearing as well as adverts for "Saloon" and "Sun Saloon" vehicles and invitations to contact Dumfries, Edinburgh, Carlisle, Kirkcudbright and Stranraer. Smaller depots also undertook private hire work, Baldnoch WRI's regular trip using a Whithorn based vehicle to Loch Lomond being an example. In the days long before tachographs, Willie McDowall, who drove the first bus from Stranraer to Whithorn for H.Brook of Stranraer, had to stop on his way back from Loch Lomond with this group to advise them that he needed to have half an hours rest as he was falling asleep at the wheel! Listed in this timetable were day, afternoon, evening and mystery tours operating from May to September. The year 1935 also signalled the start of extended tours, the following being operated from Whitesands, Dumfries : 2 day Loch Lomond - Oban - Inverary; 2 day Perthshire Highlands; 2 day East Coast Tour and 5 day Scottish Highlands.

In pre-war days, Caledonian were engaged in other interesting tours and hires. One involved the LMS Railway which regularly organised tours from Newcastle to Dumfries. Caledonian picked up the passengers and gave them a short tour around the shore road via New Abbey to Sandyhills, then back to the Station. In 1935 a further tour licence was gained operating from Moffat Station in conjunction with the L.M.S. allowing the use of up to 15 vehicles on a short excursion via Beattock, St Anns, Johnstone Bridge before returning to Moffat. Another local trip which followed the same route as the LMS tour from Dumfries was organised locally by the British Legion. Departing from Whitesands, this tour grew in popularity to the point where twenty-five vehicles were involved, the departures being "staggered", starting at 9am. A large boiler for making tea was carried on a four wheel trailer obtained from Wylies, who were grain merchants in the town. Another feature was the application yearly to the traffic commissioners for a short period licence to operate from Lockerbie to Hungry Hill for the "Point to Point" horse racing, which took place every April.

The full extent of Caledonian's operating area can be seen from this hand-drawn map taken from the company's 1932 timetable. It incorporates not only the former Harper routes together with those of other operators acquired including Farrer & Faulder's route to Brampton, but also the garages, including those at which Caledonian rented space. Within a year, the extent of the empire was to be trimmed considerably with the transfer of a number of routes to SMT.

Land was also purchased in Lewis Street, Stranraer on which a new garage and offices were built to replace the overcrowded Trade Street premises in May 1935. The land had been the western boundary of Stranraer Reformatary which closed in 1927. According to Wigtown Free Press, in October 1935 Caledonian's plan for a new garage were considered by the Town's Dean of Guild Court and accepted, the development being a large undertaking for that period. The premises were designed to allow the garaging of haulage vehicles and buses separately, separate access through different doors being built. This allowed the sale of the small Edinburgh road garage acquired with James Bell's business. Lewis Street was to prove something of a headache to Caledonian (and to "Western" to this day), because the premises were built on land which was prone to subsiding. The premises at Trade Street were retained, and leased out. Around this time, further west along the A75 a bus was garaged for a short period overnight in Gatehouse of Fleet to operate the first morning departure to Dumfries.

Profits increased further for the year ended March 1936 rising to £8486 and the company invested in further vehicles in the shape of fourteen Weymann bodied Dennis Lancet IIs, split between seven bus seated and seven coach seated variants (numbered 174-187 ; BSM820-833) and two 20-seat Thornycroft Handys (numbered 188-9 ; BSM834-5), bodied by Brush. The Thornycrofts had sliding roofs and window curtains, making them handy little private hire vehicles. An official view of one of these coaches shows Jim Calder at the side of 188 (BSM834). Despite the blind setting, these vehicles were not used on the Edinburgh service, instead assisting with the day tour summer work. The Lancets introduced large front and nearside large destination boxes with the luxury of heaters in

A line-up of twelve Caledonian vehicles on the forecourt of Dumfries railway station waiting to take passengers on a short tour of the Solway Firth as part of an LMS-organised day tour from Newcastle. Seen left to right are four ex.Carlisle & District Daimlers, four of the first batch of six Dennis Lancet delivered in 1933, two Leyland LT2s and two ex.Harpers Albions. The vehicle nearest the camera, 122 (DS1403) which had a Cowieson 20-seat body later became parcel van P6. (Jim Calder)

both the buses and the coach seated versions with the coach versions also having sliding roofs and luggage racks plus internally-sliding doors. Two of the coach seated Lancets were to have a very short life, however, being lost in a fire which destroyed Annan garage in 1939.

Services were further developed with a Kirkcudbright - Castle Douglas - Dalbeattie - Kippford route with connections advertised for Stranraer, Newton Stewart etc. One journey in either direction operated via Hardhills and Gelston. Certain journeys on the Stranraer - Whithorn service started to serve Stairhaven, and as a result, buses traversed Glenluce main street then reversed at the top of Glenluce village at Station Road, before returning back in the direction of Stranraer and turning left for Stairhaven, gaining the Whithorn road north of the Auchenmalg Inn. An additional Saturday only journey to Isle of Whithorn via Stairhaven and a short working return journey as far as the Auchanmalg Inn during the evening was also introduced, with two journeys in the opposite direction to Stranraer from Isle of Whithorn.

The popularity of the 1935 extended tours resulted in expansion in 1936 to a range of 2, 5, 7 and 10 day tours, the latter costing £12.12.0d (12 guineas). The Trossachs were added to the Perthshire Highlands tour and a new 10 day English and 5 day English Lakes and North Wales tour was added. Expansion was however limited to an extent because the company were competing with bigger operators who could negotiate better rates with hotels.

Nevertheless, what they lost in extended tour trade they gained in a flourishing summer day tour market. A variety of vehicles, including the Thornycrofts, various Leylands and Daimlers (ex.Carlisle and District) were used on these duties. Advertising continued to promote both the services and tours as follows : To the Theatre; To the Hills; To the Sea; To the Dales; To the Towns and Villages of the South of Scotland; Travel by Caledonian.

By June 1936 the Dumfries town services had evolved into the following routes : Janefield - Queensberry Square - Brasswell (Janefield Terminus was off Dalbeattie Road), with a basic 20 minute frequency Monday to Saturday; Sandside - Queensberry Square - Brasswell (Sandside terminus was Goldie Avenue, a 1930s Council Estate off Glasgow Road), Saturdays only service introduced in 1936; Sandside - Queensberry Square - Kingholm Quay (in practice this appears to have operated as two services from Queensberry Square in either direction. Introduced in 1936); Queensberry Square - Cresswell (introduced in 1936. Operated via Glebe Street, Aldermanhill, Brooms Road, Leafield Road and Hoods Loaning, operating as a circular); Troqueer - Queensberry Square. (introduced in 1936, this and the Cresswell service were a split of the Troqueer - Cresswell service); Stoop - Queensberry Square - Crichton (Quay Loaning) via Glencaple Road; Stoop - Queensberry Square - Crichton (Rosebank Cottage) via Bankend road (introduced 1936. Stoop was on the Lockerbie road heading east out of town; this served the section beyond the junction with Moffat Road, which was served by the Locharbriggs via Moffat road service).

To supplement the fleet five Tilling Stevens with Tilling 39-seat bus bodies (thought to have been numbered 190-4 and registered DB5111/3/6/7/9) were acquired from North Western Road Car Company. The buses were unusual purchases for the company, as no Tilling Stevens had previously been operated, and they were further distinguished by rear entrances which were, at the time, most unusual for the fleet. Used on local services, they only lasted for a short period of time, however, being in poor condition and were

Both the bus and coach seated variants had bodies by Weymannn, the only time Caledonian purchased coachwork from this source. Both variants seated 32, the coaches differing in having more comfortable seats, window curtains when new, a sliding roof and luggage carrier. The most noticable difference from the Lancet I was the re-designed radiator, but more observant passengers would perhaps have noticed a less smooth vehicle than the petrol engined variety.

withdrawn in 1938 for scrap.

In Carlisle until 1936 all the bus stances had been on the streets of the city centre, Caledonian services leaving from either the Town Hall or the Crescent, but as a result of the congestion caused the council decreed that the operators should use a bus station. This could be built either by the authority and rented to the companies or built by the operators themselves. Ribble and Cumberland Motor Services combined to build a bus station in Lowther Street, whilst United Automobile Services opted to drive a street between Lowther Street and Scotch Street to provide a one way bus station and the surviving major independent, Blair and Palmer built premises in Drovers Lane. Caledonian tried in vain to save money by claiming that as all the other major operators had now moved off the streets, their vehicles would not cause any congestion and they should be allowed to carry on! The Corporation, not surprisingly, rejected this proposal and Caledonian became the last to build off street premises with a combined garage and bus station which was opened in Lonsdale Street. Vehicles departed from here operating via the Town Hall. On return journies they operated straight to Lonsdale Street via Lowther Street, Victoria Place and Spencer Street. The two storey brick building held a left luggage and parcels office but no waiting room facilities for passengers. Other property developments included the opening of waiting rooms and a parcel office at the Whitesands premises in Dumfries. Also, a goods storage and haulage vehicle depot at Salisbury Street, Glasgow was leased from Whit Sunday 1936, reflecting the growing haulage trade in which Caledonian was engaged.

REVIEWING THE COMPETITION

During 1936, a detailed survey was undertaken of the independent operators plying for business in the counties of Dumfries and Kirkcudbrightshire. The document presented to the directors on 29 October of that year gave a fascinating insight into the competition which 'Caley' faced, detailing the vehicles owned, routes and services operated, the comparative receipts of Caledonian with the two operators whom they viewed as their major competitors and proposals for purchase. With the tentacles of the Western S.M.T. empire to the north running south from Girvan to Stranraer and Newton Stewart (the latter route acquired from Ayrshire Pullman Motor Services in December 1931 incidentally), from Ayr to Castle Douglas and from Cumnock to Dumfries and geographically bounded by the Solway Firth to the south, with further developments around Carlisle effectively restricted by the agreement of the early 'thirties, there was little opportunity for expansion of Caledonian's territory. Any developments were likely to be within its operating area and the 1936 report was a survey of the potential.

The first point to note is that the survey concentrated on only two of the counties covered by Caledonian. Wigtownshire is not referred to at all, the major competitor being Murray of Stranraer, who operated Stranraer town services together with the route from Stranraer to Drummore (on which Caledonian had operated briefly as described earlier), another route from Stranraer to Ervie and an infrequent route north eastwards to the small village of New Luce. Competitors in Cumberland, who ran north from Carlisle, were similarly not covered, although reference is made to Lochinvar Motor Services of Carlisle in view of their interest in Dumfries area operations. Another interesting point was the reference to Elliot of Lockerbie who operated one service between Lockerbie and Moffat. This route had originally been operated by "Caley" as a result of the purchase of Annandale Motor Co.in 1927. The report slanted towards the advantages of acquiring operators in the Dumfries area where it was felt maximum advantage could be gained.

Of the companies contained in the report, Dumfries-based three-vehicle Anderson's Motors Ltd's solitary service was not regarded as being directly competitive to Caledonian, and although the company held a tours licence from Dumfries, none had been advertsied or operated during 1936. Similarly, neither of the two services run by James Clark & Sons of Glencaple were in direct competition to Caledonian, although this could not be said of Clark's tours which radiated from Dumfries. The company, who owned four vehicles had, it was understood, recently approached James Dickson of Dumfries with a view to acquiring his tours licences and it was felt that the purchase of Clark's business would enhance Caledonian's existing operations in the leisure field. One vehicle Craik of Bankend, who operated a solitary Wednesdays and Saturdays only service did not compete with the major company on tours or private hire work whilst the four vehicle fleet of James Carruthers of New Abbey operated a service which was competitive with David Clark but not with Caledonian.

Campbell Brothers of Gatehouse whose fleet comprised four Thornycrofts operated two services, only one of which competed indirectly with Caledonian although in the Kirkcudbright area they had built up an extensive private hire connection which caused the major company some concern. A. Davidson & Son of Auchinairn, whilst not operating any tours or catering to any extent for private hires, ran a two vehicle fleet on two services, one of which competed directly with Caledonian, although somewhat surprisingly according to the report it was suggested that no action be taken to acquire this business. James Dickson of Dumfries who operated two

One of the operators reviewed in the 1936 report was Carruthers of New Abbey, though no specific recommendations to purchase were made. Carruthers had "seen off" Caledonian competition on the Dumfries - New Abbey - Douglas Hall route in the late twenties and continued to provide competition for private hire work in Dumfries. This former Alexanders Leyland is seen at Silloth on a "rural trip" in 1935. (Robert Greives Collection)

Gibson of Moffat was, and still is, the recognised operator of the Dumfries - Moffat route, despite incursions at times by Caledonian and later, Western Scottish. His smart two-tone red fleet contained this all Scottish Cowieson bodied Albion Victor in the mid '30s. (Robert Grieves Collection)

Another operator mentioned who competed vigorously for private hire and touring work was Dickson of Dumfries who had celebrated 15 years of touring in 1936, when this Leyland Cub (CSM89) with locally built Penman of Dumfries bodywork was delivered. (Robert Greives Collection)

McDonald of Corsock used the trading name of Galloway Motor Service for his route between Dumfries and Dalry via Crocketford, Balmaclellan and New Galloway, a service which Caledonian believed had potential. McDonald's Albion is traversing New Galloway High Street before reversing to return to the main Castle Douglas - Ayr road. (Robert Greives Collection)

Leylands and an Albion had no involvement in stage carriage services and confined his activities to tours and private hire work, providing strong competition to Caledonian in both these areas. William Elliot of Lockerbie's two Bedfords were both used almost exclusively on his solitary stage carriage service which did not compete directly with any Caledonian route and as he did not operate tours or, to any great extent, private hires, he was not regarded as any threat. Conversely, James Gibson & Sons of St.Anns competed vigorously with Caledonian for private hire work and additionally operated a service between Dumfries and Moffat which competed directly with parts of no fewer than four of Caledonian's routes using a fleet of four vehicles, all of different makes. Another operator covered in the report was McDonald of Corsock whose fleet comprised three vehicles and operated a solitary service which competed with Caledonian between Dumfries and Crocketford. McDonald, however, did not involve himself in tours or private hire, most of his work in these areas being sub-contracted from other operators in Dumfries.

Penman of Dalbeattie who concentrated solely on stage carriage work with one service which was competitive with Caledonian and opaerated a solitary Bedford gave the major company little or no concern whereas the three vahicle fleet of James Robertson & Sons of Lockerbie competed extensively with Caledonian for private hire work whilst posing a lesser threat with its competitive Thursdays only stage carriage service between Lockerbie and Dalton.

The report concluded that although it would be advantageous to acquire some of the businesses investigated to enable their stage carriage services to be incorporated into those already operated by Caledonian, it was more important to gain a greater control of their tours and private hire activities. The acquisition of the majority of the vehicles owned by these operators was, however, of lesser importance, particularly as a high proportion of them were regarded as being in poor condition and in the case of some companies included in the survey, it was stated tnat little purpose would be gained from their passage into the Caledonian fold. As will be seen later, some were in the event, purchased whilst others continued to remain independent for many more years.

HAULAGE AND PARCELS

Caledonian had the unusual distinction of being a bus operator and haulage contractor, operating lorries as well as a fleet of Parcels vans, all in a grey livery. A parcels service had been advertised from Caledonian's formation, albeit by the more common method adopted by bus companies of carrying packages on the routes covered by the service buses. Parcels could be deposited at the Company's parcels offices, or through the network of agents which they had established over the routes served. A double carriage charge was made for parcels carried on the Dumfries to Stranraer and Dumfries to Edinburgh services. However, in 1935, a parcel van service was inaugurated using at least one vehicle which had been converted from a bus (62 ; SM6950). This began the common practice of converting buses into parcel vans, at least nine of the sixteen vehicles which operated in the parcel van fleet were converted in this way. Albions were initially a favourite chassis for conversion and, indeed, were chosen for the first purpose built vans to be delivered in 1938. The purchase of Varries' parcel delivery service in 1935 strengthened this side of the operation and, despite the fleet always being small, the parcel van operation developed into a particularly thriving business, the fleet operating daily (except Sundays) in the mid 'thirties over five routes, four based in Dumfries and one on Carlisle : Dumfries - Dalbeattie - Castle Douglas-Kirkcudbright; Dumfries - Lochmaben - Lockerbie - Eaglesfield - Annan - Cummertrees - Clarencefield (circular); Dumfries - Annan - Gretna - Longtown - Carlisle (not Saturdays); Dumfries - Stranraer and Carlisle - Longtown - Gretna - Annan - Dumfries - Lochmaben - Lockerbie - Eaglesfield and surrounding districts.

Similarly, Caledonian also purchased some haulage businesses and mention has already been made of the purchase of Alexander Love of Wigtown in 1935. However, the purchase in December 1934 of the business of J.Bell of Dunragit, a village between Stranraer and Newton Stewart, was of equal, if not more, importance. A room was converted as an office for Bells at the Trade Street premises and the trading name was retained, haulage

vehicles showing both Bell and the Caledonian name. Albion vehicles were also particularly favoured for the haulage fleet and, as with the parcel van fleet, former PSVs were converted in some instances. Indeed, one former bus Dennis HH4109 was converted first to a haulage vehicle, then later became a tilt van in the parcel van fleet! An appendix details the known haulage fleet and indicates the fleet which existed in February 1937. At that time, transport of milk was a key activity (an area of work in which J.Bell had

The first purpose-built parcel vans were three Albion SPCL123s with drop down boards, delivered in 1938. Numbered P8-10 (DSM 603/4/24), they survived until Caledonian's demise.

focused), nine of the twenty vehicles being required for this work. Proposals at the time concentrated on upgrading older members of the haulage fleet. Steady progress was made on this and, certainly by 1943, older vehicles had been disposed of.

The general policy was that bus depots had to be capable of catering for haulage and parcel van business, staff to be capable of carrying out all duties. A regular practice at Eastfield Road, Dumfries was for conductors to become parcel van assistants, learn to drive parcel vans and then train for a haulage and PSV licence, before returning to the bus division as drivers. The following bus depots catered for haulage and parcel vans : Lonsdale Street, Carlisle; Eastfield Road, Dumfries (the "top" garage referred to as "The Haulage" being used solely for haulage and parcel vehicles); Harbour Garage, Kirkcudbright; Trade Street (from 1936 Lewis Street) Stranraer; Hayfield, Edinburgh and North Back Street, Wigtown (this depot was really a haulage base first and foremost which operated buses as well). The map gives further details;

The Wigtown to Glasgow haulage service was the subject of a detailed review in 1937 and gives an interesting insight to one aspect of the haulage operation. Two Albions (fleet numbers H20 and 21) operated the service and the proposal was to replace these with one large "oil engined" vehicle. The operation worked as follows : Vehicles departed from Wigtown at 6pm (the major commodity carried south was bread which was delivered to the Salisbury Street Depot in Glasgow at 3am). Vehicles departed from Glasgow at 3am and arrived Wigtown approx 8am, the bread being transferred onto 8.10am bus leaving Wigtown for Whithorn. Any goods for the Portwilliam area were transferred to the "small lorry" and the lorry from Glasgow would then deliver in the area of Wigtown, Newton Stewart, Kirkinner etc. Goods for Gatehouse, Creetown and Glenluce were transferred to the respective Dumfries or Stranraer parcel vans. The review recommended the re-siting of the acquired Wigtown depot to Newton Stewart, saving some 45 minutes to an hour on the round trip, an important consideration

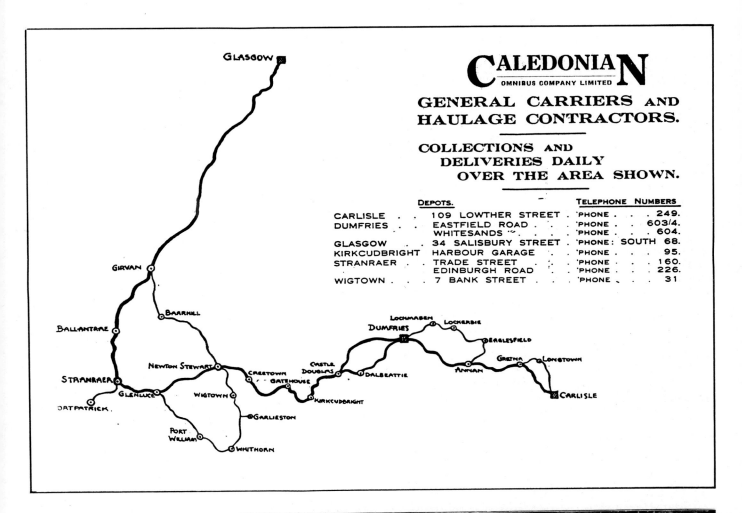

CALEDONIAN
OMNIBUS COMPANY LIMITED

GENERAL CARRIERS AND HAULAGE CONTRACTORS.

COLLECTIONS AND DELIVERIES DAILY OVER THE AREA SHOWN.

DEPOTS.		TELEPHONE NUMBERS
CARLISLE	109 LOWTHER STREET	'PHONE . . 249.
DUMFRIES	EASTFIELD ROAD	'PHONE . . 603/4.
	WHITESANDS	'PHONE . . 604.
GLASGOW	34 SALISBURY STREET	'PHONE: SOUTH 68.
KIRKCUDBRIGHT	HARBOUR GARAGE	'PHONE . . 95.
STRANRAER	TRADE STREET	'PHONE . . 160.
	EDINBURGH ROAD	'PHONE . . 226.
WIGTOWN	7 BANK STREET	'PHONE . . 31

Delivered new to the fleet in 1937, Albion SPM550 was a 4-ton truck given the fleet number H33. Vehicles were often registered by the chassis or bodybuilder, a Glasgow licensing plate being allocated on this occasion.

CARRIERS
OF   ALL
CLASSES
OF   TRAFFIC

when the law allowed 14 hours duty of which eleven hours maximum driving was permitted making the journey very tight. The subject of Wigtown v Newton Stewart for the siting of the depot was to arise again after the war. Another consideration was the transferring of goods between vehicles, especially the Dumfries bound van.

Later in 1937 the haulage firms of Learmonts Transport and McCourtie amalgamated, both operating out of Markwelltown station yard and both having offices in Galloway Street, Dumfries. Their lighter vehicles passed to McCourtie but three heavy vehicles (all Albions) were transferred to Caledonian to be numbered H28-30 (ASM83, 836 and BSM36 respectively) in the haulage fleet. A small fleet of Albion parcel vans numbered P8-10 (DSM603/4/24) with drop down tail board and canvas flaps at the rear were the first purpose built new vehicles delivered in 1938 as mentioned earlier and further vehicles were delivered to support the fleet.

CAREFUL
  OBLIGING
    CONSIDERATE

ENTRUST
  YOUR
    TRANSPORT
      TO   US

THE LATE 'THIRTIES

The 1937 purchases consisted of three Thornycroft Dainty 20-seat coaches (numbered 195-7 ; CSM602-4) again bodied by Brush and the now standard purchases of Dennis Lancets, nine with Eastern Coach Works bus bodies, complete with sliding roofs (numbered 198-206 ; CSM766-74) being taken into stock. A new service between Annan and Brydekirk was also instigated running twice daily.

The threat of war loomed heavily in 1938 and second hand vehicles were to figure more widely as events turned more serious and the company was to experience major expansion. New vehicles delivered during the year consisted of two further Thornycroft Dainties with Brush bodywork (numbered 207/8 ; DSM450/1), one Leyland Cub with Harrington 20-seat coachwork (number 209 ; DSM452 which was probably a diversion from a fellow Tilling and BAT company) and four Dennis Lancet IIs (numbered 210-3 ; DSM453-6), again with Brush bodies. 207-9 all had sliding roofs, with 209 also having a heater while 210-3 were coaches with roof mounted luggage racks, high backed seats, sliding roofs, heaters and a non standard cream side flash which swept downwards towards the rear as well as a cream rear, broken by a red waistband.

The first double deckers to be owned arrived in the shape of four ex.Bolton Corporation Leyland TD1s with Leyland style bodies built by Charles Roberts of Wakefield (numbered 214-7 ; WH2601-3/5). The arrival of these vehicles signalled the start of regular purchases of second hand double deckers and their numbers grew, forty three being in service by the end of the Second World War.

Three out of these four initial purchases had gone by the end of 1940, one being destroyed in the Annan Garage fire. With the introduction of double deckers a new variation of livery style was introduced for these vehicles, comprising the standard red livery separated by three cream bands above and below the lower deck windows and below the upper deck windows. At the same time, a grey roof was introduced, not only on the deckers but also onto the single deck fleet, the theory being that a grey roof was less conspicuous than a cream one to enemy aircraft. As double deckers arrived, their destination boxes were rebuilt where necessary to take the large style destination screens fitted to the single deckers. Fourteen ten year old Leyland Lions were also acquired from fellow Tilling and BAT operator Hants and Dorset Motor Services of Bournemouth (numbered 218-31 ; TR5944/6, RU8055/6, 8103, 8452, 8057, 8518, 7556, 8451, 8679, 5395, TR6170, RU8054). 229 had a Beadle body, the remainder being built by Leyland. Caledonian also returned to North Western Road Car, this time for more standard vehicles than the Tillings; two Leyland Lion LT5s (numbered 232/3 ; XJ827/8) acquired with the business of Goodfellow Services of Hyde in 1932 and also carrying Roberts bodywork were purchased.

Permission required to be sought from the traffic commisioners to operate double deckers and authorisation was given in July 1938 for them to operate on the following services : All Dumfries Town services; Dumfries - Thornhill; Dumfries - Sanquhar between the former point and Thornhill; Dumfries - Moniaive; Dumfries - Penpont between the former point and Friars Carse; Dumfries - Lockerbie;

The 1937 batch of nine Dennis Lancets had the distinction of being the only ones with bodywork by Eastern Coach Works (successor to Eastern Counties). First of the batch 198 (CSM 766) was photographed at the coachbuilder's at Lowestoft prior to the journey north. Sliding roofs were specified, no doubt to make them sufficiently attractive for private hire use.

The Market Square in Annan was the bus terminus until more recent times. Dennis Lancet 204 (CSM 772) sits at the bus stop between the market stalls and the bank. (Robert Grieves Collection)

During the winter of 1937/8, AEC Regal 173 (BSM173) was stranded in deep snow at Silverburn while working the Edinburgh - West Linton route. With the suspension of services, bus crews were despatched with shovels to dig their vehicles out as illustrated here.
(Douglas Harper Collection)

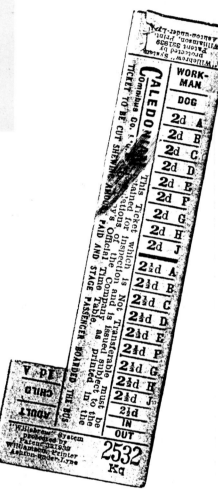

Snow could be the cause of considerable disruption in winter, especially on the Edinburgh services. Here, Thornycroft Cygnet 150 (SM9484) is stranded in a deep drift in February 1937.
(Douglas Harper Collection)

ANYWHERE TICKETS
AVAILABLE ON ANY DAY.

Anywhere Tickets may be obtained from all Conductors for use on day of issue only.

This Ticket allows the holder to travel upon any of the Company's stage carriage routes on the day of issue only, changing vehicles and routes as often as desired in the area in which the ticket is bought.

Area 1.—Dumfriesshire, Kirkcudbrightshire and Cumberland, from Ravenshall and any point east thereof on any and all routes except the Dumfries-Edinburgh routes.

Area 2.—Kirkcudbrightshire and Wigtownshire from Castle-Douglas and any point west thereof on any and all routes.

Area 3.—Dumfries Kirkcudbrightshire, and Wigtownshire from Dumfries and any part west, thereof to Newton-Stewart on any and all routes.

Tickets issued in one area are not valid for travel outwith that area.

Holders of these Tickets have no privilege over ordinary passengers, and the Company can take no responsibility for lack of accommodation, failure to make connections, or delays of any description.

Passengers wishing to take advantage of these facilities may obtain full particulars from any of the Company's Inspectors or any of the Company's Offices.

ADULTS 5/-   **CHILDREN 3/-**

A PASS FOR ONE DAY OVER THE COMPANY'S SYSTEM.
(With certain exceptions as to Area.)

EXTENDED MOTOR COACH TOURS
ARRANGED BY
The Caledonian Omnibus Co., Ltd.

CONDITIONS GOVERNING TOURS.

1.—A deposit of £1 per seat must accompany each booking, the balance to be paid at least seven days before the date of departure of the tour.

2.—Luggage is limited to one suitcase for two passengers; single passengers one small suitcase.

3.—Luggage, coats, etc., are carried at owner's risk, although every possible precaution is taken to guard against loss.

4.—Whilst every effort is made to provide single passengers with single bedrooms, no guarantee can be given that this will be so, but passengers can rest assured that suitable arrangements will be made for them.

5.—A seating plan of the coach will be kept for each tour and passengers should indicate their requirements in this respect when booking.

6.—The Company reserve the right to alter the route or method of transit should unforeseen circumstances arise, and to provide accommodation at hotels other than those named if found necessary.

7.—The Company reserve the right to cancel any advertised tour if a sufficient number of passengers is not forthcoming, but reasonable notice will be given and seats offered on any other tour which may be running.

IMPORTANT.

Owing to the sleeping accommodation at first-class Hotels being so severely taxed during the tourist season, Patrons are advised to book their seats well in advance.

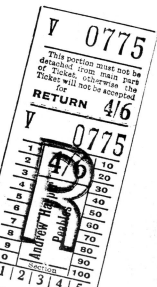

Despite the threat of war, a tours booklet was produced for the 1939 season. The opportunity was not missed to promote Caledonian routes linking the historically important centre of "Caledonia". Extended as well as day tours were advertised and seating plan for a 20-seat coach was also provided.

Secondhand vehicles were to provide much of the vehicle intake during the war. Some of the first, actually delivered pre-war, were a batch of fourteen Leyland Lions from fellow Tilling and BAT operator, Hants & Dorset Motor Services. 226 (RU 7556) rests outside Lonsdale Street, Carlisle after the war. (Garry Ward Collection)

Having specified sliding roofs on a batch of Dennis buses in the previous year, Caledonian opted for a higher specification for its four Lancet IIs delivered in 1938. 212 was the second of the batch 210-3 (DSM 453-6). All had roof mounted luggage racks, high backed seats, sliding doors and the rare luxury for those days of a heater! (Alan B. Cross)

The rear of 212 illustrates the non-standard paint scheme, with their cream side flashes and rear, making this batch of Brush bodied Lancets distinctive.
(Alan B. Cross)

Dumfries - Castle Douglas; Kirkcudbright - Dalbeattie; Dumfries - Kirkcudbright; Dumfries - Stranraer as far as Kirkcudbright; Dumfries - Gatehouse as far as Castle Douglas; Dumfries - Dalbeattie - Kippford; Dumfries - Castle Douglas; Dumfries - Carlisle via the "top road" and Lockerbie - Carlisle over the section between Carlise and Gretna only. Also, despite the threat of war, a Dumfries "sightseeing tour" had been advertised in the June timetable of that year. The lease on Roseburn Garage in Edinburgh was sold in February 1938, operations being consolidated from Hayfield. It has never been satisfactorily established whether this garage was ever used by Caledonian or indeed why they had two garages for a period in Edinburgh. On the conducting side, Bellgraphic ticket machines were introduced alongside the existing Willebrew punches. As far as the touring activities were concerned, despite impending war, day tours continued to be advertised from Kirkcudbright, Dumfries and Annan between March and October to the Empire Exhibition at Bellahouston Park in Glasgow. Also advertised was a combined Exhibition and Arrochar 2 day tour.

WARTIME AND MANY CHALLENGES

Pre-war, Cumberland, Dumfriesshire, Kirkcudbrightshire and Wigtownshire were largely agricultural areas. Caledonian's traffic had been helped by the stimulation of the agricultural by-products industry of the Scottish Milk Marketing Board, with the establishment of various creameries. Between 1939 and 1945 a total of twelve new factories, five aerodromes, one flying boat station (at Wig Bay, Loch Ryan) and twelve military camps were built. In addition, a new port at Cairnryan was constructed. Of the twelve factories, five were Ministry of Supply on production of munitions, five were supply and maintenance units of the R.A.F. and two were ordnance factories. Building of the port at Cairnryan started January 1941 and took two and a half years to complete. When completed, the port was used exclusively for the intake of military personnel and "lease lend" goods and through the war many thousands of U.S. personnel and equipment passed through this port. A railway line was built to link into the Stranraer to Dumfries line and, though freight made up the vast majority of traffic a basic passenger service was operated for troops to the bridge over London Road in Stranraer.

Before looking at the impacts of this development on Caledonian, however, we should briefly examine the economy of the areas they served and how this was affected by wartime development. In Dumfries, the Arrol Johnston factory had ceased car production in 1931. This, combined with a decline in the cloth industry, resulted in considerable unemployment until wartime preparation reversed the trend. The derelict motor works at Heathall became a RAF maintenance unit and Dumfries aerodrome was built nearby by the purchase of Tinwald Down Farm (at one time, the site of the Dumfries Racecourse) by the Air Ministry. Annan's major employer with a staff of some 600 was the Engineering firm of Cochran & Co., which had originated in Birkenhead, producing boilers at Newbie, a village west of the town. This work continued in the war, augmented by assisting in the manufacturing of tanks and later some units for "Mulbery" harbours for use in the Normandy invasion. A Ministry of Supply Factory run by I.C.I.Explosives was erected at Powfoot, called the Broom Camp again a few miles west of the town, where over 2000 people were employed.

Between Annan and Dumfries on the "low" road, the Cummertrees area had offered considerable potential in pre-war years. General Brook, founder of the large thread manufacturing firm, bought Kinmount Estate and initiated an ambitious scheme to convert the area into a resort. Success depended on the building of a sea wall to contain the erratic ebb and flow of the Solway Firth in Powfoot Bay. Though the project was abandoned some houses were built at Powfoot and some limited summer trade developed, but perhaps the most curious legacy was the building of 15 terraced houses to a very English style intended for summer development. The population that did settle were transported to the many Ministry of Supply or I.C.I. factories. The villages of Gretna, Eastriggs and

Dornoch had grown largely with the outbreak of World War I with the erection of huge munitions factories at Longtown, Mossband and Eastriggs. The population of the area decreased between the wars then began to increase again dramatically with the impending Second World War. To the south west of Dumfries a munitions factory (again operated by I.C.I) was established near Dalbeattie. Further west, the Wigtown and Whithorn area also had a concentration of wartime facilities, of which more later. In the extreme west Stranraer district had Air Stations at West Freugh (the largest in the area), Castle Kennedy, Corsewall, North Cairn and in Loch Ryan, where two squadrons of flying boats were stationed there for a time and used in the early stages of the "Battle of the Atlantic". In addition, construction of military port was started at Cairnryan and completed by spring 1942, as mentioned above. This activity resulted in the Caledonian passenger fleet expanding from 116 vehicles in 1939 to 167 in 1945, a growth in the fleet of nearly 50%. At the beginning of 1939 five double deckers were owned. By the end of 1945 forty were operated according to a Company war record document; actually, forty three were in use by then. Before the war, the conducting staff was evenly split between males and females. By 1945 all the conducting staff were females, four drivers and four inspectors also being females. Having been restricted in its development, the preperations for war and the war itself were to result in Caledonian's biggest expansion within its own operating territory. Initially, additional buses were required to transport workers engaged in the construction of these many developments; when the factories were built, this often simply changed to transporting the factory workers themselves.

The Company reflected more of its Tilling and BAT parentage when two Bristol L5Gs with Tilling style rear entrance ECW bodywork (numbered 242-3 ; ESM537-8) arrived in 1939, the first of this entrance layout bought new. The vehicles still carried the large BET Federation style destination boxes, although fitted at the front only, complete with sliding roofs. Another "odd man out" was a Bedford WTB with Duple 20-seat bodywork (numbered 241 ; ESM 484), purchased for extended tour work but stored for a while before being pressed into service. Secondhand purchases were five 1928 Leyland Titan TD1s, with Leyland lowbridge bodywork and open staircases (numbered 234-8 ; TM3744, 3824, 3843, 3846 and 3735) and two 1930 AEC Regents with Short lowbridge bodies from Eastern National (numbered 239-40 ; VX4902 and TM6307) and five Leyland Titan TD1s with Leyland bodies from Keighley-West Yorkshire (for the sum of £40 each and numbered 244-8 ; WW7861-3, 8358/60) and four TD1s with Leyland highbridge bodies from Wilts and Dorset Motor Services of Salisbury (numbered 255-8 ; KR1729/31/33, 6531).

The collection of secondhand stock from various locations throughout the country became a fairly regular occurance during the

By then in Western colours, this Leyland highbridge-bodied Leyland Titan TD1 was the last of four vehicles acquired from Wilts & Dorset Motor Services. 258 (KR 6531) was repaired by Carlisle coachbuilder James Bendall and Sons during the war and fitted later with a 'COVRAD' replacement radiator, probably at the same time as being re-engined with a Gardner diesel unit in 1948.

The first moves towards Tilling buying policy came in 1939 with the delivery of two ECW-bodied Bristol L5Gs, the first Bristols in the fleet. Having specified similar Gardner engines in its Dennis Lancets since 1936, the new arrivals were not as 'non-standard' as might at first appear, although the rear entrance styling certainly was. Caledonian clung to BET practice with the fitment of a large destination box, however, as illustrated by the second of the two vehicles, 243 (ESM538). (Eastern Coach Works)

A definate 'odd man out' was 20-seat Duple-bodied Bedford WTB 241 (ESM484) which would have been a useful private hire and touring vehicle had the declaration of war not consigned it to more mundane duties. It signalled the delivery of numerically the last new vehicle for three years. (Duple).

war and Jim Calder told an interesting story about some of the pitfalls of this activity. He volunteered with other drivers to travel down to Chelmsford to collect the vehicles acquired from Eastern National. The group of seven were given railway tickets and instructions on what and where to collect the stock. On arrival at Chelmsford they were directed to the back of the garage where seven forlorn vehicles awaited them. Before any attempts were made to start them, three of the vehicles had flat tyres to be pumped up. When all was ready and the vehicles duly fuelled, they set off in convoy, Jim Calder driving the Short bodied AEC Regent. This highbridge vehicle was almost his downfall in Cambridge when the roof vent became entangled in a length of bunting which had been strung across the street and tied through an upstairs window to a dressing table. The bus stalled and had to be hand cranked after disentangling the garland from the bus. Meanwhile, the convoy had continued on, unaware that one of their group was stranded, but after giving chase, he eventually caught them up. The double deckers were concentrated in the Dumfries, Annan, Gretna, Longtown and Carlisle areas to serve the burdgeoning military and Government establishments like Mossband Military and Naval distribution stores and 14 MU (Carlisle Aerodrome). From Dumfries, they regularly operated to Lockerbie as well as the busy Dumfries town services, especially the Locharbriggs town service, some journies on this route being extended to Heathall RAF works, as well as Dumfries to Annan via the "high road". At least two double deckers were drafted into Stranraer during late1942/early 1943 in

Annan garage was burnt out in May 1939 with the loss of seven vehicles. The former Greenknowe Church had changed little, structurally, on its conversion to a bus garage with only the frontage being altered to allow the creation of an access point.
(Garry Ward Collection)

Fire completely destroyed the Annan Garage in May 1939 also destroying seven vehicles viz ; Three 1928-9 Leyland Lions (222/3/8 ; RU8103, 8452, 8679); two 1936 Dennis Lancets (182/3 ; BSM828/9) ; one 1937 Thornycroft Dainty (195 ; CSM602) and a 1930 Titan TD1 (215 ; WH2602). The cause was never established although a smouldering cigarette end was supected. By the time Jim Calder and J.M.Harper arrived on the scene from Dumfries, the

The last competitor on the Carlisle - Longtown road finally succumbed in December 1939, with the takeover of Lochinvar of Carlisle. The distinctive fleet with their large fleetnames and tartan waistbands were a familiar site around Longtown and, on Sundays, Gretna. Their Garage at Longtown provided much needed space for the growing traffic to the military establishments and munitions factories in the area. HH 3105 was a 1926 Albion PKA26 which had been sold before the takeover, but four other Albions and a Dennis Lancet survived to be operated by Caledonian.

The parcel van service was restricted from September 1939 to conserve fuel. P12 represents a bus conversion carried out after the war in 1946, the work on this 1930 Leyland Lion LT2 entailing basically a stripping of the interior and pannelling of the sides, with access doors being provided at the rear. The destination box was retained, a useful reminder that parcels could be carried on vans like this or on bus services. (Alan B. Cross)

garage was well ablaze. The fire chief remarked that they were starting to get the fire under control but enquired where the petrol tanks were. The reply was that he was standing on top of them, which caused very swift movement! Buses were quickly drafted in from Dumfries for start up of the services the next morning. The premises were virtually totally replaced in the 1939-41 period by a more "purpose built" garage.

All tours (day and extended) ceased in 1939, and in addition the Parcel van service was subject to restrictive services from Saturday 16th September and the details are reproduced to illustrate the extent of the operation;

Parcel, Van P9 : Monday - Dumfries to Stranraer delivering and collecting at Kirkcudbright, Gatehouse, Creetown, Newton Stewart, Wigtown, Whithorn, Portwilliam and intermediate villages; Tuesday - At Stranraer; Wednesday - Stranraer to Dumfries collecting and delivering at Portwilliam, Whithorn, Wigtown, Newton Stewart, Creetown, Gatehouse, Kirkcudbright and intermediate points; Thursday - At Dumfries; Friday - As for Monday; Saturday - At Stranraer. *Parcel Van P10* : Monday - From Dumfries as for van P9 on Wednesday; Tuesday - At Dumfries; Wednesday - From Dumfries as for van P9 on Monday; Thursday - At Stranraer; Friday - From Stranraer as for Monday; Saturday - At Dumfries. P9 and P10 will work alternate weeks. *Parcel Van P8* : Monday - Dumfries to Dalbeattie, Castle Douglas and return Friday, to Dumfries circular serving also intermediate inclusive; villages en route; Saturday - Dumfries to Kirkcudbright via Dalbeattie and Castle Douglas, returning to Dumfries via Castle Douglas, serving intermediate

villages en route. *Parcel Van P11* : Monday - Dumfries to Carlisle via Lockerbie, Annan and Gretna serving intermediate villages en route; Tuesday - At Carlisle; Wednesday - From Carlisle via Gretna and Annan and direct to Dumfries; Thursday - Dumfries to Annan via Lockerbie, returning direct to Dumfries from Annan; Friday - As for Monday; Saturday - At Carlisle. *Parcel Van P6* : Monday - From Carlisle as for P11 on Wednesday; Tuesday - As for P11 on Thursday; Wednesday - As for P11 on Monday; Thursday - At Carlisle; Friday - As for Monday; Saturday - At Dumfries. P11 and P6 will operate as above alternate weeks. *Parcel Van P2* : Spare as required at Dumfries. Collection and delivery in Dumfries; Monday to Friday inclusive. Each morning, the van operating the Dumfries, Lockerbie, Annan and Carlisle Service will deliver and collect in the following district in Dumfries : Hoods Loaning - Gorrills Limited; English Street - Morton Bros. and Wright Bros.; Loreburn Street - R.Morrin and Sons; Munches Street - W.B. Anderson, W Grieve and Sons; Loreburn Street - W.W. Ross; Queensberry Street - Solway Co., J.W.Ferguson and Son, and Armstrong, Ironmonger; High Street - Rankin, Dinwiddie, Macgowan and Binn Limited; and, in addition, any other orders received for goods in premises in above area; On completion of calls, to return direct to Eastfield Garage via English Street, Leafield Road and Brooms Road. On Tuesday and Thursday only, Messrs. D.Hunter & Co., Brooms Road, Dumfries, - for Lockerbie and Annan traffic. All other collections will be for goods for all van areas. Van operating Dalbeattie and Castle Douglas Monday to Friday : Delivery and collection in the following area; Bank Street - Maxwell and McNish;

Leyland Titan WW 8605 was one of eight TD1 models purchased from Yorkshire Woollen District in 1940, together with six similar vehicles from Glasgow Corporation and a solitary Leyland Lion from Ribble Motor Services. Numbered 259, with Caledonian, it lasted a further three years after the takeover of Caledonian, being sold in 1952. (Alan B. Cross)

The haulage fleet operated under the control of the Ministry of War Transport during the hostilities. Albion ML55 H8 (VS 2498) is seen outside Salisbury Street depot in October 1943. Despite the enforced austerity the vehicle still carries a streamlined paint scheme and various embellishments on its radiator, the star being particularly popular in south and west Scotland on buses and trucks and is occasionally still seen. (Douglas Harper Collection)

Photographs of accidents were often taken for insurance purposes. This wartime view shows an unidentified Dennis Lancet II, probably one of the 1938 batch, overturned at Skippers Bridge near Langholm. The bus swerved to avoid an oncoming truck and tumbled down to the river's edge; tragically lives were lost. A young Michael Hayton was sent to assist in the recovery - he noticed all but the destination blind glass had been broken and remembers even that being smashed as they tried to recover the bus. Despite the serious damage it returned to service. (Jim Calder)

Irish Street - Marr; Maxwelltown - Payne, Carnation Co., etc.; Whitesands - C.O.C. Office and obtain there any further 'phoned orders received wither through the Whitesands Office or Eastfield Office for collection on return journey to Eastfield and, in addition, Leafield Road - Magneto Co. On Tuesday and Thursday only - Messrs. D.Hunter & Co., Brooms Road, Dumfries, or traffic for Dalbeattie - Castle Douglas Area. Saturdays - All deliveries and collections as required for traffic for Dalbeattie, Castle Douglas, Kirkcudbright Area. *Stranraer Van* : Mondays, Wednesdays and Fridays only - D.Hunter & Co., Brooms Road, Dumfries - traffic for all areas.

The final competitor on the Carlisle - Longtown road was purchased when Lochinvar Motor Services were acquired in December 1939, though the application had been made for the licence in May of that year. The name Lochinvar is associated with the Longtown through Walter Scott's poem about a young Knight of this name who stole his bride from the Grahams of Netherby, a village some 3 miles from Longtown. They began services with Albion 14 seaters progressing to bigger 30 seaters, the first of the larger vehicles being purchased in 1926. They ran from a terminus between the Town Hall and Robertsons (later to become Binns),

vehicles operating in red with a distinctive bright red tartan band and had a a registered office at Eden Bridge, Carlisle. Four Albions, and a Dennis Lancet were acquired, together with services from Carlisle to Longtown via Blackbank on which they had competed with Percival's and a Carlisle - Gretna service on Sundays (Lochinvar had a contract for supplying newspapers into Gretna and there was a special run on a Sunday morning). Lochinvar had also previously operated a daily return journey between Longtown and Newcastleton, which connected at Longtown with the Carlisle service, but this had ceased before the takeover. Also acquired with the business was a garage at Longtown, which was to prove invaluable as a base for serving the mushrooming Military and Government establishments. Up to this time, Caledonian had garaged a vehicle at the Auction Mart overnight in the town. In the same year, Caledonian began a re-engining programme, replacing the petrol engined units with Gardner oil engines. First to be treated were the two Leyland Lion LT5s acquired from North Western Road Car Co. (232/3 ; XJ 827/8), which, together with Lion LT5 152 (SM9502) were re-engined with Gardner 4LW units. The pace of conversion would have been much quicker had wartime shortages not frustrated their plans.

The delivery of sixteen Bedford OWBs in 1942/3 gave some relief to the hard-pressed fleet. Many were employed transporting workers to the multitude of factories and military establishments throughout Caledonian's operating territory, but some were employed on services, particularly post-war. All were withdrawn immediately by "Western", most seeing subsequent service with contractors. 280 (FSM 451) saw service with Loch Lomond and Loch Katrine Motor services, linking with the pleasure sailings on both lochs.

Purchases continued apace in 1940; nine TD1s with Leyland lowbridge bodies were purchased from Yorkshire Woollen District, Dewsbury (numbered 259-67 ; WW8605, HD4360, WW8606, HD3698, 3700-1, 4361-3) six similar vehicles came from Glasgow Corporation (268-73 ; GE2454/88/94/84/87/58) and a further Leyland Lion PLSC3 (numbered 274 ; TE4563) came from Ribble Motor Services (although it was new to Furness Motor Omnibus Company). The company managed to convert two of the batch of Titans received (264/7) to oil engines, this time Gardner 5LW.

The War Department visited during 1940 to requisition vehicles and Caledonian, knowing that the war department representatives had a reputation for requisitioning the most modern vehicles in the fleet, ensured these would all be out on the day of their visit to Edinburgh. This worked to an extent, the first four selected being vehicles over ten years old but the last two were a mere four years old, being selected as they returned to the garage. The vehicles requisitioned were : 46 and 50 (SW 2551 and 6743), two of the original 1927 Leyland Lions bought new, 134 and 139 (DS1594 and DS1690) 1930 Thornycrofts acquired with Harper's business and 184 and 186 and 1936 Dennis Lancets (BSM830 and 832).

The Kent coast was evacuated in 1940 with the real threat of invasion and, as a result, the major operator East Kent found themselves with a surplus of vehicles. Caledonian were ready

takers, providing higher capacity replacements for the vehicles requisitioned by the war department. They arranged for the hire of a mixture of Leyland Titans late in that year and Caledonian drivers were involved in the collection, which took 2-3 days to complete. With sign-posts being removed as a wartime measure, the journey was doubly difficult. Both petrol engined and diesel engined vehicles were hired at the rate of £1.15.6d per bus per day. A total of seven vehicles were collected, two petrol engined Titan TD1s JG1412 and JG1621 of 1930/1 respectively, fitted with Leyland L27/24R bodies and five Leyland Titan TD5s of 1938 with Brush L27/26R bodies. The TD5s are remembered for their anti-splinter netting covering the windows, as well as their excellent condition; not surprisingly, the vehicles were well liked by Caledonian staff. They ran for Caledonian for over a year and a half, their return starting in July 1942. The East Kent vehicles were the last arrivals for over a year, no new or secondhand vehicles appearing in 1941, reflecting the general "drying up" of vehicle availability.

Wartime timetables removed route maps, but nevertheless reflected a number of interesting changes. The Lockerbie - Bankshill

Former Eastern National AEC Regent 239 (VX4902) was the other vehicle given new Roe bodywork in 1942. Built virtually to peacetime standards, the only hint of its wartime origin was the white-painted wing tips and guard rails and its grey roof. Its registration number plate and headlamps are still to be fitted, but the destination blind is already in situ and set for the Edinburgh - Moffat - Dumfries route. (Chas.H.Roe)

The second of two vehicles which were despatched to Roe of Leeds in 1942 for fitting with a body built to pre-war design was Dennis Lancet I 254 (EPD594). It's livery was also of peacetime standards and even included lining out, although its fleet name was of the type fitted after the war which was originally not outlined.   (Chas.H.Roe)

short workings were extended to the hamlet of Puddockhole by 1939. A service between Carlisle and the city boundary at Kingstown was advertised in the June 1939 timetable; in practice the service was simply a summary of the Caledonian routeswhich served Kingstown on their way north. All except the Rockliffe/ Castletown services operated through Kingstown and by virtue of their licences were allowed to pick up within the city boundary. A peculiarity of these licences was that buses operating from the City Boundary on the Longtown route charged 1/5d to the city, a relic of Percivals days, whilst buses running in from Dumfries and Lockerbie charged 1d. This caused considerable arguments between passengers and conductors and to try to reduce confusion Longtown buses displayed a red board in the nearside window to differentiate vehicles on this route from the Lockerbie and Dumfries services. However, the arguments continued and not just between conductors and passengers......... Ribble operated the local service between the City Centre and Kingstown, having acquired this route from an independant called Foster. A dispute arose between Ribble and Caledonian around the carriage of "point to point" passengers within the city boundary. The dispute ended with Caledonian agreeing to a 2d minimum fare between Kingstown and Carlisle, which at last removed the confusion for intending passengers and, no doubt, encouraged them to use the Ribble local services. The Carlisle - Longtown service had one Market day Saturday only journey in either direction diverted to the east off the A7 via Jerriestown and Barrackstown, operating from 1939 until 1946/7. At other times, residents simply walked to the stop at Westlinton Cross Roads or Blackford Church. Another diversion not marked in the timetables for security reasons was the deviation of the 6pm bus to Longtown, which travelled up the Gretna road from Kingstown to serve 14 MU RAF Carlisle. The purpose was to pick up workmen, after which the bus returned to the normal route via Harker Road Ends where more MU workmen would be picked up from Number 3 Site. This diversion could, on occasions, be pointless as the the bus was full leaving Carlisle, and indeed if it did stop some workmen simply shoved the conductress aside in pure frustration and crammed into the bus.

Some examples of the Caledonian service operations in Carlisle during the war follow. The 6pm buses were always busy; the blackout meant that most shops closed at 5.30pm and shop assistants and shoppers, as well as workmen made for the departures to Longtown, Gretna and Langholm etc. A "blind eye" was turned by the friendly inspector at Carlisle to overcrowding, which is more than could be said for of one particular conductress, who was notorious for the practice of stopping people getting on and so many complaints were received that she was sacked on at least three occasions. She never took these sackings seriously, however, and always turned up for work the next day! The overcrowding was resolved to an extent by giving priority to workers who possessed 12 journey tickets; shoppers were made aware of the priority and started to travel home on earlier buses. Despite the tribulations, the public generally appreiciated the efforts the company made. With the exception of the conductress mentioned, staff were very pleasant; the inspector called Ernie who ran Carlisle depot is recalled as being like a "pleasant Sergeant Major". Further west in the Annan area, Irish Navvies were employed to build the I.C.I. Broom Camp and were transported by "Caley" to the camp until the

construction of a platform on the line between Annan and Dumfries. One double decker conducted by the late Sid Young had over 100 on board, the navvies refusing to wait for the second bus.

The Leyland Cub 209 (DSM452) was garaged at Lockerbie during the war and Dumfries crews met up with it when providing workers transport to the Broom Camp. This involved a layover for shift changes and the bus was very popular because it possessed a heater. However, the staff through the notice boards received a straight-forward message indicating that the running of an engine on layover was not permitted; fuel supplies were scarce! As war tightened its grip, the petrol pump at Penpont was requisitioned by the Land Agent Scottish Command later in the war to illustrate the point.

Service changes during 1940 involved the Edinburgh - Moffat via Biggar being cut back to Biggar; the service was never reinstated, the section linking Abington and Moffat using the A74 being abandoned. Also, by November 1940, the Dumfries - Moniaive service had some of their journeys routed via Newtonairds, other journies continuing to serve Burnhead. The Company was also involved in the distribution of evacuated children to Reception Centres in the Southern Counties of Scotland at the outbreak of war. A "considerable" number of vehicle journeys were made from the railway stations carrying children evacuated from Glasgow.One operation involved the collecting of evacuees from Locharbriggs Station on the outskirts of Dumfries and transporting them to a hall at Crocketford on the Castle Douglas Road, where the children were served tea and distibuted to new families. Similarly, the evacuation of Norway took place in 1940, Dumfries becoming a reception centre for the 2000+ evacuees. Civilians were brought to the Burgh in large numbers, the Burgh eventually becoming the Ordnance Headquarters of the Norwegian Army and Norwegian soldiers were also billeted in the District. Caledonian was extensively involved in their transportation.

In the Dumfries area, Mrs. Lauder, who was a conductress during the war recalls looking out for regular passengers on the country roads at night. Locations were also called out to passengers. More severe problems were encountered with the fog which could lie in the Dalveen Pass north-west of Thornhill on the Edinburgh route. She would lean out the door with a hooded torch, with a finger poised on the bell to indicate to the driver when he was too close to the side of the road. Some conductresses also had small hooded lamps, which they affixed to their uniform to allow them to see more clearly the tickets they were punching. Incidentally, they had small metal plates made to keep the tickets flag in their racks; bent tickets would not slot into the Willebrew punch! Heavy snow could also reek havoc to the operations and in the winter of 1940, snowdrifts stopped the operation of the Dumfries - Edinburgh via Dalveen Pass route. Staff were reallocated and one duty was the Dumfries - Dalbeattie route. However, the outbound bus got stuck at Kirkgunzeon one Saturday night and the inbound bus had to turn back to Dalbeattie where the crew and bus were stranded for a week! On the property side, the old Stranraer garage at Trade Street was let on the 7th February 1941 to the Ministry of Works and on the plus side 7 Castle Terrace, Edinburgh was purchased in June with the intention of moving from the rented premises next door. However, this was immediately let to the Womens Voluntary Service.

The original Weymann coach bodies removed from 170-3 were sturdy enough to be re-fitted and that from 171 was bodied onto a second-hand AEC Regal acquired from Blake of Dunstable, via wartime allocation, in 1944. 299 (TM 8807) headed a line of four vehicles, a post-war Bristol L5G and two Dennis Lancets, awating departure from the Castle Terrace terminus in Edinburgh in October 1948. Note the curious mixture of headlamps on 299. (Douglas Harper Collection)

When Bill McGowan started at Wigtown in 1943, there were four PLSC3 Lions (58, 60, 61 and 98 registrations SM6963/6/7 and 75 respectively), the latter being an ex.South of Scotland machine. Other vehicles were LT5 Lions numbers 151/2 (SM9501/2), plus Lioness 104 registered SM7018 (another ex.South of Scotland vehicle), two Albion lorries H14/6 (OS3890/5) and one parcel van P12 (SM8318), the Carlisle van at that time being P13, former Leyland Lion bus 55 (SM6920). Number 152 was known locally as the "Bomber", due to the noise from its Gardner 4LW engine which had been fitted prewar as part of the re-engining programme which involved installing Gardner oil units in place of the original petrol engines. When diesel engined vehicles were garaged at Wigtown, they had to be sent to Whithorn for refuelling, a diesel pump not being installed at Wigtown until after the war. Both 151/2 had longitudinal seats to allow a greater carrying capacity, but also to allow them to be put into use as emergency ambulances for which, thankfully, the need did not arise. Later, they received 153/4 (SM9503/4) Lions with new bodies fitted in 1943 and known locally as having "Bristol" bodies (see later for details). Buses 232/3 were transferred to Wigtown later in the war and were again used on early shift work having self starters, one being based as a "sleeper" at Newton Stewart. Bill McGowan started as a garage store attendant sweeping out, refuelling and washing vehicles (if there was time for the latter). He learnt to drive by shunting the buses around, the first bus he drove being Lioness 104, which had originated with South of Scotland Motor Company. On the subject of seating changes, quite a few single deckers were re-seated during the war to increase their capacity. Leyland Lions 47/8 and 71/2 had their layout changed to 30 longitudinal seats by the end of 1943 to enable a further 30 standing passengers to be carries whilst Lion 99 became a 31-seater, 64 had its seating increased to 32 and AEC coaches 163-5 together with Thornycroft Cygnets 166/7 were converted from 28 to 32 seats.

As an illustration of wartime activity around Whithorn and Wigtown, there was an Anti-Aircraft force at Burghmuir, an RAF Aerodrome at Baldoon, and RAF camp at Kidstall and a Territorial Camp at Burrow Head which had opened in 1938. I.C.I. had a munitions factory at Carsegowan producing nitro-cellulose; this plant, in common with many others was on 24 hour production, requiring buses to support every shift changeover. Allocation of vehicles was important where buses were required for early morning runs where only the driver was available; the key requirement was for a bus with a self starter. Thus, AEC Regal 164 (SM9978) was kept at Whithorn for these early morning shift run to Carsegowan. At that time the other Regals in the batch, which had once been the pride and joy of the Edinburgh run were at Annan (163 ; SM9977) and Stranraer (165 ; SM9979).

Caledonian were also involved in the regular troop movement from Stranraer to Burrow Head with a requirement for up to eight buses. Connections were also made with trains at Whithorn station at the terminus of the line from Newton Stewart, again needing up to eight buses. Indeed, the station platform at Whithorn had to be lengthened to allow for the speedy unloading of larger troop trains. On one trip to Burrow Head from Stranraer with Willie McDowall at the wheel the bus was literally half filled with soldier's kit. The bus faltered in the icy conditions on the climb up the Rocks of Garchie near Auchenmalg Inn. The bus was emptied of soldiers and kit and they pushed the vehicle up the hill, before clambering back in to resume their journey. Traffic between Baldoon RAF Camp and Newton Stewart was particularly heavy with service personnel seeking entertainment. Though the Whithorn line carried some of the traffic through the nearest station at Kirkinner, much passenger traffic was carried on the buses. So full were some of the vehicles at weekends that the conductor sat on the nearside mudguard! At the same time, the driver would also have a passenger in his cab and on one occasion, 32-seat AEC Regal 164 had 99 tickets issued on one of these runs. The Annan run with a double decker from the Broom Camp pales into insignificance by comparison. Whithorn and Wigtown could have made good use of double deckers but they stayed in the eastern area where the need was judged to be greater.

Blackout conditions created their own particular problems as the following story illustrates. Whithorn Main Street is a wide thoroughfare which narrows at either end. At the southern end the road narrows due to property on either side. A white line was painted around the property and adjacent pole on the east side of the road to guide traffic into the narrow outlet. However, this did not stop one bus filled with Service personnel from RAF Kidstall Camp clattering into the poll at the side of the house one night. Willie McDowall and his family had moved into this house and his daughter well remembers the loud noise and his reaction. He realised immediately what had happened, dropped the book he was reading and ran outside. Fluid was pouring onto the road from the coved in front of the bus and after quickly helping the driver out of his cab and assisting passengers out of the bus he ordered the family out of the house, suspecting the fluid to be petrol. In the event, it turned out to be water from the damaged radiator!

At Stranraer depot vehicles and drivers were away from Stranraer for as much as a week at a time with military personnel. Destinations were kept secret until the drivers reported for duty. Operation closer to home included a service from Stranraer to the Wig Bay RAF Depot at Solburn via Auchneel and Craichmore, leaving Stranraer at 9pm and returning from Solburn at midnight. The service transported locals to dances at the Officers Mess and, as a matter of interest, continued after the end of the war. In September 1942, the Tilling and British Automobile Traction Company was broken up, Caledonian becoming a subsidiary of Thomas Tilling Ltd. The grouping of the two organisations had been an uneasy one and differences of opinion around policy, not helped by alternating chairmanship between Tilling and BET every year had contributed to the split. Its impact was little, if any, on Caledonian which had more immediate pressing matters.

Some relief was received by the hard pressed fleet with the delivery of three "unfrozen" vehicles, as part of the authorization given by the Ministry of War Transport for the building of vehicles on which work had begun when production was frozen or for which sufficient stock was held to allow building to take place. A Dennis Lancet II with Strachan bodywork (one of a total of twenty Lancets released, most being bodied by Strachan with utility bodywork, numbered 277 ; FSM435) and two Bristol L5Gs (of a total of fifteen, numbered 275/6 ; FSM380/1) with East Lancashire Coachbuilders

A poor quality photograph is the only one which has been discovered of one of the 1942 Bristol L5Gs with its original East Lancs body.

The first of two Thornycroft Handys was posed for a publicity shot, supposedly operating on the Edinburgh route, though they never strayed north-eastwards on services to the capital.
(K.A.Jenkinson Collection)

bodywork, in this case to full peace time standard, made up the three. The Bristols were part of an order for five placed by Rotherham Corporation; Caledonian received two, Aberdare Urban District Council received one and Rotherham received two. The allocation of Bristol and Dennis chassis was a sensible move, even if the bodywork carried was new to Caledonian. The body of the Lancet was also to peactime standards, using a destination box display identical to the style supplied to Aldershot and District.

Further allocations of vehicles were twelve of the utility Bedford OWB chassis fitted with S.M.T. 32-seat bodywork (numbered 278-89 ; FSM449-54 and FSM506-7/14-17) reflecting the important war work with which Caledonian was engaged. The Bedford OWBs were primarily intended for use on workers transport, two known to have been based in Lockerbie, four in Annan with some at Dumfries, as well as Carlisle, Moniaive and Penpont. Despite their wartime grey livery and wooden slatted seats they were welcomed by drivers, having light steering and being easy to drive. Caledonian probably requested an allocation of single deckers, rather than double deckers, in the belief that the latter would only be required for the duration of the war for transport of workmen to the many factories and military establishments. One run was from Dumfries via Shore Road to Dalbeattie, three times daily to the Dynamite factory. Other important workers journies were to the I.C.I. Broom Camp at Powfoot and the dynamite factory at Drungans. Lockerbie had two important workers services, one being via Corrie, Wamphray, Ecclefechan and Eaglesfield to I.C.I. Broom Camp and the second operating via Ecclefechan, Eaglesfield and Brydekirk to I.C.I. Drungans. The latter service involved a night shift duty where the crew, in theory, deposited their passengers at Drungans, then returned to Eastfield Road where they were expected to assist in cleaning out buses. More often than not, a sleep was managed on the bus instead, if they could get away with it! The Bedfords at Moniaive and Penpont outstations were driven by lady drivers, one of the regulars at Penpont being 283 (FSM454). Their main duties were transporting schoolchildren, operation of the Thornhill Station - Penpont - Moniaive service and the Penpont - Kier - Dumfries service, as well as carrying shift workers to the I.C.I. Factory at Drungans. One frightening incident involving one of the OWBs was recalled by May Davers, one of the female drivers at Penpont during a return journey from Thornhill Station. The train had been late and as she "put her foot down", one of the front wheels flew off. Her reports of a squeeling wheel at lunchtime had been dismissed; reports after that incident were listened to carefully! The two OWBs allocated to Carlisle had as one of their main duties a run to take Polish refugees to work from Hallburn Army Billets to a quarry between Roadhead and Newcastleton.

A total of 30 buses were allocated purely to war workers transport. Twelve AEC Regent ST-type double deckers were hired from London Transport, the first five (ST239, ST398, ST605, ST762 and ST778 ; GH552, GK3118, GK5444, GK5605, GK5630 and GK5636 respectively) arriving in August 1942, with the remaining seven arriving in November (ST380, ST387, ST421, ST424, ST454, ST501, ST585 ; GK3026, 3120, 3095, 3094, 3080, 5306 and 5407 respectively) costing £408.12.8d per month. They operated unnumbered on, amongst other duties, Dumfries town services, especially the Locharbriggs route and workers services to the aerodrome beyond Heathall and on the Lockerbie route, a couple of the vehicles being garaged at Lockerbie for a period. The regular allocation of double deckers resulted in the roof at Lockerbie garage

having to be raised. They kept their London Transport livery and fleetname, destinations being provided by means of paper stickers in the nearside lower deck window, a common practice to this day. The STs are remembered on the "plus side" for their good condition, though on the negative side for having no cab door, bomb proof gauze on the windows on both decks (with notices inside advising they were there for passengers protection) and poor climbing ability. The hiring of the STs allowed the return of the East Kent Titans, TD1 JG1412 and TD5 JG9926 being returned in July, the other TD1 JG1621 was returned in September, whilst the remaining TD5s JG9924/8 were despatched home in October and the last, JG9925/7, went back south in November.

Caledonian continued to be short of vehicles during 1942 due to ever increasing military and wartime factory transport requirements. To further assist, six Dennis Lancet Is of 1933/4 vintage with Eastern Counties B34F bodywork were hired from West Yorkshire Road Car at £25 per bus per month, five of the six coming from the Northern Ireland Road Transport Board to whom they had been on loan since April 1941, the sixth coming from the NIRTB back via West Yorkshire. The loan was officially from 9th November 1942. All six were still in West Yorkshire livery when received with their fleetnames painted out in black. Two of the Lancets (YG4704 and YG3060) were returned to West Yorkshire Road Car in December but the remaining four were retained and purchased from West Yorkshire for the sum of £150 each in September 1943. The vehicles were numbered 295-8, registered YG3043, 4700/1, 5723. Two Leylands were also hired at the same hiring rate as the Lancets of West Yorkshire from United Automobile Services for use at Carlisle, operating from December 1942 until June 1943. The vehicles were United's LL1 (TY4671), a Leyland Lion PLSC3 with Leyland 31-seat bodywork new in June 1928, and which had originated with County Motors of Stakeford and LT4.2

The oldest of the four ECOC-bodied Dennis Lancet Is purchased from West Yorkshire Road Car Co., 295 (YG3043) passed with its sisters to Western SMT in 1949 only to be withdrawn from service during the following year. Fitted by Caledonian with a BET-style destination box, it is seen here in Darlington soon after its sale to J.Maude of Richmond in 1951.   (K.A.Jenkinson Collection)

ECOC-bodied Dennis Lancet I YG4700, one of six buses of this type hired by Caledonian from West Yorkshire Road Car Co. is seen here in Northern Ireland where it had been on loan from March 1942 until its arrival with Caledonian in November of that year. Still wearing its original owner's red & cream livery to which a grey roof had been added, and with its fleet name painted out, it retained its metal 'bible-type' destination board holder in its front roof dome. (K.A.Jenkinson Collection)

Leyland Tiger 172 (BSM 172) was one of eight Tigers rebodied with Eastern Coach Works bodies which had actually been built pre-war and stored in kit form at Dumfries until their fitment in 1942. The high nearside front window was built to suit fitment on the Bristol L5Gs on which these bodies were originally destined for. The photograph taken at Whitley Bay in 1946 makes an interesting comparison with that of sister 170 (BSM 173) with its original body. *(Roy Marshall)*

A Leyland Tiger TS4 was acquired from Grey Green Coaches of London, numbered 301 (JJ 8823) and fitted with what appeared to be a Alexander body of mid' 30s origin. *(Roy Marshall)*

(DC9385), a Leyland Lion LT1, also with Leyland bodywork which was new in July 1929 and had originated with Smith Safeway Services Ltd of Middlesborough. Local operator James Clark and Sons of Glencaple also hired their bus SC4334, a Leyland bodied Lion LT1 built in 1929 which had originated with SMT. This was hired between December 1942 and March 1943.

The acquisition of this variety of second hand stock must have been challenging to say the least to Caledonian's engineering department at Eastfield Road. Apart from the general policy of converting petrol engined machines to oil engines which had started in 1939, the company was forced to embark on a large scale programme of overhaul, rebuilding and, in some cases, rebodying of both the second hand vehicles acquired and their own fleet. Dependant on the condition of the vehicles and the PSV examiner's requirements, the treatment varied but the aim was always the same; to keep the maximum number of the fleet on the road. The Government had decreed that certain coachbuilders were permitted to carry out rebuilding and, in some cases, rebodying work. One of these, Croft Engineering of Glasgow became heavily involved with Caledonian in both these types of activity and continued its association after the war. With Caledonian's own workshops overstretched and no doubt lacking much of the raw material required to carry out extensive rebuilding work, the company turned to a number of coachbuilders to assist them to keep their fleet on the road. The extent of rebuilding depended on the condition of the bodywork, but one general rule followed was the removal of side destination indicators from single deckers fitted with this layout during rebuilding, whilst second hand double deckers had their destination blind apertures rebuilt to take the large destination

screens. In general, vehicles rebuilt were also repainted into wartime grey livery with at least four different shades being applied depending on the coachbuilder involved. The major rebuilding and rebodying programme started in earnest in 1941 and, where supplies allowed, conversions to oil engine continued.

TD1s 235/6/8 (TM3824/43 and 3735) were sent to Pickerings of Wishaw for rebuilding in 1941; at the same time, 235 had its Leyland petrol engine replaced with a Gardner 5LW unit in 1941. The two AEC Regents 239 (VX4902) and 240 (TM6307) had AEC 6-cylinder engines fitted in August and October of that year in place of their petrol units. 240 had its body completely rebuilt at Dumfries, amounting to virtually a new body being constructed, the only complete rebuild known to have been carried out at Dumfries. Having received an oil engine, 239 (VX4902) was despatched to Roe, followed in 1942 by Dennis Lancet 254 (EPD594) for the fitment of new and very stylish Roe bodies to full peacetime standards (apart from the obligatory masked lighting and white painted mudguards). The body on VX4902 was very similar to that fitted on pre-war West Riding TD4s and was the only double decker with five-bay bodywork in the fleet during the war. Three coachbuilders were involved in the rebuilding work for that year. Pickering rebuilt Leyland Lion 50 (SW 6743) which had been returned by the War Department the worst for wear, together with 99 (SM7208) and TD1 237 (TM3846). Croft Engineering repaired Lions 46, 48 and 54 (SW2551, 6741 and SM6919) respectively and Willowbrook rebuilt Dennis Lancets 157/62 (SM9971/6) and rebodied TD1s 262/4/7 (HD3698, 3701 and 4361) respectively. The rebodying allowed the seating capacity to be increased from 51 to 55, which must have been some help, whilst further measures to

increase capacity were taken, this time by increasing standing room. Finally, AEC Regal 164 (SM9978) received a Gardner 5LW unit. One truck also received attention, H34 (BGB165) being repaired by Penmans of Dumfries.

The principle applied by C.Bloomfield, Chief Engineer of that period, was that where a regular problem was encountered preventative action should be taken to ensure this did not occur on other vehicles in the fleet. Some actions were pretty desperate as material shortages bit hard; petrol engined vehicles were known to be running temporarily on three cylinders. An example of a persistant problem was the cracking of the differential housing which resulted in the "prop shaft" dropping onto the road in extreme cases. The company's own blacksmith produced metal supporting ties and a programme of fitment to batches of vehicles was instituted. To illustrate another example, Dennis Lancets were found to be prone to suffering chassis breakages towards the front and strengthening plates were fitted as they visited Eastfield Road. Gardner-engined vehicles were considered to be particularly valuable and incidents involving damage to them were viewed very seriously. One such incident occured at Annan Garage where a Gardner engined Titan parked outside overnight refused to start. The bus was found to be frozen solid and, after consultation with Eastfield Road, the water jackets were removed and the vehicle was towed in an attempt to start it. Efforts to unfreeze the radiator proved very difficult and, after much scratching of heads a solution was found by sealing two thirds of the radiator tubes and, combined with the fitting of blanking plate using a flattened out cardboard box used for transporting cigarettes, refitting the radiator to the bus. The vehicle was forced to run in this manner for two months until the radiator could receive more permanant attention and, as a result of the origins of the blanking plate, was referred to by the workers at the Broom Camp as "the Woodbine Bus". As they became available, the more modern "COVRAD" replacement radiators were fitted to the Titans which had been fitted with Gardner engines. The Coventry Radiator Company produced them for Titans, and Lions built in the period 1928-1932, some of their Lion fleet also receiving these in later years. Radiators were a particular cause for concern, the Scottish Metal Works being involved in working "flat out" in reconditioning radiators. The major problem in Winter was that of freezing, anti-freeze being unknown in those days. Drainage of the radiator was never altogether successful, as some water remained in the radiator tubes. Such was the backlog of work at the Metal Works that Caledonian sent along two of their own mechanics to assist. Sub-depots were allocated mechanics to assist their operation, one duty being 2 days at Lockerbie and 3 days at Annan one week, then 3 days at Lockerbie and 2 days at Annan the next week.

Some of the "defect" reports from crews could be alarming; one report came into Eastfield Road advising that the rear bench seat of a bus was regularly wet during and after rain, despite their being no obvious sign of leakage from windows. Further investigation uncovered the fact that the rear wheel arch was rusted

through and water from the rear tyre was splashing through! Equally, not all maintenance exercises went according to plan; one "decker" returned after rebodying lost its back axle on the first night back into service on the Dumfries to Lockerbie road. Brake testing was undertaken on a set route, which involved the climbing of Bankend Road near the hospital and the descent of Stonehouse Loaning. Skid marks all over the road provided evidence of the testing! One problem with testing was the need to remember not to negotiate the bridge at the bottom of Eastfield Road with a double decker. One vehicle out on test was stopped just as it began to scrape the roof of the bridge and had to be extracted by letting the air out of all the tyres!

Four further Bedford OWBs this time with Duple bodywork arrived (291-4 ; FSM623-6) in 1943, easing the vehicle situation and allowing the hirings from United and Clark to be terminated. An eleven year old Dennis Lancet carrying a B32R body by its previous operator, United Counties was acquired, the vehicle having been new to J.Meadows and Son, Barton Seagrove and passing to United Counties in December 1938 (290 ; NV1361). The pace of rebuilding and rebodying hotted up further in 1943. Croft Engineering repaired and rebuilt Leyland Lions 53, 57, 60, 61, 64-6, 98, 101, 218, 219 and 224 (SM6918, 63, 66, 67, 8315-7, 6975, 7012 and RU8055-7 respectively), converting 64 from 30 to 32 seats at the same time. Croft also repaired Thornycroft 149 (SM9335) and Dennis Lancet II 210 (DSM453), as well as Albion truck H17 (OS4069). Two local coachbuilders were employed, with James Bendall and Sons of Carlisle rebuilding Titan 258 (KR6531), whilst Penman of Dumfries rebuilt Dennis Lancet I 161 (SM9975) and also repaired Albion truck H26 (YS9146). A longer journey was made by Lancet IIs 177-8 and 187 (BSM 823/4 and 833 respectively) and Titans 256, 259-261 and 263/4 (KR1731, WW8605, HD4360, WW8606 and HD3700 and 4362 respectively) which travelled to Willowbrook for rebuilding. Tha batch of Dennis Lancets starting at 174 all had their internally-sliding doors altered to slide externally during their rebuilding except for 180 (BSM826) which retained its original feature. Burlingham of Blackpool were also involved, rebuilding Lancet I 160 (SM9974). Leylands 153/4 (SM9503/4), 170-3 (BSM170-3) and 232/3 (XJ 827/8) were sent to ECW for rebodying. These ECW rebodies have been the subject of much speculation over the years, principally because in the case of 170-3 no record could be found of body numbers allocated to Caledonian at the time. Also, the style of bodywork carried on these rebodies had not been produced since 1940 and body information from ECW, which had been evacuated to Irthlingborough in Northamptonshire away from the vulnurable east coast, was "patchy". Photographs show a high nearside front window of the design fitted to prewar Bristol L chassis and similar to the two supplied to Caledonian prior to the outbreak of war (242/3 ; ESM537/8). Herein lies one of the clues; the company in fact placed an order for a total of ten Bristol "L" chassis with ECW, but only the two vehicles 242/3 were actually received. The balance of eight chassis were never received but the bodies remained on order

The body from 173 was fitted to another secondhand AEC Regal acquired in 1944 (300 : GF481) which had originated with London Transport.   (Alan B. Cross)

and arrangements were made to have these supplied in CKD (completely knocked down) form. On arrival, the kits were stored in an old furniture van in the haulage shed at Eastfield Road, Dumfries. The kits were then transported back south late in 1942 to Irthlingborough and built up onto the eight chassis, 170-3 receiving 33 seat rear entrance bodies and the remainder 32-seat bodies. Indeed, regular progress payments in surviving Caledonian ledgers record these as "rebuilds", no doubt emphasizing the assembly. At the same time the original Eastern Counties body of 154 was fitted to Leyland Tiger 102 (SM8910), its Leyland body being scrapped. One oil engine conversion was carried out with a Gardner 5LW unit being fitted to 217 (WH2605).

Of necessity service developments continued to be kept to a minimum but one development was the extension in 1942 of the Queensbury Square to Sandside service through to the new Council housing development to the north of the town at Lincluden every ninety minutes. A couple more service developments took place in 1943. The first was a curiosity which appeared in the timetable for one seaon only, detailing a Rockliffe - Kippford - Dalbeattie service running once in either direction leaving at 8am Monday to Saturday, returning 5.24pm ex Dalbeattie Monday to Friday and 12.14pm on Saturday, perhaps initiated to assist in the movement of workers form these rural districts. The service disappeared from the timetable in 1944. The joint service with S.M.T. between Dumfries and Edinburgh via Moffat became Saturday only, no doubt to assist in fuel conservation on a strategically less important route. The terminus was also switched a year later to St Andrews square, the main departure point for S.M.T. services.

Petrol rationing was introduced in 1942. Indeed, a timetable of that year clearly explained the situation; "restricted supplies is one of the main difficulties confronting the operator today" and asked for help, appealing to the public not to stop the bus at intermediate points and avoid delays by queueing "in an orderly manner". Passengers were reminded "that a running engine in a stationary bus uses almost as much petrol as a moving one". Despite petrol rationing an official company document relating to the war record indicated that there had been no reduction in services due to petrol shortages. However, some pruning of non essential services had taken place, the Dumfries - Edinburgh via Moffat service being an example. The increase in "car mileage" at the same time was given as 90% per car mile, illustrating the increase in volume of traffic.

In common with other Tilling companies, Caledonian converted a number of vehicles to operate on producer gas, five being so converted by the end of 1943. Tilling management announced that "Caley" would have fourteen vehicles converted but this proved to be wildly optimistic. Although, regretably, records have not survived of which vehicles were modified to run on producer gas, it is understood that a maximum of seven were converted. One Lancet was converted by incorporating the producer unit into the rear of the bus. It is believed that the vehicle concerned was 178 (CSM824) which would had to have involved the replacement of its Gardner diesel unit with a petrol engine. However, the unit caught fire and the vehicle was converted back to a standard layout, with trailer. Four Lancets were converted, together with one Leyland Tiger (102, SM8970 - ex.South of Scotland Motor Company) and two Leyland Lion LT2s (believed to have been 70 ; SM8851 based at Carlisle and 73 ; SM8853 at Dumfries). Guidelines issued at the time suggested that operators should allocate converted vehicles to routes which avoided hills and which had turning circles at either end of the route. The recommendation was also that long layovers should also be avoided. To concentrate the vehicles near depots

Another bus to be rebodied by Croft was Leyland TD1 244 (WW7861) which, like several others, retained its original radiator although it had been fitted with a Leyland oil engine in place of its original petrol unit in 1946. Just visible in the background is similarly rebodied TD1 269 (GE2488) fitted with a replacement Covrad radiator.   The location and date is Carlisle depot, June 1950. (Alan B. Cross).

which could service the requirements of this form of propulsion, the buses were placed on the Dumfries - Annan - Carlisle route, a service which did have a number of hills, admittedly not severe and the Dumfries - Lockerbie service. Eighteen gas producer trailers were obtained from Bristol Tramways and Carriage Company and some were stored at the Gretna depot. The reversing manouvre at Whitesands was avoided by turning the buses in the wider portion of the road south of the bus stands and parking the buses facing upwards towards the town. Similarly, at Carlisle the vehicles could be turned within the garage. The converted vehicles proved extremely unpopular, being underpowered and temparamental. One story is told of a driver struggling with the gas trailer one day at Eastfield Road and, when asked by the manager if he was having difficulties, throwing the poker at him and suggesting that he should have a go! Such insubordination, it must be emphasized, was rare. The units were certainly a trial to staff and passengers alike. One "gas bus" was also allocated to the Brasswell - Janefield - Troqueer local service in Dumfries, starting at 9.30am. A standard bus maintained the service until this time, allowing the gas bus to be prepared for service. The service had two problems for which the official operating guidelines recommended avoidance. Firstly, the bus had to be reversed at both Brasswell and Janefield terminus; the former was relatively easy being a large farmyard entrance off the A75, but the latter was quite another matter. The bus had to be reversed from Dalbeattie Road into Park Place, a "blind" manouvre because the gas trailer could not be seen. Driver's caps were removed, ties loosened and sleeves rolled up for this difficult process under the directions of the conductress! On the plus side, drivers and conductors/conductresses were teamed up with "their bus" and the regular driver was given instruction on how to manouvre the vehicle and trailer. However, when the regular crew member was on holiday or sick, those unfortunate enough to have to provide cover had a very difficult time, as the majority had no training on these buses. To try to simplify the process, the Chief Engineer, Mr.Bloomfield, had a white line painted in the roadway to help in "lining up" the bus for the reversing manouvre. The second problem was a fairly steep climb to Troqueer up St Michaels' Bridge. Drivers not used to the gas powered buses would slow to a speed where it was quicker to walk. This resulted in a tap on the bulkhead window, signalling the need for the conductress to lean out of the door and switch on the petrol supply from the autovac until the hill was surmounted. Passengers would often prompt the conductress themselves with a request for the switching on of the "special fuel!". Some drivers just gave up, ran out of fuel and called the depot to be rescued in sheer desperation. Conducting was less arduous, although Mrs.Lauder, a conductress on this route, recalls her feet being toasted after a shift, caused by the heat given off from the floor area around the front bulkhead. Even the regular driver who could "coax" 30mph out of the bus when others were struggling to get 15mph had difficult days. When the gas producer was proving temperamental the timetable became impossible to maintain and in

situations where they were hopelessly behind schedule and "packed to the door", drastic action was occasionally called for. Mrs Lauder recalls that on their way out to Brasswell, where large queues were observed at Kirkowens Street and Noblehill waiting for the bus to return to Dumfries, the driver induced a backfire resulting in flames shooting from the gas trailer. Intending passengers quickly set off on foot for town, deciding that walking would be much safer! The trailer could extract its own particular brand of revenge. Mrs.Lauder's regular driver had been been given a new overcoat one day, his old coat complete with metal buttons on which the Caledonian name was proudly embellished, being replaced with one with plastic buttons as wartime shortages dictated. Being a gentleman who was always very smartly turned out, he was most upset about the poor quality buttons, but nevertheless happy to have a new coat to replace the one which had literally fell apart. On the same day, the gas producer started to become troublesome and outside St Michaels Church he stopped to give it some attention. The contraption back-fired covering him in a cloud of smoke and, worse still, throwing hot fuel onto his new coat, resulting in holes being burned into it! Nevertheless, despite these tribulations, statistics produced at the end of the war gave 51,919 miles operated by producer gas vehicles and a calculated 8,650 gallons had been saved, the average fuel consumption of the petrol engined vehicles being 6.5 miles per gallon. In mid September of 1944 the Government authorised the abandonment of gas producer powered vehicles and, in common with many other operartors, Caledonian quickly re-converted the vehicles and staff and management breathed a sigh of relief.

Secondhand purchases continued apace in 1944. Three AEC Regals were purchased, one coming from T.W.Blake of Dunstable (299 ; TM 8807), one from Tilling of London (302 ; ELY529) and one from the unusually named Loch Katrine Steamship Company of Callander, the latter bus having originated with London Transport (300 ; GF481). All three were rebodied with secondhand bodies from Caledonian's 170-3 (BSM170-3) which had been held in store. TM8807 is known to have had the body from 171, GF481 the body from 173 and ELY529 the body from either 170 or 172. A Leyland Tiger TS4 was also acquired from George Ewer's Grey Green Coaches (numbered 301 ; JJ8823), again being rebodied allegedly with a secondhand Leyland body but there is also speculation that the chassis was fitted with an Alexander body from the mid 'thirties.

Glasgow Corporation supplied the secondhand double deck intake in 1944, consisting of Caledonian's first Albion double deckers; four Venturers of 1935/6 with Glasgow built Cowieson bodies (303-6 ; YS2003/7/95 and 2100) and two fourteen year old TD1s, again with Cowieson bodies (numbered 307/8 ; GE7235 and GG907), the Leylands arriving in May and the Albions in November. Two of the London Tranport STs were returned in October as 1944 drew to close when the pressure eased a little (ST380 and ST454), with four more being released in February (ST239, ST605, ST763 and ST778), with a further two in June (ST387 and ST421), the final

Foden R6 H40 (UJ 499) was inherited with J. & J. Scott's haulage business in 1939. After serving as a truck, the vehicle was converted into a breakdown vehicle in 1946. Also photographed in October 1943 in Glasgow, the vehicle carried a mixture of masked and unmasked lights. (Douglas Harper Collection)

four being released in September/October (ST424, ST501 and ST585 in September with ST398 following in October).

Rebuilding, rebodying and re-engining continued. Leyland Lion 100 (SM6782) was re-engined for a second time, this time with a Gardner 4LW unit in place of its previous oil engine (presumably Leyland) which had been fitted in 1937. AEC Regals 163 and 165 (SM9977/9) were re-engined meanwhile with Gardner 5LW units and TD1 255 (KR1720) also had a 5LW engine fitted and was rebodied with a new 51-seat utility body by Croft. TD1s 217 (WH2605) and 269/72 (GE2488/7) were also rebodied by Croft with similar bodies. In addition to rebodies, Croft rebuilt Thornycrofts 207/8 (DSM450/1), as well as Lion 230 (TR6170) and overhauled Lions (226/7 ; RU7556 and 8451) and Albion haulage vehicle H39 (DSM971). Eastern Coach Works concentrated their efforts on the rebuilding of the entire batch of 1937 Dennis Lancets 198-206 (CSM766-74), together with the four Lancets bought from West Yorkshire 295-8 (YG3043, 4700/1 and 5723), plus 1938 Lancets 211-3 (DSM454-6). Burlingham only carried out one rebuild on Thornycroft 166 (SM9980), whilst Willowbrook rebuilt Lancets 174/9/81/5, (BSM820/5/7/31).

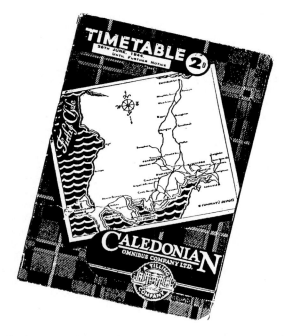

Despite the war and paper shortages etc., Caledonian continued to produce its timetable book, this issue being dated 26 June 1944.

Further acquisitions in 1945 brought four TD2s built in 1932 from Plymouth Corporation, two with Weymann bodies and two with locally built Mumford bodies (309-312 ; DR9843/4/52/48). That completed the purchase of secondhand double deckers increasing the number from four in 1938 to forty three in 1945. Numbers 309-11 were sent to ECW for rebuilding and 309 gained a Leyland oil engine together with unrebuilt 312; the return of these vehicles allowed the releasing of the last of the last of the ex.London STs. AEC oil engines were fitted into recently acquired AEC Regals 300 (GF481) and 302 (ELY529) and Lion LT5s 151/3/4 (SM9501/3/4) were re-engined with Gardner 4LW units. Number 151 was also overhauled by ECW and rebuilds were carried out on AEC Regals 165 (SM9979), Lancet 290 (NV1361) and TD1s 270/1/3 (GE2494, 2484 and 2458). Croft rebuilt Thornycroft 150 (SM9584) and overhauled TD1 307 (GE7235), whilst rebodying sister 308 (GG907) with a new 51-seat body. These two vehicles which had arrived in the previous year are remembered for their "rubbish" condition on arrival, reflecting no doubt their hard life in Glasgow throughout the war years. Despite having an obvious case for obtaining allocations of new double deckers as far as is known, Caledonian made no attempt to obtain them and continued with the policy of rebuilding, rebodying and re-engining acquired stock, as well as their own vehicles bought new. Croft also rebodied TD1s 244/5 (WW7861/2) with new 51-seat bodies. Willowbrook carried out two rebuilds of Lancets 175/6 (BSM822/3) and one rebody of AEC Regent 240 with a new 53 seat body. This vehicle had been rebuilt with what was virtually a new body by Caledonian's own workshops in 1941. Haulage vehicles received the attention of Penmans with Albion H20 (VS2637) being overhauled.

In 1944 some further service pruning was initiated when the Kirkcudbright - Castle Douglas - Dalbeattie - Kippford service disappeared. However, during January, a number of services had extra journies added. The Dumfries - Penpont service had a Saturday only single journey short working introduced between Penpont and Porterstown. An additional Dumfries to Castle Douglas service was introduced together with a Sunday only extra journey between Dumfries and Stranraer and additional journies on the Dumfries - Carlisle, Dumfries - Lockerbie and Carlisle - Longtown services. Dumfries town services gained one extra Saturday only run to Brasswell, Janefield, Lincluden, Crichton and Troqueer. Two extra Wednesday only journies between Dumfries and Dunscore and two extra Sunday only journies between Carlisle and Rockliffe were introduced. In the east, one extra Edinburgh to Biggar run and extra Edinburgh - Lamington services with a Sunday only extra to Abington were initiated. Also, the first morning departure from Moniaive was extended to the Dumfries LMS station if required by passengers. In addition, some Sunday journies via Newtonairds were introduced the remainder running via Burnhead.

Brief mention should also be made of the haulage fleet operation during the war. The fleet was a controlled undertaking under the Ministry of War Transport Scheme and in this capacity the company's vehicles covered the British Isles and Northern Ireland extensively, carrying MOWT fleet numbers in addition to their Caledonian numbers. One vehicle was included in the Scottish contingent sent to the continent in 1945 for conveyance of essential foodstuffs and was based and worked in Belgium and Holland. Also, much nearer to home, as part of the MOWT MWT7 area work, they delivered foodstuffs to stores throughout Wigtownshire.

A view of the interior of Claythorn Street showing the loading bays and distribution points. Albion H8 is seen complete with canvas covers, standard livery and small headlamps shortly after the garage was opened.
(Douglas Harper Collection)

PREPARING FOR PEACE

Although the company continued to concentrate much of their efforts on war transport, during 1945 an extensive review was undertaken of the company's operation by H.H.Merchant, who was shortly to be appointed to the post of General Manager. Their long time General Manager J.H.Martin moved on to East Kent during 1945 to be succeeded by J.S.Gavin who only served for a year before H.H.Merchant's appointment. The report, published in June 1945, reviewed future potential developments when the war ended. On the public service side, Merchant recommended that further development should be shelved until the political climate was clearer. When the position came up for review a number of operators were targetted for takeover; R.Murray and Sons, Stranraer, Carruthers of New Abbey, Clark of Glencaple and Elliot of Lockerbie, the latter two having been considered in the 1936 report on independents. The acquisition of these operators was viewed as giving the company a virtual monopoly and with the opportunity to generate additional revenue from their established excursion and tour work.

On the haulage side the review was split into two; "Bulk" and "Smalls". The "Smalls" work had profitable services operating from Glasgow to Dumfries, Newton Stewart and Stranraer. The company was looking to expand in the Edinburgh area, possibly by the purchase of a small haulage business, particularly in the Leith area to allow a link up between Edinburgh and Glasgow and Edinburgh and Dumfries. Only small businesses were recommended for purchase to give a footing in the districts. A review of potential tie ups south of the Border was also recommended, although caution was expressed until the attitude of further expansion of haulage was tested with the parent Tilling Group. The haulage business of Hopkirk of Moffat was recommended for purchase. Similarly, the parcels collection and delivery service in Carlisle was viewed as capable of development, with acquistions of small haulage businesses recommended to give a footing in Cumberland. The aim was to eventually link up with the Dumfries and Glasgow/Edinburgh services.

Premises and major bus stances were reviewed. Dumfries Town Council had put forward plans for the construction of a broad footpath at the Whitesands Bus Stance in Dumfries. This attractive location at the side of the River Nith had always been the major departure point for country services. Effectively, it comprised of a surfaced area with a footpath at the rear and vehicles had to reverse into the surfaced area. The Town Council, following the recommendation of the Regional Traffic Commisioner, had put forward plans for the construction of a broad footpath with barriers, queueing rails and fixed departure points with suitable destination boards (the existing process involved reversing into any spaces that were available; departure points were not fixed by space, other than some provision for independants). The major advantage was that the tricky manouvre of reversing would be eliminated, this being particularly difficult as the vast majority of traffic had to move into the wrong lane to face the traffic before the reversing manouvre could be made. Vehicles not required immediately would be parked further down the "Sands", being brought forward to the stand 20 minutes before departure time. One problem was that to give an adequate number of departure points, the footpath would require to be extended beyond the present limit, which was not favoured by the Town Council. The decision was taken that the burgh surveyor should proceed with the plans and provide estimates, following which the footpath would be constructed and reversing and direct pull-in tried before erecting tne barriers. Over the years there has been much talk of providing a bus station; the developments outlined above finally came to fruition in late 1991.

A seperate haulage depot was recommended in Dumfries and this later came to fruition on the north side of town, but by then the haulage fleet had passed to the nationalised British Road Services. Haulage vehicles continued to use the top shed at Eastfield Road. Merchant recommended the building of the seperated depot on spare land at Eastfield Road with access being gained near the Recreation Hall. The report indicated that the main workshop roof had been heightened to accomodate double deckers and further work was being put in place to heighten the rest of the garage. At Annan, the report recommended that spare land owned by the railway should be acquired at the rear of depot. This was to come to fruition much later in "Western" days (see subsequent chapters). Office accomodation for the depot inspector and a messroom had been provided. Longtown was reported to be in very poor condition and a rebuild or move nearer town was suggested, again being addressed much later. The need for Gretna was recommended to be kept under review. Lonsdale Street in Carlisle was inadequate; more space was required, due to the garage having become more of a bus station during the war; this statement is curious in that this was part of its intended use. Suggestions were made that adjoining property owned by Dias & Co. be acquired; part of the area could then be used to give seperate access for haulage The inadequate garage space required a number of measures not referred to in the report. Vehicles were parked on waste ground at "The Sands", adjacent to the River Eden on the north side of the City during the day and near to the County Garage, where garage space had originally been rented incidentally. In particular, vehicles used to transport personnel to 14MU were parked there. This parking area and the peripheral Bridgewater Road continued to be used until 1981. Space at the Viaduct Garage in West Walls was also rented for four to five buses during weekdays and continued to be rented until the early 'sixties, when the building was demolished, together with the Queens Hall, for the construction of a Tesco store. Buses could not be garaged there on a Saturday, space being given over to cars with the result that a few vehicles (generally, the elderly PLSC Lions in postwar days) were garaged at United's premises in

R. Murray and Sons of Stranraer was one of the operators targetted for takeover in the 1946 review. The business projected an image of a big operator, publishing quality tour guides and using a fleetname style very similar to that used by the Alexander empire. Operating a mixed bag of vehicles, Albion WG 528 had originated with Alexanders and was operated on the range of routes spreading from Stranraer. (Roy Marshall)

Carruthers of New Abbey was another operator identified for possible takeover. Their smart chocolate and yellow liveried fleet was a familiar site on the Dumfries-New Abbey-Rockliffe route. Amongst the early post-war fleet was this Harrington-bodied AEC Regal bought new in 1946 (SW 6893) which had arrived at Dumfries and was about to cross the road to park up. The main points of the route were carried on the metal window louvres. (Alan B. Cross)

The Lewis Street premises at Stranraer were built in 1936 to replace the cramped Trade Street Garage. Photographed in 1947, the seperate access to the haulage depot on the left can be seen. A late '20s Leyland Tiger can be seen together with Bedford OWL truck delivered during the war. (Douglas Harper Collection)

Peter Street. This practice had ceased by the time Western took over in 1949. Despite all these arrangements, the bus station/ garage was still overcrowded.

To move a little forward in the story to illustrate the point, in 1947 stern measures continued to be required to get vehicles in. An extra line of vehicles was created by "shoe-horning", which involved reversing buses in, under guidance, as close as possible to those on the nearside, the last line just leaving sufficient room for the driver to leave through the cab door. If the procedure was not carefully carried out, the driver had to clamber via the window over the bonnet. All the buses had to be left with steering straight-ahead, because arrangement of a last-in-first-out sequence was impossible. The early morning chore consisted of bringing in one of the street parked vehicles (which had the engine running all night in winter; fuel supplies having eased sufficiently to ensure avoidance of the Annan "freeze up" incident again), and towing the buses out driverless. As 14MU work dwindled post war the requirements for this practice ceased, no doubt much to the relief of the company staff.

Returning to H.Merchant's report, his opinion was that the garage at Penpont should be re-located a couple of miles eastwards to Thornhill, where the main through traffic could be catered for and haulage development could be assisted, a move which was never made. The Trade Street premises at Stranraer had been let to a local haulage contractor prior to the war; during the war and at the time of the report the garage was still in the hands of the Ministry of Food. The recommendation was that, on decommission, the premises be returned to use by the haulier or be used by Caledonian for their own storage, although repairs to the house would require to be arranged by the Ministry. Stranraer Town

Council had been agitating for some time for barriers and shelters at the main departure point at Port Rodie; the company's attitude was to avoid the expense. The shelters were later built and it is believed that the company made a contribution to their construction and erection. No development of Lewis Street was contemplated; adequate spare land was available for expansion, though reference was made to building on built up land and the need to watch for structural defects. One development proposed was the replacement of the rented enquiry and parcels office at Port Rodie as the space was inadequate. Regretably, that inadequate space was tolerated until its closure in the seventies.

Whithorn garage was viewed as unsatisfactory, being basic, lacking drainage and with no facilities for staff. Negotiations were reported to be taking place with the Church Authorities for the purchase of a Church Hall near the centre of the town (St Johns' church) which it considered to be suitable for both both PSV and haulage usage. Again, nothing came to fruition, although negotiations reached the valuation stage. The building eventually becoming a garage with petrol pumps fronting onto the road, a function it still performs today. If the premises in Whithorn were viewed as unsatisfactory those further north at Wigtown were viewed even less enthusiastically and the proposal here was to re-site the depot at Newton Stewart. Again, they had no staff facilities and a supporting letter complaining of this situation by the Transport and General Workers Union was apparantly intended for use in an attempt to influence the Ministry of Works and Buildings to grant a licence to carry out the work. The proposed move to Newton Stewart was well progressed by June 1945; a site had been found and purchased in Church Street, close to the bus terminus at Dashwood Square on the site of the old outdoor Curling Rink and

A very rare view of the "unsatisfactory" Whithorn garage, with Leyland Lion 152 (SM 9502) sitting outside in 1947. Having been re-engined in 1939, its destination blind had been rebuilt to the larger BET Federation style and, within two years, it would be receiving a new ECW body.
(Douglas Harper Collection)

Wigtown garage was also photographed in 1947. The planned move from these premises in North Back Street, inherited with Love's haulage business, was thwarted by the refusal of planning permission to site a garage at Newton Stewart. Leyland Lion 71 (SM 9502) had been rebuilt in similar fashion to 152 and would also be rebodied by ECW.
(Douglas Harper Collection)

plans for a composite depot had been prepared and reviewed by the Crosville Motor Services architect. Bill McGowan remembers being told to report to a hotel in Newton Stewart one morning during the war and collect the architect; throughout the day he acted as his assistant and was sworn to secrecy by his superior! Planning permission was applied for to the County Council, but floundered on the proximity of the depot to the local Penninghame Primary School. This must have been a bitter disappointment to the company, but no

further effort was put into finding an alternative site. They retained ownership of the land, passing it to Western S.M.T. on their acquisition, who eventually sold the plot in the 'fifties. Overnight garaging of one bus with McKeands continued at Newton Stewart, the Western S.M.T. vehicle on the Girvan - Newton Stewart service also being based there overnight.

The garage at Dunragit near Stranraer inherited with Bell's business was highlighted for close examination. Under peacetime

Dennis Lancet 210 (DSM 453), a 1938 Dennis Lancet model, sits inside Hayfield Garage in Gorgie Road, Edinburgh in the late '40s. No development of this garage was necessary, ample room being available for any expansion.
(Douglas Harper Collection)

A successful move was made in Glasgow during 1946 to new spacious premises in Claythorn Street, after some initial difficulties with planning permission.
(Douglas Harper Collection)

conditions the need for maintaining this depot was to be reviewed, its major purpose being milk collection in the area. The Hayfield garage in Gorgie Road, Edinburgh had a much reduced PSV operation during the war and was reported to have ample room for their needs. The premises at Castle Terrace had been intended for expansion and, as detailed earlier, the adjoining premises at number 7 had been acquired with this in mind. Number 7 had been occupied by the W.V.S. but proposals were made to convert this when available to make a waiting room and provide staff facilities. The chairman was to be approached with this proposal, but this in fact never happened and the premises were ultimately transferred to the British Transport Commision Advert Division, when "Western" absorbed Caledonian. Incidentally, this became the office for "Scotland's Magazine", formerly the SMT magazine which Travel Press and Publicity produced.

In Glasgow the 5 year tenancy of the haulage depot in Salisbury Street was due to expire in February 1946 and, given that the premises were too small, premises in Claythorn Street had been purchased and plans drawn up for alterations. An application to the Ministry of Work and Public Building for a licence to initiate the work had been refused because the Ministry of War Transport (Road Haulage Division) would not give their support. The Regional Transport Commisioner in Edinburgh and the Ministry of War Transport were approached and the Commisioner indicated approval of a modified scheme. On approval, alterations were rapidly made and the premises were quickly occupied, of which more later. Regarding traffic, concern was expressed at the impact on revenue of the closure of most of the I.C.I. factories involved in

wartime production, possible redundancies and fleet reductions were mooted. Also mentioned in the report was the requests from Tilling that route numbers should be shown and a temporary arrangement be introduced as soon as possible. As most of fleet had large indicators the company decided to have blinds incorporating the service numbers. Ironically, service numbers had actually started to appear in the timetables in 1944 despite not being displayed on destination blinds at that time! Brief mention was also made of the plan to use Eastern Coach Works only for the rolling stock repair programmes for 1945, although this did not happen in practice. Final comments dealt with the likelihood that surplus vehicles were thought to be likely after the war. These comments were understandable, given the statistics which the company had produced on their wartime activity which showed that 75 Factory and workers buses per day were required, on average carrying 5000 people per day.

Other interesting facts drawn from the statistics were : Forty three vehicles held against invasion standby, with drivers on 24 hour call; No single deck buses were converted to ambulances (although longitudinal seating converted vehicles could be quickly adapted); Prewar conducting staff consisted of approximately 50% male and 50% female. In 1945 there were 100 female conductresses. Four women had graduated to female inspectors and four were employed as drivers; Buses were housed at their garages throughout the war; no vehicles were outstationed in fields away from the towns, as happened with other operators who's territories were in areas of strategic importance.

THE POST-WAR BOOM

It is interesting to note that H.Merchant's reference to the need for possible fleet reductions to the fleet after "normal conditions" had resumed. In practice, very few vehicles were withdrawn between 1945 and 1949 with the exception of the Thornycroft Daintys and Cygnets, and more of the Leyland Lion PLSC3s. A postwar boom was experienced, with a public keen to travel; petrol rationing continued and new cars were relatively scarce (unless you were prepared to pay a substantial premium). As an illustration of the growth of the company, in 1932 passengers carried totalled 2.75 million. In 1946 this had increased to 12.5 million. Over the same period, the miles covered had increased form 2.5 million to 4 million. The company was progressing well through the rebuilding programme and this continued into 1946 and 1947 (of which more later), resulting in the fleet, though ageing in profile, being in good condition, aided considerably by the very high standards to which Caledonian were again able to maintain the fleet after wartime shortages.

To deal with breakdowns and heavy recovery work, the Foden lorry H40 (UJ499) was transferred from the haulage fleet, no doubt hastened by its involvement in an accident near Thornhill, which resulted in it leaving the road and twisting the chassis members into a bow shape. What would have constituted a "write-off" in other

companies, simply provided another challenge to the engineering staff. On return to Eastfield road the vehicle was stripped and a brick framework was built around the chassis members. Portions of the damaged vehicle body and any other heavy items were then piled onto the chassis. Fuel was then poured into framework created and ignited and the the combined force of intense heat and heavy weight helped to straighten the chassis members out! The vehicle was then fitted with a jib and block and tackle for lifting purposed. A removable platform was also fitted to allow the vehicle to double as a "tree-lopper", an important requirement now that double deckers were the norm. Previously, recovery of vehicles involved the attaching of tow ropes to members of the fleet (a Thornycroft being remembered on this duty in particular).

In common with operators throughout the country, fleet replacements concentrated on buses rather than coaches. A single Bristol L5G with ECW B35R bodywork (313 ; GSM120) arrived in August 1946, part of an order for ten, the remainder of which arrived between March and June 1947 (314-322 ; GSM121-9). Evidence of increased Tilling influence was the introduction of a new style of destination box, with a shallow ultimate destination box above a deeper larger box which carried information on intermediate points and, at the side just forward of the rear entrance a shallow ultimate

Early postwar deliveries were focussed on buses by necessity, tour work being undertaken often by pre-war vehicles. Dennis Lancet 199 (CSM 767) would not have not have been as arduous to travel on to Whitley Bay in 1946 as might seem; despite its rougher diesel engine, comfortable seats and a five speed gearbox would have made the journey reasonable, if not luxurious. (Roy Marshall)

destination box. A full destination box was carried at the rear but not used and was suitably panelled over. The paint scheme also reflected Tilling practice, with the cream being extended above the window surrounds to a band above. A red roof replaced the previous grey roof which had been widely applied to single deckers. The arrival of the Bristols allowed the release of seven Lion PLSC3s to fellow hard pressed Tilling operator Crosville Motor Services in

1946/7 on loan (numbers 53/6-9, 221 and 231 ; SM6918/48/63-5 and RU8056/54 respectively) with Southern Vectis receiving a Thornycroft Dainty (207 ; DSM450). All were returned by the end of 1948, except one which was disposed of by Crosville (53; SM6918). A start was made on repainting the utility Bedfords (and other vehicles) out of grey as paint supplies eased and at least one had its seats recovered in blue and gold moquette.

Having received one Bristol L in 1946, a further nine were delivered in 1947, complete with standard ECW bodies. First of the batch 314 (GSM 121) is at Lowestoft prior to delivery.

The first Bristol L delivered postwar could be identified by the different style of sliding windows. The whole batch, including the pre-war and wartime Bristol Ls rebuilt and rebodied to postwar standards lasted until 1960 with Western SMT. Their good condition guaranteed ready takers after their withdrawal. (Roy Marshall)

The post-war boom in passenger traffic compensated for the run-down of the military establishments as illustrated by this September 1949 line up of five buses about to leave Castle Terrace, Edinburgh at the start of the local holiday. Headed by Bristol L5G 314, three Lancets and an AEC make up this group, with Douglas Harper's Morris 8 staff car parked on the left outside the company's office.   (Douglas Harper Collection)

The rebuilding and rebodying programme continued together with re-engining. Three coachbuilders were involved in the postwar work, Portsmouth Aviation, ECW and Croft, the former coachbuilder being a new choice for Caledonian. Other Tilling Companies were making use of Portsmouth Aviation for rebodying as well as the rebuilding which Caledonian required, although they tended to be geographically much closer, Wilts and Dorset being an example. Interestingly, the rebodying work went to Croft, no doubt reflecting the better availability and geographical proximity of this coachbuilder, but the work for 1946 was concentrated on the first two companies. Vehicles converted to diesel engines were Leyland TD1s 244/70/1 (WW7861, GE2494/84) and Leyland TD2s 309/10 (DR9843/3) which were fitted with Leyland oil engines. AEC Regal 299 (TM8807) received an AEC oil engine, Leyland Lion LT2 73 (SM8854) received a 4LW engine, whilst TD1s 261/3 (WW8606 and HD3700) received 5LW engines. Leyland Lion 65 (SM8317) was re-seated from 30 to 32 seats, whilst Eastern Coach Works rebuilt TD1s 246/8 and 268 (WW7863, 8360 and GE2454) as well as Dennis Lancet 158 (SM9972) and AEC Regals 163/4 (SM9977/9), with Portsmouth Aviation rebuilding Lancets 159 and 277 (SM9973

and FSM435). The latter vehicle was only five years old, but the unavoidable use of poor quality timber during the war hastened the need to rebuild relatively youthful vehicles.

Route developments were chiefly concerned with serving of small communities not already served, sometimes by diverting or extending existing services or in other cases developing new routes. However, an early postwar development was the introduction of a new Dumfries town service to the west end in 1946 which operated as a circular between Queensbury Square and Maxwelltown Memorial via St Michaels Bridge, Pleasance Avenue, New Abbey Road, Rotchell Road, Troqueer Road and back over St Michaels Bridge. Other developments in 1945-7 were : In the Stranraer area - Service 60. Certain journies on the Stranraer - Lochans - Portpatrick service were diverted via the hamlet of Awhirk from 1946. This changed again after one year to a diversion via High Three Mark and Awhirk; Service 61. Stranraer - Kirkcolm - Ardwell Shop. (Extended to North Cairn on Saturdays only in 1947. Ardwell shop was purely a collection of houses, North Cairn was even more sparse, culminating in a lighthouse); Service 65. Stranraer - Auchenree - Portpatrick (a new service introduced in 1946). In the Newton Stewart area : Service 64B. Wigtown - Kirkcowan - Newton Stewart (a new service introduced in 1946 on Tuesdays, Fridays and Saturdays, extending to Newton Stewart on Fridays only); Newton Stewart - Monrieth via Wigtown, Wauphill, Kirk of Mochrum and Portwilliam (a new un-numbered service on Sundays only introduced in 1947). In the Dumfries Area : Service 15A. Dalbeattie - Kirkcudbright (one journey in either direction on Saturdays on diverted at Dundrennan to serve the coastal hamlet of Netherlaw from 1946); Service 18C Dumfries - Newtonairds Station via

Crosville Motor Services were the main recipient for Caledonian's surplus vehicles with seven elderly Leyland Lion PLSC3s being loaned. All were numbered by Crosville, 53 (SM 6918) carrying Crosville fleet number B253 and having its Caledonian fleetnames etc. painted out in this view at Rhyl. They ran for around a year before returning north.
(Dr. J. Roberts)

Irongray (was introduced in 1947 operating on Wednesdays and Saturdays only with two journies operating in either direction); Penpont - Druidhall - Belstane (a new un-numbered service introduced in 1946 with two journeys on Saturdays only. This service only operated for a brief period of time. The route covered was the same as that provided for a school journey during the week. It re-appeared in 1949 as a Penpont - Glenairlie Bridge service). A minor service which disappeared in 1946 was the Sundays only Moniaive - Glencairn Church service. In the Annan area : An Annan local from the Market Square to Silverlaw Factory via Newington Road, Butts Street and High Street replaced later by a revised route via High Street, Lady Street, North Street and returning via Newington Road, Butts Street and High Street running Monday to Saturday in 1948. In the Carlisle area : Service 48 Carlisle - Evertown (A new service was introduced 1946 operating on Saturdays only); Service 49 Canonbie - Newcastleton (A new service was introduced in 1945 operating on Saturday and Sundays only; Service 51B Carlisle - Cliff - Longtown (A new service was introduced in 1947 operating on Saturdays only).

The most unusual purchase in 1946 was the long established Oughtons Restaurant in Church Place, Dumfries. Interestingly, no reference is made in Merchant's report of any proposal to move into this side of the trade. The management clearly had a go ahead outlook, the purchase being made with an eye to the potential of the touring coach trade which started to "find it's feet" after the war. The restaurant was bought as a "going concern", although its wartime use had been as Norway House, providing accomodation for Norwegian refugees. Oughtons' were an old established concern going back to 1874 and after refurbishment adverts were quickly placed inviting people to book social events, wedding receptions etc in the suitably named "Caledonian Rooms". By 1947, not only a full service of coffees, snacks, lunches high teas was offered, but also an orchestra on Wednesdays and Saturdays, as well as a lounge bar. On Whit Sunday 1946 the Salisbury Street premises in Glasgow were vacated and the move was made to 36 Claythorn Street. Some rationalisation was achieved with the garaging of vehicles at Solley's Castle Douglas premises ceasing in that year.

A late 'fifties view of Oughtons Restaurant in Church Place, Dumfries purchased in 1946 and transferred to Western SMT in 1949. (Garry Ward Collection)

Croft were involved in a considerable amount of rebodying in the 1947 rolling stock repair programme. The bodies were by then being produced to full peace-time standards and though they were rather plain they were well proportioned. The rebodying concentrated on some of the Titans which had not already received major attention to their bodywork and the Albions acquired from Glasgow Corporation and, at the same time, introduced a simplified double deck livery with the cream band below the lower deck windows being abandoned and a red roof being applied in place of the original grey in similar style to the Bristol Ls. Tilling style "two aperture" destination boxes were carried at the front and, for the first time on double deckers, at the side as well. Titan TD1s 235-7, 247, 257 and 265 (TM3824, 3843, 3846 and 3735, WW8358, KR1733 and HD4361 respectively), TD2 312 (DR9848) and Albions 303-6 (YS2003/7/95/100), all received new 53-seat bodies. 235-7

With the arrival of the Bristol Ls, Caledonian were able to provide some relief to hard pressed fellow Tilling Group operators, albeit with old or non-standard vehicles. In the latter category was Thornycroft Dainty 207 (DSM450), loaned to Southern Vectis on the Isle of Wight in 1947. This vehicle still had its white wing edges, a throw back to wartime days. (Garry Ward Collection).

had been the first to be rebuilt in 1941 by Pickerings, but clearly their bodywork had deteriorated to such an extent that a rebody was considered necessary, though two out of the three had to wait another year before receiving a diesel engine. Portsmouth Aviation carried out their final rebuilds for Caledonian on Tiger TS4 301 (JJ8823) and AEC Regal 302 (ELY529). Gardner engines were fitted into Leyland Lion LT2s 71/2 (SM8852/3), which received 4LW units and TD1s 262/5/8 which received 5LW engines.

In common with the whole of the country the winter of 1947 caused major disruptions to Caley's operation, snowdrifts as high as a double decker being encountered, with staff working 14 hour days to dig out buses. Caledonian took delivery of its first ever new double deckers with the arrival of two Bristol K6Bs with ECW L27/28R bodies in 1948 (323/4 ; HSM642/3). No corresponding double deckers were withdrawn, acknowledging the ongoing need for this type after the wartime expansion. The vehicles were unusual in also being the first Bristol engined machines in the fleet and two similar K5Gs should also have been delivered. However, when completed in January and March 1949 respectively, the two vehicles (325/6 ; HSM644/5) were loaned as part of the arrangement where the newly nationalized Tilling Group diverted 180 Bristol K6A and K5G deckers to London Transport to assist them in overcoming a severe vehicle shortage. As no Bristol engined vehicles were to be involved, the transfer of the two Gardner engined vehicles is oft quoted as the paradox of a transfer to an operator who had a lower proportion of older vehicles than the operator who had ordered them. One wonders if Caledonian having had intimation of the intended loan quickly changed their order for 323/4 from Gardner to Bristol engines to reduce the impact! It is probable, however, that the better availability of the Bristol engine unit was the real reason. The vehicles were on loan for a year, returning in February 1950, after the takeover. All four vehicles carried the standard livery of two cream band and Tilling style destination boxes which were, like the single deck Bristol Ls, also carried at the rear but panelled over.

Reference has been made above to the nationalisation of the Tilling organisation. This took place in September 1948. Caledonian had displayed Tilling buying practice rigidly since the war taking only ECW bodied Bristols and adopting the Tilling style of destination. One of the first outward signs of nationalisation was increased interavailability of British Railways and Caledonian tickets on the Newton Stewart to Whithorn service and further evidence was all subsequent rebodying work being placed with ECW from 1948. Older single deckers which had not been part of the rebuilding programme, were rebodied and renumbered at the same time. First to be rebodied were two Dennis Lancets 180 and 219 (BSM826 and DSM453) which received new 35-seat rear entrance bodies, very similar to those being fitted to new Bristol Ls. At the same time, the vehicles were renumbered 352/3. One Leyland Lion 48 (SW6741) was re-seated again to 32 from the longitudinal 30-seat configuration which it had operated in during the war, whilst many of the Bedford OWBs delilvered during the war were sent to Croft for

Caledonian's first ever new double deckers were two Bristol K6Bs with ECW lowbridge bodies delivered in 1948, of which 323 (HSM642) was the first. Their delivery introduced the Bristol K and Bristol engines to Scotland and had the added distinction, together with their two Gardner-engined sisters, of being the only Bristol Ks delivered to an operator north of the border.

Two Bristol K5Gs should have followed the pair of K6Bs, but both were instead diverted direct to London Transport as soon as they were built. Indeed, they never actually ran for Caledonian due to not travelling north until after the Western SMT takeover. Here 326 (HSM645) is seen in London Transport service near the end of its period of loan in February 1950. (Alan B. Cross)

repairs; 281-2/4-7/91-4 ; (FSM452-3, 506/7/14/15 and 623-6) and at around the same time, OWBs 280-9/91-4 were downseated to 25. Much progress was made in the re-engining of vehicles, Leyland Lion LT2 70 (SM8851) was re-engined with a 4LW unit and TD1s 236-7, 245-8, 256-9, 266, 272 and 273 (TM3843/6 WW7862/3, 8358, 8360, KR1731/3, 6531, WW8605, HD4362, GE2487 and 2458 respectively) were fitted with 5LW units. In the same year, the eighteen gas-producer trailers which had lain unused (and unwanted!) since 1944 were disposed of to Connor (breaker) of Dumfries.

In 1949 the final rebodying work under Caledonian ownership was completed. Four Leyland Lion LT2s (numbers 70-73 ; SM8851-4) which were already eighteen years old were rebodied, this time with 31-seat rear entrance ECW bodies and renumbered 346-9. Three had already been re-engined (73 in 1946 and 71/2 in the following year, number 70 being the last of the four to be re-engined with a Gardner 5LW engine in July 1948); in typical frugal fashion the original Leyland body on 70 was considered sturdy enough to replace the original Leyland body on 130 (DS1477). Two Lion LT5s of 1932 (151/2 ; SM9501/2) were also rebodied with similar new ECW 33-seat bodies, obtaining new numbers 350/1. Four Bristol L5Gs completed the rebodying

exercise, the two 1939 examples and the two 1942 examples (242/3 ; ESM537/8 and 275/6 ; FSM380/1 respectively) receiving 35-seat rear entrance bodies, as usual by ECW. At the same time, their high "shield-type" radiators were replaced by those of the lower postwar PV2 style, making them virtually identical to the post-war deliveries, other than the obvious indications of older registrations and new numbers (the vehicles were renumbered 354-7 respectively). It is interesting to note that single deckers rebodied in the postwar years

Rebodying older vehicles continued after the war, Leyland Titan TD2 312 (DR 9848) receiving a new body to full peace time standards built by Croft Engineering in 1947. The bus is parked at Castle Terrace, Edinburgh whilst allocated to Edinburgh, one of the few double deckers based there for a time. (Douglas Harper Collection)

The new ECW bodies on the Leyland Lions looked neater, helped by the fitment of the COVRAD replacement radiator. 348 (SM 8853) was one of six Lions rebodied. The side destination indicator quickly fell into disuse under Western ownership and the large Tilling style destination blinds were progressively reduced to the top ultimate box over the years. (Ian Maclean)

Leyland Titan 236 (TM 3843) illustrates the plain but quite attractive Croft post-war body style fitted to Caledonian vehicles. The two piece ultimate and intermediate destination box is illustrated, as is the simplified post war paint scheme, with red replacing the grey roof and two cream bands. (Alan B. Cross)

were all renumbered into a series from 346 to 357, whereas the double deckers retained their original fleetnumbers after rebodying. Perhaps of more tangible interest to the company was the increase in costs of new bodies since the war, the Croft Engineering double deck bodies costing £2,300 each.

Further route developments in 1948/9 were : Dumfries Town service 9 High Street - Hardthorn Road. Introduced 1948 and operating via Terreagles Street (an interesting restriction was put on the licence; when "Queen of the South" football club were playing, buses were routed via Laurieknowe, Albert Road and Victoria Avenue to regain Terreagles Street. This was under the order for "regulation of vehicular traffic in connection with football matches held in Palmerston Park."); Queensberry Square - Locharbriggs became Lincluden - Queensberry Square - Locharbriggs in 1948.

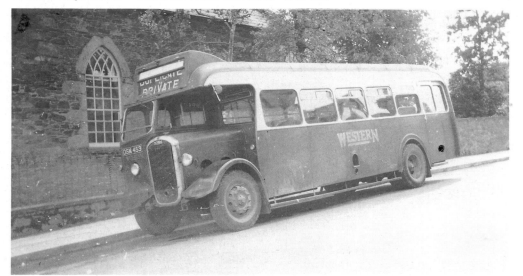

No photographs have been uncovered of the rebodied Dennis Lancets and Leyland Lions in Caledonian colours. Seen in Western SMT days at Newton Stewart is 353 (DSM 453), one of two Lancets rebodied with standard ECW bodies. The ECW body did not sit comfortably on the Lancet with its high offset radiator position, which required a different style of drivers front window. The bus is in Stewart Street, one of a number of layover points used over the years for vehicles operating school journies. (Roy Marshall)

240 (TM 6307) came to grief whilst operating from Edinburgh garage, a burst tyre causing it to overturn. After rebuilding, it returned to service and passed to Western SMT in 1949. (Douglas Harper Collection)

Further extensions were made within Lincluden along Lincluden road to the junction with Criffel Road in 1949; Other amendments to the town services involved operation of a Janefield to Cresswell and a Brasswell to Troqueer service, the Queensberry Square to Locharbriggs and the Janefield to Brasswell services ceasing; Service 45B. Annan - Kirkpatrick Fleming via Creca service was introduced as a Friday and Saturday only service in 1948, replacing the Annan - Creca district circular service; Service 22 Stranraer - Dumfries limited stop. Perhaps the most interesting of all the developments, this new service introduced in 1948 ran on Sundays only with one journey in either direction. This left Stranraer at 10-30am taking 3 hours to reach Dumfries in comparison with the service bus time of 3 hours 45 minutes. A connection was provided from Wigtown at Newton Stewart. The bus returned from Dumfries at 5pm. The service was introduced for people visiting the Dumfries and Galloway Royal Infirmary, Cresswell Maternity Home and Lochmaben Sanatorium; 21G Stranraer - Castle Kennedy - Glenluce via Limekiln introduced in 1948; 52A Carlisle - Scugg Gate - Nook Gate. Introduced 1949 with one journey in either direction on Saturdays only; Newton Stewart - Isle of Whithorn via Grange of Cree launched 1949 with two journies on Saturdays only. This diversion had been introduced to replace a service which had been given up by Willie Bell of Wigtown who had a garage and taxi service, as well as one bus. A contract was held to carry workers to the Bladnoch Creamary, as well as operation of a service from Newton Stewart to Wigtown via Grange of Cree; 15B Kirkcudbright - Townhead introduced 1949 and operated on Fridays only; 10D Annan - Powfoot. Introduced 1948 and operated on Fridays only, a short period licence for operation on specific days had been granted for this service from 1947; Un-numbered service Dumfries - Dumfries and Galloway Royal Infirmary was introduced in 1949; Un-numbered works service introduced Eastriggs - Broom I.C.I. Factory; Annan - Langholm and Carlisle - Langholm services had certain journies in Langholm extended to David Street in 1949; Service 19 Dumfries - Penpont, (became Wednesdays, Saturdays and Sundays service and was extended on Saturdays only via Belstane to Glenairlie Bridge in 1948. This re-established the Belstane extension which had operated briefly after the war and also gave useful connections with some of the Dumfries to Sanquhar journies). Other special services introduced in 1948 and early 1949 were : Dumfries - Torthorwold via Collin and Racks operating on the second and fourth Sunday of each month and other Sundays as required; Drumlanrig Castle - Thornhill (Morton Church) via Carronbridge, Burnbrae and Gaitlawbridge on Communion Sundays and other Sundays as required; Dumfries - Carlisle express, serving 14 MU RAF Carlisle HQ and 1,2,3 and 5 sites for military operation.

In February 1949 licences for a new range of extended tours were obtained, this aspect of the operations having been suspended during the war : Highlands, Edinburgh and Loch Ness (5 days); John O Groats (7 days); Loch Lomond, Oban and Inverary (2 days); Perthshire Highlands and Trossachs (2 days).

Caledonian's final acquisition was the tour licences and haulage contracts of John Dickson (Transport) Ltd. in May 1949. No vehicles passed to Caledonian with the acquisition. For the record, the tour licences (all from Whitesands, Dumfries from April to September) were as follows : Boreland Glen; Sweetheart Abbey; Hoddam Bridge; Shalloch Glen; New Galloway; Gatehouse; Carlisle; Melrose; Water of Ae; Edinburgh; Douglas Mill; Ayr and Girvan; Edinburgh and Forth Bridge; St Marys' Loch and Peebles; Ullswater and Keswick; Auchecastle; Jedburgh; Milton; St Marys' Loch and Hawick; Ellisland; Eaglesfield (for Eaglesfield Show).

The Hayfield garage in Gorgie Road, Edinburgh was closed on 3 January 1950 when the allocation was transferred to the SMT depot at New Street, operating as a separate unit for a further six months before the services were amalgamated with those of SMT. (Douglas Harper Collection)

THE TAKEOVER

When the S.M.T. group sold out to the British Transport Commission in 1948, Caledonian and its large neighbour Western S.M.T. came under common ownership for the first time. With Caledonian being the only Tilling owned company based in Scotland, the opportunity was taken to transfer the operation to the ownership of the company to S.M.T's local subsidiary. Though Caledonian's operating territory was fairly extensive geographically it was small in relation to vehicle size. The decision was taken to absorb the Caledonian into Western S.M.T. as part of the exercise which the latter was going through to absorb its other subsidiaries at that time, namely W.R.Dunlop and Greenock Motor Services, both of Greenock and Rothesay Tramways, which operated in the outpost of the Isle of Bute. The actual date of the sale was 31st December 1949.

At the time of takeover, Caledonian's licences were used to operate the following services, which Western S.M.T. inherited : Service 1,2,5A Locharbriggs-Queensberry Square-Lincluden; 3B Queensberry Square-Stoop; 3C,3D Queensberry Square-Crichton; 4,7 Janefield-Queensberry Square-Cresswell; 4,6 Brasswell-Troqueer; 8 Queensberry Square-Maxwelltown Memorial; 9 High Street-Hardthorn Road; 10 Dumfries-Carlisle; 10,10A Dumfries-Annan via Cummertrees; 10,10B Carlisle-Annan; 10,10B,10C,54, 54A Carlisle-Gretna; 11A Dumfries-Annan via Dalton; 12 Dumfries-Edinburgh via Moffat; 13 Dumfries-Edinburgh via Thornhill; 14 Dumfries-Kippford via Dalbeattie; 14,14A Dumfries-Dalbeattie; 15A Kirkcudbright-Dalbeattie via Auchencairn; 16 Dumfries-Lockerbie; 17 Dumfries-Moniaive via Holywood; 17A Dumfries-Dunscore via Holywood; 18 Dumfries-Moniaive via Newtonairds; 18A Dumfries-Dunscore via Newtonairds; 18C Dumfries-Newtonairds Station via Irongray; 19 Dumfries-Penpont; 20 Dumfries-Sanquhar; 20,20A Dumfries-Thornhill; 21 Dumfries-Stranraer; 21,21A,21B Dumfries-Castle Douglas; 21,21C,21D Dumfries-Kirkcudbright; 21,21E Dumfries-Gatehouse; 22 Dumfries-Stranraer (Express); 21,30B,30D Kirkcudbright-Castle Douglas; 30B,31,31A Castle Douglas-Dalbeattie; 14,31 Dumfries-Haugh of Urr-Castle Douglas; 35 Thornhill-Moniaive; 35A Thornhill-Penpont; 38 Lockerbie-Annan via Brydekirk; 39 Lockerbie-Annan via Bankshill; 43 Annan-Silverhill; 44 Annan-Moffat; 45 Annan-Langholm; 45,45A Annan-Canonbie; 45B Annan-Creca-Kirkpatrick Fleming; 46 Annan-Newbie; 47 Canonbie-Newcastleton; 48 Evertown-Gretna; 50 Carlisle-Langholm; 51 Carlisle-Gretna via Longtown; 51A Carlisle-Longtown; 51B Carlisle-Longtown via Cliff; 52 Carlisle-Corner House Inn; 52A Carlisle-Penton Bridge Inn; 52B Carlisle-Nook Gate; 53 Carlisle-Rockliffe-Castletown; 54,54A Carlisle-Lockerbie; 60 Stranraer-Portpatrick; 61 Stranraer-Ardwell Shop; 62 Stranraer-Whithorn; 62,62D Stranraer-Auchenmalg Inn; 63,64 Isle of Whithorn-Whithorn; 63B Whithorn-Portwilliam; 64 Newton Stewart-Isle of Whithorn; 64,64A Newton

This view of Bristol Ks 324 and 325 illustrates the rear destination boxes which were panelled over form new and the different liveries carried in June 1950. Former Caley 324 still carries the Caledonian livery while 325 which never ran for the company illustrates the Western livery and fleet number DB878. Soon afterwards the Western fleet numbers were centred on the cream band above the lower deck rear window and encased in a new style of garter. (Alan B. Cross)

Stewart-Whithorn; 64B Newton Stewart-Monrieth; 64C Newton Stewart-Wigtown via Grange of Cree; and 65 Stranraer-Auchenree-Portpatrick. In addition, a range of works services were operated, the main operations being Nithsdale Factory-Lincluden; Whitesands-

A front view of the two vehicles illustrates the different liveries. Though 324 was still in Caledonian livery it had gained a Western fleetname above its Caledonian number. The bus was about to leave Whitesands on the former Caledonian route to Sanquhar in June 1950 shortly before the route was extended to Ayr. (Alan B. Cross)

The coachshop at Dumfries quickly set about repainting the fleet, but as a temporary measure many of the vehicles simply had a Western fleetname applied. A complication which delayed painting was where paper advertisements still had a period of their contract to run. 235 (TM 3824), one of the Titans rebodied postwar by Croft sits outside Lonsdale Street Carlisle waiting to take its turn in the bus station. (Alan B. Cross)

Early repaints into "Western" colours carried the standard red livery, darker than the Caledonian shade, together with three cream bands, but without the cream advert panels which were just beginning to appear in 1950. A few adverts, such as the ubiqutous "Shop at Binns" one were placed on the cream bands initially, before the fleet numbers were moved to this position, complete with garter and the advert panels were introduced. (Alan B. Cross)

Drungans; Nithsdale Factory-Brasswell; Wolsey Factory-Lincluden; Wolsey Factory-Brasswell and Eastriggs-Broom Camp, as well as a service from Dumfries High Street to Park Farm Showground on Agricultural Show days etc. On the leisure side were the excursions and tours licences from Kirkcudbright; Dumfries; Annan; Thornhill; Penpont; Gretna; Lockerbie; Moniaive and Whithorn.

AEC Regal 300 (GF 481) had still to receive its Western livery and fleetname in this view at Eastfield Road. An advert for the Caledonian Parcels service is still carried below the rear window of its second Weymann coach body, traces of which can still be seen in areas like the side flash trim. (Alan B. Cross)

Bristol K5G 326 (HSM 645) was photographed in June 1950 after its period in service with London Transport. Though painted in Caledonian colours, it never carried their fleetname or numbers. More K5Gs are believed to have been on order at the time of takeover. (Alan B. Cross)

S.M.T. inherited and operated the following services from the licences gained : 12 Dumfries-Edinburgh via Moffat; 13 Dumfries-Edinburgh via Thornhill; 13,13A Edinburgh-Biggar; and 28 Edinburgh-Broughton.

The vast majority of vehicles were transferred to Western S.M.T. and numbered in the fleet directly after the vehicles absorbed into the main fleet from former subsidiary Rothesay Tramways Co. Ltd. The Leyland Lion PLSC3s were unlicensed at the time of takeover and were disposed of by Caledonian. Orders had been

placed for vehicles prior to the takeover for delivery in 1950 and the orders are believed to have been for 4 Bristol K5G/ECW; 6 Bristol L5G/ECW buses and 9 Bedford OB/Duple coaches. The orders were re-allocated to other Tilling members; one K5G each is believed to have been re-allocated to Western National and Southern National, with the other two being switched to Southern Vectis. The L5Gs are believed to have been shared equally between Crosville and United Counties. It is interesting to speculate that Caledonian would appear to have been intending to promote the tours side of their business again with the order for OBs.

THE EARLY 'FIFTIES

The total Caledonian area was placed under the management of one District Traffic Superintendent and an Area Manager, both of whom were based at Dumfries, a sensible move which helped to retain loyalty. Jim Calder was appointed to the former position (a post he held for twenty years until his retirement in 1970), whilst J.M.Harper was appointed Area Manager (having been "Caley's" Traffic Manager since 1945). The Caledonian vehicles were allocated numbers from 772 to 910. Western had initiated the practice of applying two suffix letters preceding the fleet number. The first letter indicated the garage from which the vehicle operated, but in the case of all the Caledonian garages, Western took the

simple expedient of lettering all vehicles "D" for Dumfries area garages. On paper, allocations were maintained for each garage within the territory. Thus, depots as far apart as Carlisle and Stranraer had a recognised allocation controlled from Dumfries, as had been the process in Caley days. The second letter indicated the chassis type and the Caledonian vehicles acquired were lettered appropriately. The principle used was that single deckers received the first letter of the chassis make and double deckers of the same make received the last, but this process immediately created exceptions where the code "B" was already in use for Bedford single deckers and the last letter "D" was already in use for Leyland

All but one of Western's Leyland Tiger TS8 specials built in 1939 were transferred into the area, DL 163 (AAG 102) serving for a time at Stranraer. A prominent board advertises the relatively new owners of the Caledonian garage. British Road Services retained the left hand portion of the garage and one of their trailers can be seen behind the bus. (A.J.Douglas)

Some of the first vehicles transferred into the area were a batch of 1946 AEC Regent II's from Cumnock garage, bringing with them the newly introduced cream advert panels. Some were allocated to the long Dumfries - Stranraer service after permission had been gained to operate double deckers west of Kirkcudbright.   (Alan B. Cross)

In the reverse direction, former Caledonian vehicles strayed north on services and hires. Dennis Lancet DS841 (CSM 770) is seen at St Enoch Square in front of the long since demolished station. (E.Shirras)

double deckers. The following codes were thus applied; L = Leyland single decker; S = Dennis single decker; B = Bristol single or double decker or Bedford Single decker; A = AEC single decker; D = Leyland double decker; N = Albion double decker; and C = AEC double decker. As an example, former Caledonian Leyland Titan double decker 880 carried DD880 : (Dumfries area allocated LeylanD decker numbered 880).

Regular visitors to the north on the newly extended service to Ayr from Dumfries were the two Bristol K6Bs. Former Caledonian 323 is seen leaving Ayr shortly after the extension of the route and as its former Caledonian blind did not carry an Ayr destination or a suitable one for the complete return journey south, a plentiful supply of paper stickers were resorted to.   (E.Shirras)

The first vehicle moves involved the speedy disposal of the Bedford OWBs to the regular purchaser of the bulk of Western's vehicles, Millburn Motors of Glasgow. Despite being purchased principally for transporting war workers, the Bedfords had continued to give service postwar in the outposts like Penpont and Wigtown. Though they had all been allocated fleet numbers (DB777/9-82/5-8 : FSM453/506-7/514-5/623-6), none were repainted into Western livery and their departure started in June 1950, being completed by the end of the year. Numbers had also been allocated to the thirteen buses operating from Edinburgh garage, seven OWBs (DB773-6/8/83/4 ; FSM449-52/4/5-7), four elderly Lions (DL801-3 ; SM8315-7, 805; DS1477), a Tiger (DL804; SM8910) and an AEC Regal (DA812 ; ELY529) but in the event they passed to S.M.T. and were quickly disposed of.

The disposals in the first year comprised the solitary Cub (DL806 ; DSM452), which had been allocated a number but, like the OWBs, never carried it and the remaining two Thornycroft Daintys (DSM450-1), plus the solitary Bedford WTB, (ESM484) which had been allocated DB772. Numbers 772-4 were re-allocated to a couple of prewar Bedfords and an Albion Victor absorbed into the main fleet from Rothesay Tramways. Also sold were the Lancets (DS790/1/4/6-800 ; SM9972/3/6, NV1361 and YG3043,4700/1, 5723). Though most were elderly vehicles, their disposal seems more related to the drive to remove petrol engined vehicles from the fleet, which by then numbered very few. AEC Regent IIs were drafted in from Cumnock (which had just received new Regent IIIs) to replace these single deck vehicles, reflecting the ongoing growth in postwar traffic which was to continue longer than in parts of more affluent England.

Western had been quick to apply for permission to operate double deckers from Kirkcudbright westwards to Stranraer, allowing the Regents to be allocated to the long Dumfries to Stranraer route, with two (DC311/2 ; BAG125/6) being allocated to Wigtown for operation of the Newton Stewart - Isle of Whithorn services and some also being allocated to Stranraer. The AECs displaced the Bristol L5Gs which had operated on the Stranraer service from new. Having disposed of a number of petrol engined vehicles, a 1947 Bedford OB was transferred from the former Young's fleet, providing a useful private hire coach (DB2161 ; XS6185), being one of the first vehicles allocated to the region to wear Western's black and white livery. In 1952, a 1937 Bedford WTB (DB773 ; VS3906) also appeared and stayed for a couple of years before sale, ironic considering the speedy disposal of Caley's own WTB.

Though they would no doubt have liked to, the company did not have new vehicles available to allocate to the Caledonian territory. The Scottish Bus Group companies were under pressure due to overall "over ordering". Western still had a large number of AEC double deckers on order as well as 100 Leyland PD2s, all of which were cancelled. How these would have helped the fleet! However, though the majority of the vehicles inherited were old and, indeed, most of the Caledonian fleet was fully written down at the time of

LPA37 H28 (ASM 83) had been inherited from Learmonts Transport in 1937; by 1950, the vehicle was being stripped for spares.   (Alan B. Cross)

After permission was granted to use double deckers west of Kirkcudbright, a regular allocation of such vehicles was based at Stranraer, Whithorn and Wigton garages for a full range of duties for which Leyland DD897 (HD4361) was one of a number of ex.Yorkshire Woollen District Leyland Titans received. Its post-war Croft body was donated to an ex.London Transport Guy Arab a year after this view was taken at Newton Stewart in 1953. (R. Marshall)

acquisition, their overall condition was very good as a result of some very thorough rebuilding.

The standard Western livery was applied to vehicles (complete with cream advert panels between decks on double deckers from late 1950/early 1951). Caledonian fleet names began to disappear quickly, in some cases by simply applying the "Western" fleetname to the original livery. Ex.Caley 153 LT5 (SM9503) was the first bus seen in Newton Stewart on a Dumfries - Stranraer service in Western colours carrying its new number DL857 and a few passengers remarked how Western had lovely buses in comparison to Caledonian!

The most obvious changes which became apparent to former Caledonian Staff (apart from the repainting of the vehicles) was the steady changeover to Western uniforms and the equally steady changeover for conductors to Setright Insert ticket machines These "punches" were not entirely strange to all members of the Caledonian staff. Discussion used to take place with the Western crews who operated south to Newton Stewart on the merits of Caledonian's Willebrew punch versus the Setright Insert. Bill

McGowan issued 50 singles and 1 return ticket in eight minutes on the journey between Palnure and Newton Stewart. This was on a duplicate on the Dumfries to Stranraer service which had to move swiftly as the service bus had to wait in case any passengers were going on to Stranraer.

The paint shop at Eastfield Road was kept fully occupied as vehicles were repainted in full Western livery. An early casualty of the switch over was the beautiful Caledonian Omnibus Company legend carried over the enquiry office at the Whitesands. The brass nameplate was rescued from scrap and stored up in the rafters at Eastfield Road by Willie McGrath, who later became Chief Engineer at Dumfries. Recently removed, the nameplate has been superbly restored by Michael Hayton and will form one of the exhibits at the planned Albion Museum at Brasswell on the outskirts of Dumfries. The comprehensive facilities at Eastfield Road remained intact, with the full overhaul and repair work continuing as well as repainting. One exception was the overhaul of engines which was centralized at Kilmarnock. Initially, former Caledonian area vehicles continued to pass through the "shops", but later other Western depots sent vehicles down for overhaul and repaint, especially Ayr, buses often being sent down "on service" to Dumfries and replaced on the northbound journey by newly overhauled and repainted machines ready for return. The workshops were renowned for the quality of their repaints in particular, as well as their individuality; in the seventies when vehicles were turned out with cream wheels, Dumfries repaints could be distinguised by a red band around the outer ring of the wheel! As the Caledonian fleet had been subject to thorough rebuilds little remedial work was needed, even on the

oldest members of the inherited fleet. Some minor changes instituted were the fitting of sliding windows into many of the Dennis Lancets, in place of the original "half drop" type. The coach-building side of Eastfield Road, which had developed considerable expertise over the years, was employed on the building of a half-cab body fitted with recovery equipment on an AEC Matador chassis, one of several purchased by Western SMT after the war. When completed, the vehicle replaced the Foden recovery wagon converted by Caledonian.

Ex.Caledonian vehicles stayed very much in their homeland, no transfers to other garages taking place. No doubt the thought of northern area drivers grappling with the unfamiliar centre throttle of a Dennis Lancet was enough to discourage any thoughts. However, in reverse, a steady stream of vehicles came south from Western's garages to replace time-expired vehicles. Nevertheless, Caledonian vehicles did stray north on service, Dennis Lancets forming duplicates from Girvan to Newton Stewart and the elderly Titans operating the Dumfries to Glasgow service on busy summer Saturdays, as did the occasional Dennis Lancet and Bristol L. The Bristol K6Bs were also regulars on the Dumfries - Ayr route.

The inheritance of such a geographically large territory must have proved difficult, to say the least, for Western's management, especially as they had been in the throes of absorbing their subsidiary companies, together with amalgamating some 140 vehicles from Youngs Bus Service and their associated Paisley and District Omnibus Company operation in the north into their fleet. However, some compensation was gained with the inheritance of

The last batch of Guys received from London Transport were eight delivered in 1953. Their original bodies were immediately removed and were replaced by post-war Croft bodies taken from pre-war Leyland Titans. After its transfer to Dumfries, DY1048 (GLF661) is seen carrying the body previously fitted to DD897 (HD4361) which had been modified by the fitting of a bulbous front dash panel neccessitated by the protruding Guy radiator. (R.F.Mack)

All-Leyland TD1 DD893 (WW8606) served Western for just over two years until its withdrawal in 1952 by which time it had given twenty-three years of service, nine of which were with Caledonian. (R.F.Mack)

Carlisle garage, which provided a servicing and fuelling point for vehicles on express duties to Lancashire and London. Some minor cost savings were achieved in garage rent as well. Western had started to garage their buses on the Dumfries and Stranraer services at Caledonian's depots from 1940. Prior to that, the vehicles had been garaged with the South of Scotland Motor Company in Dumfries and, after their acquisition by Caledonian, the Dumfries Motor Company Limited in English Street. In Stranraer, buses had originally been garaged with the Stranraer Cooperative Society and later with local operator R.Murray & Sons at West End Garage.

On the Property side, the haulage depots at Dunragit and Claythorn Street, Glasgow were transferred to the Road Haulage Executive in September 1949. At Stranraer, the Road Haulage Executive arranged to pay rent for the use of the left hand portion of the garage through the newly formed Road Services (Caledonian) Limited until 1972. The parcel van and lorry fleet passed to the Road Services Division at the same time. In reverse, Wigtown garage which had originated as a haulage depot was also transferred to the Road Haulage Executive, though buses continued to be garaged there alongside the trucks. At Dumfries, land was

acquired just north of the Dumfries to Stranraer railway line on the Glasgow road, where a spacious new haulage depot was built, allowing Eastfield Road to revert to operating as a bus garage only. The Edinburgh premises passed to SMT, except 7 Castle Terrace which passed to BTC advertising division in December 1949.

Though Western had experience in seasonal catering facilities at Ettrick Bay on the Island of Bute, they had not been involved in the running of a restaurant. An early appraisal convinced the management that they should dispose of the business and authorization was granted in July 1951 to seek advice from the Hotel Executive as to the best method of selling the establishment. Three years elapsed before the restaurant was offered for sale in October 1954 a further ten years elapsed before the business was

Three years after the takeover, the region received its first new vehicles with the delivery of four Guy Arab UF's, carrying Alexander centre entrance bodies and commonly known as the "Bombers". Two of the batch, including DG 971 (EAG 473) were reseated from 36 seaters to 30 seaters, fitted with toilets and operated on the Glasgow - London service. The Station yard site at Lockerbie was a stopping place for express services for many years, parking bays being assigned for "Western" and Ribble vehicles specifically; in practice, the High Street was used in busy times. (J.C.Gillham)

Croft bodies had also been fitted post-war to the four Albions acquired from Glasgow Corporation, but as the chassis were not as old as the Titans, being built in the mid-1930s the bodies remained on them until the batch were withdrawn in 1957. Two of them (DN873 and 874, YS2007 and 2095 respectively) illustrate both the differences in radiator, DN874 being one of the two re-engined with Leyland units and fitted with COVRAD Leyland radiators and the also the slight differences in bodywork, the two with Leyland radiators being fitted with opening upper deck window vents.   (Ian Maclean)

Few former Caledonian double deckers found new owners. Croft-rebodied Leyland TD1 DD866 (WW7861) was one of the lucky ones, gaining an extra lease of life as a contractor's bus with Marine Engineering of Bridlington with whom it is pictured here still in full Western livery.   (R.F.Mack)

sold to Reo Stakis in 1964! Early efforts to sell the surplus Trade Street premises in Stranraer were equally unsuccessful and the property continued to be leased out until final sale in July 1959.

Despite little scope existing for major route development, some tidying up, together with a few extensions and route variations, were instituted. One of the first moves by the new company was to apply for permission to operate double deckers on routes west of Kirkcudbright, as mentioned earlier, in March 1950. As a result, elderly Titans, especially former Caley vehicles TM3824/4 were

early visitors duplicating the Dumfries to Stranraer route, especially on summer Saturdays, and Stranraer garage received a regular allocation of deckers, including some of the "HD" Titans in early days. On the debit side, operation of the two Dumfries-Edinburgh services was taken over by SMT completely.

In the extreme west, the railway passenger services on the branch lines from Stranraer to Portpatrick and from Newton Stewart to Whithorn were early closure casualties. Railway passenger services to Portpatrick ceased on 6 February 1950, Western introducing new departures, three starting from or terminating at the Stranraer Town railway station, including an early morning departure at 6-40am to Portpatrick. In the same area, a Stranraer to Cairnryan South Deep working was also introduced, chiefly to serve the dockyard, whilst in the following year an express service from West Freugh RAF Station to Glasgow was granted to coincide with weekend leave together, with a similar service from Cairnryan (Ladyburn Camp) to Glasgow St Enoch for civilian workers. The Whithorn branch passenger workings ceased later in the year on 23 September 1950.

To cope with increased passenger loadings two AEC double deckers were drafted in as mentioned earlier and stationed at Wigtown garage, though they had to layover outside the depot, which was only capable of accommodating single deckers, like Whithorn. As with the Portpatrick service, new departures were introduced and again certain journies were extended to and from Dashwood Square up the hill via Stewart Street and Station Road to Newton Stewart station, including a new 6am departure from the Station to the Isle of Whithorn. At the same time, certain journies were diverted between Isle of Whithorn and Whithorn via Portyerrock; Caledonian had been in the process of applying for the latter variation at the time of takeover in December 1949, the application being withdrawn and re-applied for by the new company. Less successful was an application in February 1950 to operate one Wednesday only service between Wigtown and Newton Stewart by

Another view at Carlisle illustrates the use of the lane at the side of the garage for departures, due to the relatively restricted area within. DY1002 (HGC 140) was one of the ex London Guys rebodied by Alexander in 1952/3 forming one of nine allocated to the area. Leyland Tiger TS7 DL862 (BSM 170) and a Leyland Lion rebodied with a post-war ECW body illustrate the former Caledonian stock still operating in the area. (Ian Maclean)

a circuitous route via the hamlet of Malzie, this licence being refused. Buses operating from Wigtown and Whithorn were also frequently used on Saturday nights to carry the population to dances and, less frequently, when sailings to the Isle of Man were made from Garlieston. Another early route development was the linking (at last) of Caledonian route 20 from Dumfries to Sanquhar with the Ayr to Sanquhar service, also in 1950, to form a through route. The new service was re-timed to give an hourly service in conjunction with the Dumfries to Glasgow service, between Dumfries and Cumnock. Both these operated by the main road route using the A76 beyond Auldgirth, whereas the former Caledonian route had operated via Dalswinton and Kirkton. A new service was introduced between Auldgirth and Dumfries via these villages, connecting at Auldgirth with some of the "main road" journies in either direction. Certain journies were extended to Thornhill at the same time, to provide duplication at busy times and licences were also granted for a service on the last Sunday of the month between Chanlochfoot and Penpont Church via Druidhall and Holm of Drumlanrig, as well as

between Keir and Durisdeer via Penpont and Thornhill in connection with dances and concerts. In the following year, one return journey from Penpont to Thornnill via Holm of Drumlanrig, Burnsands, Farthingbank, Drumlanrig Park and Queens Drive was also initiated.

After much agitation over a period of years by Langholm area residents, a Saturdays Langholm to Lockerbie service was also started in 1951, to connect with, the Lockerbie to Dumfries routee, allowing Langholm residents to visit patients at the County Sanatorium at Lochmaben and hospitals and nursing homes in Dumfries. Despite earlier successes in gaining express workings from Cairnryan to Glasgow, the company failed in its application for a weekend express service from Claddyburn Camp, Cairnryan to Glasgow, with R.Murray and Sons gaining the licence in December 1951. Murray's were judged to be in a stronger position, having operated this as a private hire for a period. More successful, however, was an application for an express service to carry civilian workers from Cairnryan to Glasgow at weekends granted in the same month.

The region received its first new vehicles in 1952 in the shape of four Guy Arab UFs with Alexander centre entrance bodies (DG970-3 ; EAG472-5). Seating varied, DG970 and DG973 having 41 seats whilst DG971/2 had 36 seats. Within the year, 971/2 were fitted with toilets and reseated to spacious 30 seaters to compete with newly introduced services operated by Northern Roadways from Glasgow and Edinburgh to London. The availability of a large number of double deck vehicles with 5LW engines from London

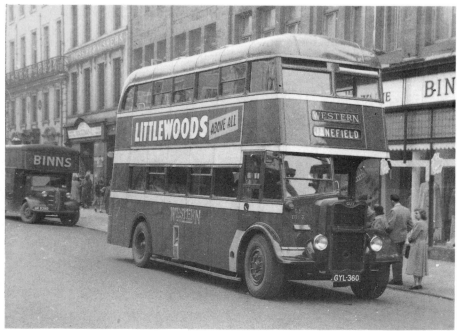

DY1027 (GYL360) was one of the five ex.London Transport Guy Arab IIs with NCME bodywork of a batch of tewnty five which were allocated to Dumfries in 1953. Picking up in the town's High Street, these buses were similar to Western's own Guys as well as those inherited from Youngs of Paisley, many of which served in Dumfries in later years as replacements for the ex.London vehicles after their withdrawal in 1957/8.   (Ian Maclean)

Ex.Youngs Bus Service Guy Arabs started to trickle down to the region in 1952, DY2135 (XS5547) being the first from this source. Its wartime Massey body had been replaced with a new ECW highbridge body as illustrated in this view outside the former Caledonian parcel and enquiry office at Whitesands, Dumfries. (A.Richardson)

Transport had been noted by the Bus Group management. However, their chassis would require overhaul and the bodies would need to be replaced according to their assessment. Western quickly received an allocation of these vehicles which were pressed into service painted but unnumbered and carrying their original utility bodies. In some cases at least their destination layout had been rebuilt to accommodate an illuminated fleetname panel above the single box, a practice brought by W.Young from Youngs Bus Service when he became chief engineer with Western. Within a year all but three of the original batch had been despatched to Walter Alexander for new 53 seat lowbridge bodies and nine of them were transferred down to the Dumfries and Galloway area on thrie return from the coachbuilders (DY999-1007 ; GLL590/6, GXE552, HGC140/3/6-8, GYL335), DY1000 and DY1002 later gaining the more powerful 6LW engine.

Mention is made above of the fitting of illuminated panels above the destination box although only a few Caledonian vehicles received this layout, most retaining their original layout which, as they came through for overhaul or accident repair, were reduced to a single line aperture by painting over the remainder of the box. Side destination indicators fell into disuse and were similarly treated on entry through the coach shop. Two batches which did receive the illuminated panel were the most recent deliveries, the Bristol Ls and Ks, though even some of these missed out. The Dennis Lancets, with their large "BET Federation style" layout would have lent themselves to fitment of a the panel but, as they were earmarked for early disposal, they remained with a reduced layout until the last were withdrawn in 1957. The Croft bodied Titans did, however, qualify for treatment, no doubt based on their relatively new bodywork and they survived on fitment to the ex.London Guys, of

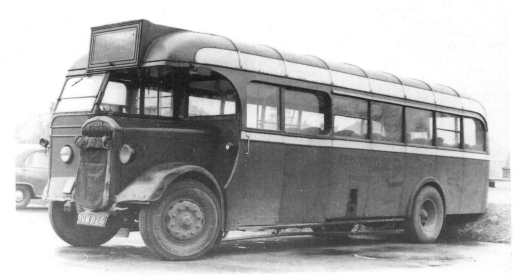

Many of the ex.Caledonian single deck vehicles saw further service after sale by "Western", including DS831 (BSM 824) which passed in 1955 to T.F.Rooney and Sons (Contractors) of Wallington.

Like the TS8 specials, Western's complete batch of Guy Arab saloons with Guy 32 seat bodies ended their days in the Dumfries and Galloway region. The first of the batch, DG395 (BSD 576) sits inside Lockerbie Garage, with an ex Youngs Guy Arab. (A.Richardson)

which more later. The Croft-bodied Albions were also similarly treated. No further effort was made to convert existing vehicles when, in 1956, new deliveries started to carry three track number displays and timetables began to carry service numbers again (for the first time since the war in Western's case).

Service developments continued; a variation of the Dumfries to Lockerbie service started via Locharbriggs, Amisfield Sheildhill and Templand in 1952, providing some compensation for the loss of the Dumfries - Lockerbie passenger service, another early rail casualty. The third Wednesday in each month was a whole day holiday in the Machars district around Newton Stewart and Whithorn. An express licence was obtained by Western in 1952 to compete with a local small operator, McKeand of Newton Stewart (where Western garaged their "sleeper bus"!) who had, enterprisingly, obtained a licence for a service to Glasgow from Newton Stewart to coincide with this holiday. Western's service started from Whithorn numbered 59F and, despite the timetable, picked up at road ends as well as the official points of Whithorn, Kirkinner, Wigtown and Newton Stewart. They also stopped regularly at a cottage at the side of the Newton Stewart to Girvan road, where the driver would blow the horn and await the lady locking up. Fresh baked scones were regularly given to the crew as a "thank-you" for this additional service! In the same year the Stranraer to Dumfries express service was extended to Carlisle on Sundays only, but this extension ceased in the latter part of 1953 and was replaced by one Saturday only express return journey by the direct A76 "High Road" from Dumfries to Carlisle, stopping at Annan and Eastriggs only. This service had also disappeared within a year! A Moniaive to Castlefern service with two return journies on Saturdays only was introduced but, similarly, was short-lived, disappearing in 1954.

In Wigtownshire, a Portwilliam-Eldrig-Mochrum-Portwilliam circular was introduced with three journies on Saturdays only. At the same time, the Newton Stewart - Wigtown - Wauphill - Portwilliam - Monrieth - Whithorn service, which had run on Sundays only was revised to operate as far as Portwilliam and increased with journies on Thursdays to Sundays. This replaced a Saturday only service given up by Crawford of Portwilliam. Indeed, as passenger loadings steadily fell off on their own services Western's Wigtownshire operation gained some compensation as smaller operators ceased. Provision of buses for dances was still important in the fifties and work was inherited from McKeand of Kirkinner and Smith of Creetown, the latter providing buses from his home base into Newton Stewart. Other operators from whom work was inherited included McCubbin of Kirkcowan and Tom Crawley of Portwilliam.

Returning to 1953, a small number of new Guy Arab 1Vs with "new look" tin fronts and nicely proportioned NCME 53 seat lowbridge bodies formed only the second small batch of new vehicles for the area since acquisition on receipt in 1953. DY1014-6 (ESD212/6/7) were allocated to the Dumfries to Stranraer route, displacing the Regent IIs onto other services. The pace hotted up with the acquisition of further Guy Arab IIs from London Transport, this time carrying metal framed NCME bodies built to peacetime

standards. Being in better fettle and fitting in with very similar vehicles bought new by Western and operated at Ayr, the requirement to rebody these vehicles was avoided. Five of the batch of twenty five were allocated initially to the area; DY1027/9/35/45/6 (GYL360/75/93/429/30). To complete the busy 1953 vehicle movements a further eight Arabs with utility bodies dating from 1943-5 were obtained from London (DY1048-55 ; GLF661/92/7/9, HGC151, GXE568, GYL317/406). This batch had their bodies removed at Kilmarnock and were then moved down to Eastfield Road where an interesting body transfer was arranged. Ever frugal, the company organised the removal of the sound batch of Croft bodies fitted new in 1947 to the elderly Caledonian Titans at Dumfries and their placement onto the Guy Arabs. This clever piece of economic rebodying involved the fitting of an insert put between the radiator and windscreen to partially conceal the longer engine compartment built to accommodate Gardner 6LW engines This piece of the conversion was carried out by Robertsons Metal Co. of Dumfries.

The body transfers involved the following; the body from DD897 to DY1048; from DD910 to DY1049; DD886 to DY1050; DD884 to DY1051; DD882 to DY1052; DD881 to DY1053; DD883 to DY1054 and from DD890 to DY1055. The elderly Leyland chassis were then broken up for scrap. As well as double deckers, a trickle of Guy single deckers with Guy rear entrance 32 seat bodies also began to arrive from the north in 1953 and by 1957 the whole batch of ten had arrived in the district (DG395-404 ; BSD 576-585). These allocations, together with the start of a steady trickle of ex.Youngs and Paisley and District wartime Guy Arabs (DY2135 XS5547 being the first in 1952, preceded by two of Western's own Arabs DY206/7 ; ASD404/5 which had been rebodied with new ECW bodies in 1951), allowed the withdrawal of Caledonian's older vehicles, the Titans in particular. Full details of the withdrawal of Caledonian vehicles are given at the back of this book in the fleet list. Although the majority of vehicles were sold to the usual outlet, Millburn Motors, a few of the older vehicles were officially "sold at Dumfries". It has been possible to trace a few of these as the details will show. While few double deck Caley vehicles moved to subsequent operators, due to their age and the availability of more modern second hand stock, a comparatively large number of quite elderly single deckers saw further service in a variety of roles, a testimony to the standards of maintenance by Dumfries.

Route developments were less intense in 1953; a local service between Annan and the curiously named Back of Hill was started. On the negative side, as passenger loadings began to drop, certain services were trimmed, the changes at first being relatively minor. The Wigtown-Kirkcowan-Newton Stewart service was cut back to Kirkcowan with connections being offered to Newton Stewart. In its hey day, the service could boast three full single deckers, carrying passengers to the "Pictures" at Newton Stewart. However, traffic was gained with the building of Chapelcross Nuclear Power Station near Annan on the site of a former wartime aerodrome, Western providing some of the workers vehicles.

In 1954, the vacated Moniaive garage at Dunreggan was sold, whilst Wigtown passed back from British Road Services to Western

ownership in July 1954 and the garage became purely a bus operating base for the first time in its existence.

MODERNISING THE FLEET
The late 'fifties and early 'sixties

The first reasonable quantity of new vehicles arrived in 1955 when ten Guy Arab LUFs (DG1116-25 ; GCS201-210) with Alexander 44 seat bus bodies were allocated to operate on the Dumfries - Stranraer and Dumfries to Carlisle routes. The trade press carried a feature on these vehicles, with a company spokesman stating that they were being introduced on the longer runs to improve passenger comfort. Verdicts from passengers over the years, incidentally, suggested that they had extremely hard seats and were very uncomfortable! Be that as it may, drivers appreciated their speed, over sixty miles an hour being possible in fifth gear. Two of them (DG1124 and 1125) were allocated new to Carlisle for use on the Glasgow to Dumfries route, which had been extended to run through to Carlisle together with the Ayr to Dumfries service without the need to change buses. Double deckers were precluded from the main Dumfries - Carlisle route due to a low bridge at Cummertrees and, as a result, single deckers were substituted, Cumnock garage using AEC Regal IVs which had been converted from 30 seat London service coaches. The licence for the service actually allowed double deckers to be used as far south as Clarencefield and then from Powfoot Road End to Carlisle, thus permitting 'deckers to provide duplicates over these sections. The services had been linked in response to the threat of an application by an Annan operator for a through service from Annan to Glasgow. No doubt the experience of McKeand gaining an express licence from Newton Stewart to Glasgow on whole day holidays had triggered them into speedy action. In practice, passengers for the through journey were relatively few, a direct link from Carlisle to Glasgow using the A74 being offered on the Lancashire stopping services. The schedules resulted in Cumnock's Regal IVs being used by Carlisle every second day and Cumnock making use of the Carlisle based Guy LUFs, the vehicles returning to their home base the next day. On receipt of the LUFs, the three Arab IVs delivered in 1953 were transferred to Johnstone. Secondhand arrivals were four further ex.London Guys which had originally been allocated to northern garages (DY1022/32-4 ; GYL296/380/91/2).

During that summer, the 1952 Guy UFs were allocated to the newly introduced Carlisle to London service, which ran through to Whitehaven on Fridays and Saturdays in July and August. A duplicate day coach operated in Summer from Carlisle to London, together with a summer season evening departure. A "Dumfries Pool" of drivers for the London service had been created in similar fashion to the original Kilmarnock and later "Johnstone Pool" to provide experienced drivers from the region's garages to operate the London services. Caledonian's last elderly Titans were withdrawn in the same year and by then considerable inroads had been made into the fleet of Dennis Lancets, as well as removing from the fleet the Tigers and Lions which carried the wartime built ECW bodies. New vehicle deliveries to the area remained relatively scarce, Western's management having to concentrate on re-stocking their northern garages, where intensive operation was taking its toll on wartime vehicles and where considerable public pressure was being felt for more modern machines.

The position was further complicated by the acquisition of Glasgow Corporation services in the Paisley area, firstly the bus services in 1955 and then, subsequent to the Suez crisis, the abandoned tram routes in 1957. Some relief was obtained by cascading more ex.Youngs Guy Arabs DY2140-50 (XS5650-

Leyland LT5A DL23 (VD3431), new in 1934, was one of twenty such vehicles acquired by Western from Central SMT in 1946. Its original Leyland body was immediately replaced by new Brush coachwork before its entry into service on the company's newly-resumed coach services including Glasgow - London. It is seen here in 1955 after its transfer to Dumfries garage on a private hire duty at Windermere.   (K.A.Jenkinson Collection)

9/709)and DY2285-7 (XS5719-21) having arrived by June 1958, no doubt the quality of Eastfield Road's maintenance had a bearing on the retention of older vehicles in the south, together with the less intensive operation away from the Dumfries town services. The region also received a batch of AEC Regals in 1955 after rebodying with Brislington Body Works 55 seat bodies (DC275/6/80/90/303/6/8-9 ; BAG73/4/8/88/107/10/2-3).

Private hire and day tour work had been in the hands of a mixture of Arab UFs plus a motely collection of Leyland Tiger TS7 and TS8 specials, DL21 (CS5269) and DL47-9/51 and DL110-12 (CS2005/21/2/7, CS5250/5/63) respectively being the TS7s drafted in after rebodying in 1950 with new Alexander C35F bodies and

G974 (EAG476) was one of a large batch of centre entrance Alexander-bodied Guy Arab UF coaches delivered in 1952 for use on the London service and private hire duties. With a sun visor above the windscreens and painted in Western's white and black livery, these coaches looked quite attractive.   (K.A.Jenkinson)

Portions of the Eastfield Road depot yard remained unsurfaced until the 'sixties. One of the ex.Youngs Bus Service Guy Arabs, DY2287 (XS5721), which had been rebuilt with a metal panel replacing the upper deck front opening vents, partly obscures an ex.Caledonian Leyland LT5. The 'Local' panel above the Guy's destination screen was used chiefly on Greenock area town buses, but did appear on a few ex.Youngs vehicles operated by its subsidiary Paisley & District. Its use was appropriate in Dumfries as well, however, as the Guys generally operated here on town services.   (Ian Maclean)

TS8 Specials DL169-74 (AAG108-13) rebodied with new Alexander C39F bodies in 1950. In addition, the ex.Youngs Bedford OB supported this work until its sale in 1954, together with a solitary Leyland Lion acquired in 1946 from Central SMT and rebodied with a new Brush body (DL23 ; VD3431), one AEC (DA575 ; CAG 803) which was drafted in during 1951, followed by two similar vehicles from the same batch DA577/9 (CAG806/8) in 1955 and a TD4 rebuilt as a TS7 and fitted with a new Burlingham C33F body (DL554 ; YS2028) which appeared in 1953. Further rebodied TS8 Specials were cascaded from northern garages between 1953 and 1958 (DL162-8/75-81 ; AAG101-7/14-6/20/3), resulting in all but one of the batch reaching the south. To this selection two new underfloor engined MW6Gs were added (DT1395/1400 ; LCS205/10) fitted with new Alexander DP41F bodies in 1958, followed a year later by a batch of two year old LS6Gs with similar bodies (DT1274-83 ; JSD910-9) from Greenock. In exchange, Greenock received all but two of the Arab LUFs, the odd men out being transferred to Kilmarnock. To support the bus fleet, a further breakdown vehicle arrived from Kilmarnock in the shape of D30 which had been converted from ex.London Transport Guy Arab GYL382 which had served as bus Y919 for four years from 1953. By 1958 all of the large fleet of Lancets had also gone together with all the Leyland Lions with post-war ECW bodies, and all that was left of the former Caley vehicles were the Bristol Ks and Ls including the four pre-war and wartime machines which had been rebuilt and rebodied to postwar standard in 1948.

The land on which the proposed Newton Stewart garage was to be built was sold in 1955, whilst the premises at Whithorn, which had struggled on in a poor state since H.H.Merchant's report in 1945 recommended demolition and re-siting were finally dismantled in August 1955 and the ground was sold in the following year. The fuel tank was moved down to Whithorn Station, the railway line still existing to carry freight traffic only. An office was rented from the

DL170 (AAG 109) was one of the TS8 specials drafted into the area after rebodying by Alexander in 1950. Wearing dual purpose cream and red livery, they provided handy private hire vehicles and were attractively finished inside with coloured light shades and comfortable seating. In later years, all but one of the batch were repainted into red bus livery.   (R.F.Mack)

More modern coaches, though still secondhand to the area, were two AEC Regals, one of which was DA579 (CAG808) also carrying Burlingham 33-seat coachwork, which arrived in 1955, joining another of the batch which had been sent south in 1951.

Whithorn Station became the base after the demolition of the Glasserton Street Garage in 1955. Tiger TS8 DL166 and Guy Arab DG400 are parked at the side of the station. (J.C.Gillham)

Ten Guy Arab LUFs with Alexander 44-seat bodies were delivered in 1955 and were used initially on the Dumfries - Stranraer and the new Carlisle - Dumfries - Glasgow through service. DG1124 (GCS 209) was one of two allocated new to Carlisle to operate the latter service and is seen prior to entry into service. (Ian Maclean)

numbers allocated were based on Western's system and, thus, did not conform with the old Caledonian numbers abandoned in 1950; for example, the Dumfries - Stranraer service carried service numbers in the 21 series in Caledonian days, but 76 under Western. The old Caledonian numbers had actually survived for a number of years on the destination boxes of ex.Caledonian vehicles, where they had not been rebuilt. One service which "might have been" was an express service between Glasgow, Ayr and Castle Kennedy. Licences were obtained to operate to this former wartime aerodrome to connect with an air service operated by "Silver City Airways" between Castle Kennedy and a base near Newtonards in Northern Ireland in the mid 'fifties. However, the capacity of the planes carrying two cars and some ten passengers never justified start up of the bus service and the air service fizzled out after a few years.

In 1957 one late Saturday only journey numbered 91D was introduced beyond Langholm to Ewes, but disappeared a year later. Further minor pruning in the east saw the 67A Stranraer-Auchenree-Portpatrick service cut back to Auchenree. In the following year, the 76A Dumfries to Stranraer express service was reduced to one Sunday only return journey. The 74B Penpont to Glenairlie Bridge service was amended to terminate at Burnsands, whilst a new Penpont to Thornhill service via Burnhead, Tibbers, Durmlanrig, Holestane Bridge and Carronbridge numbered 73E started operating on Wednesdays only was introduced for the benefit of people going to the cinema in Thornhill. Increased TV ownership even in rural areas "killed off" this service in 1961. A new route 76Y also started operating from Dumfries via Drumsleet and

British Railways Board for the depot inspector and vehicles were parked in the open in the yard.

The year 1956 heralded one new service between Dumfries and Dalry via Corsock operating on Saturdays only, with short workings to Corsock on Wednesdays only. Numbered 76G, a 76X variation via Lochfoot also operated. This service had been operated by McDonald of Corsock at the time of the 1936 Caledonian route review. Route numbers were re-introduced during that year, although the number of vehicles in the area capable of carrying the route number was very limited for many years. Indeed the numbers did not even appear in the timetables until 1957. The service

A solitary Leyland Titan TD4 rebuilt to TS7 standard and fitted with Burlingham 33-seat coachwork arrived in 1953 to boost the coach fleet. DL554 (YS2028) had strayed south to Lancaster when this view was taken. (S.E.Letts)

Lochfoot to Haugh of Urr, with short workings to Lochfoot numbered 76Z. This service operated over the old "Military Road" and complimented the Dalbeattie service on one flank and the Stranraer service on the other. Also, the Annan "local" 88 to Silverlaw was extended to the new council estate at Newington. On completion of Chapelcross Power Station, workers service 87E was introduced between Annan and the Plant to which an Eastriggs - Chapelcross service number 87F was added in 1959, followed in 1960 by service 81E from Dumfries via Lockerbie, Ecclefechan and Gauls Bridge to the Power Station and a Carlisle - Gretna - Chapelcross service. The Chapelcross services were also regrettably short-lived, ceasing by 1961. Although Clark of Glencaple still operated the main service, Western began operating a service 76F from Dumfries to Shawhead in 1960.

The old Harbour Garage at Kirkcudbright was demolished in 1957 and a new one built, whilst in the following year proposals were made to erect a new garage at Gretna which was deferred for a year due to British Transport Commission capital constraints. The

The first Bristol MW6Gs arrived in 1958, DT1400 (LCS210) being one of the first seen here at Ardrossan on a private hire duty. Although route numbers had been re-introduced in 1956, these vehicles were the first in the Dumfries and Galloway region capable of displaying them. (R.Marshall)

DS832 (BSM825) represents one of the last Dennis Lancets to be withdrawn in 1957. The bus is reversing into the right hand exit door of Carlisle garage with assistance from the conductress. (S.E.Letts)

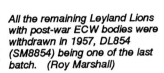
All the remaining Leyland Lions with post-war ECW bodies were withdrawn in 1957, DL854 (SM8854) being one of the last batch. (Roy Marshall)

proposal included the transfer of vehicles from Longtown and the consequent demolition of the garage and sale of land. The proposal dragged on, planning permission to build a garage on the existing site being refused. As a result, land was purchased in Annan Road in 1962 but no progress was reported in 1963. Six vehicles continued to be kept at Longtown, though they had to brave the elements as the old garage had been demolished in 1962. A local firm, Irving & Sons, approached the company with a view to purchasing the 1.5 acres of land which would have been surplus when Gretna garage was built. The intention was to rent the land back from Irving until the new garage was built, but the scheme foundered due to planning difficulties.

The period 1959-63 demonstrated a determined effort to improve the age profile of the Dumfries and Galloway region fleet. In 1959, three new Leyland PD3s DD1540-2 (MSD404-6) with Alexander 57 seat lowbridge bodies were delivered for operation on the Dumfries - Glasgow route, their delivery coinciding with the stopping of through running. In practice, this had already been happening when double deckers were allocated to the route. Their arrival brought the first double deck vehicles with platform doors to the region. The Leylands were also used on the Dumfries - Ayr and Dumfries - Stranraer service. Following these in 1960 were the last batch of Guy LUFs built for the home market, bodied with the usual Alexander DP41F bodywork (DG1548-55 ; MSD412-20). More new

By 1958 only the Bristol Ls and Ks remained of the fleet inherited from Caledonian. DB813 (ESM837) and DB814 (ESM 538), the two 1939 deliveries sandwiching an AEC Regent originally operated from Cumnock. The rebuilding and rebodying of the Bristols post-war made them indistinguisable from the younger counterparts, other than the registration number, and Western treated them as post-war vehicles, withdrawing all the Ls in 1960. (Roy Marshall)

caused some concern. Railways in the area at the time of Caledonian's start up comprised the line from Carlisle which branched off the main Glasgow line to Dumfries. From there, passenger services radiated westwards through Castle Douglas, Gatehouse and Newton Stewart to Stranraer, with a branch to Kirkcudbright. North-eastwards from Dumfries, one line extended to Lockerbie, gaining the main Glasgow line there and another line headed north up the Nith Valley to Sanquhar, Cumnock and Kilmarnock, whilst a light railway branched off to serve Moniaive (of which more later). In the west, a line branched from Newton Stewart to serve Wigtown and Whithorn, with a branch to Garlieston, the latter having been a very early casualty in losing its passenger service. From Stranraer, one line headed south to Portpatrick whilst another line turned north for Girvan and Ayr. In June 1929 the Stranraer to Girvan route was further extended to Glasgow, a distance of 86 miles, when a joint service was inaugurated with the BET controlled Scottish General Transport Company, by then based in Kilmarnock, who operated under the fleet name of Scottish Transport. The agreement for operating this service provides an insight into the complexities of joint running arrangements. The dividing line of the companies areas was the coastal resort of Girvan, Scottish Transport being responsible for all mileage and the revenue north of the town with "Caley" (as the company quickly became locally known) being responsible for all mileage and revenue south of that town. Any mileage imbalance was chargeable at 8d (3.5p) per bus mile , but could be "run off" i.e. the company with the shortfall in miles could make this up in mileage rather than remunerating the other. Through tickets were available, each company's conductors carrying a batch of the other's tickets and waybills. Two waybills required to be filled in over the route to record the sale of each companies' tickets. "Caley" cashed in the Scottish Transport's takings at the British Linen Bank at Stranraer , whilst Scottish Transport was to cash "Caley" takings at the Commercial Bank of Scotland branch in Paisley, suggesting that Scottish Transport's Paisley garage was responsible for operation of the Glasgow-Stranraer service. The Bank slips were then forwarded to each company. Through tickets were advised and cash adjustments made monthly. No local passengers could be carried between Turnberry and Girvan, although it appears that this was irrelevant, as the route did not operate between these two points, the agreement originally drawn up perhaps referring to a previously proposed route. The joint route south of Ayr was via Crosshill and Dailly to Girvan (for one return journey), the remainder operating direct from Maybole to Girvan. In October 1929 all journies were routed via Crosshill and Dailly. South of Girvan the main service operated direct through Lendalfoot, whilst a connecting bus served Pinmore and Colmonell villages before connecting with the through service back on the main road at Ballantrae. Advance booking of tickets was possible at locations where extra buses could be provided if required, namely Stranraer (Caledonian), Ayr, Kilmarnock and Glasgow (all Scottish General Transport). Midland Bus service also operated five through journeys between Glasgow and Stranraer with "extras" to Girvan in competition with Scottish Transport and Caledonian. This service had actually been inaugurated two months before the joint service although this operated at different times and followed a different route over certain sections south of Ayr, travelling via Maidens and Turnberry to Girvan, then direct on the A77 over Kennedy's Pass through Lendalfoot to Ballantrae. The original proposed route of Caledonian and Scottish Transport may have been changed as a result of Midland establishing their service over the same route. Relationships with Scottish Transport were obviously quite cordial from the start, as Caledonian arranged for the repair and overhaul of a couple of vehicles in their first year of operation (Leyland SM4681 and TC5273), as well as regularly purchasing "stores" until Scottish Transport's formation into Western S.M.T. in 1932.

The road traffic act of 1930 resulted in Caledonian having to apply in common with all operators to the newly formed Traffic Commissioners to operate the routes they were running. The days of uncontrolled running over competitors routes ceased, although competition still existed over routes which had more than one licensed operator. As a result, takeovers were increasingly used by Caledonian as a means of obtaining a monopoly on routes, as will be seen as the company's history unfolds.

During 1930, the High Street premises in Dumfries were vacated in favour of the Whitesands premises which by that time consisted of a house, hall and offices which were converted for use

A timetable was produced in June 1929 for the Stranraer - Girvan - Glasgow route, introduced jointly with Scottish General Transport. The Glasgow terminal point was George Square but had moved by 1931 to North Frederick Street.

Although the timetable implied a through service, in practice vehicles had a layover at Stranraer before continuing to Portpatrick. 'Anywhere' tickets were an early form of unlimited travel ticket, valid in specified areas.

as an enquiry and parcels office and staff canteen. Initially rented, the buildings were purchased in 1932. The attractive location had one particular disadvantage in that the River Nith, which flowed behind the stances could, on occasion, flood the bus stance area. Jim Calder never remembers the flood waters reaching the Whitesands office but there were occasions when the buses had to be moved up the "Sands" due to flooding of the bus parking area. In the west, Port Rodie enquiry office and staff room was established in Stranraer in March 1930 around the corner from the main departure points.

The accounts up to March 1930 showed a healthier upturn in profit to £1,530, allowing a dividend of 3% to be recommended by the Directors. However, comment was made that the revenue was being depleted by competition from an associated S.M.T. company from April 1929 over 57 miles of their operating territory. This referred to competition from John Sword's Midland Bus Service over the Girvan - Stranraer section of Caledonian's Glasgow route and over the whole of the Sanquhar to Dumfries route. Competition over these routes was to influence events later in Caledonian's life, of which more later. A further development was the purchase of James Clark of Lockerbie in June 1930 for £761. He ran a service between Lockerbie and Annan using two vehicles, a 26 seat Thornycroft and a 20 seat Bean in maroon and cream livery, both of which were taken into stock with the purchase. Arrangements were made with the L.M.S. railway to rent standing space at the forecourt of

to Newton Stewart via Twynholm, Gatehouse of Fleet and Creetown four times a day. Although this service was acquired, together with two Albions for £1200 (the family business being keen users of this chassis), they retained their other service from Castle Douglas to Carsphairn via Dalry and New Galloway. Known as the "Mail Run" as mail was carried on the service, the service operated over the same route which Midland Bus Service covered on their longer Ayr to Castle Douglas service. A considerable amount of traffic was generated on this route from the building of dams for Hydro Electric generation, of which there were a number being built in the 'thirties at Clatteringshaws, Loch Ken and New Galloway. Local passengers on this rural route had an interesting method of hailing their bus; for those whose properties were just off the main road, yellow flags were handed out by Solleys. On seeing a flag displayed the driver would stop his vehicle, give a hoot on the horn and await the appearance of the intending passenger; many a potential soaking from waiting for buses in exposed spots must have been avoided by this novel idea. Unfortunately for Solleys, just as Caledonian had competed heavily with them on the Newton Stewart route, so did Sword's Midland Bus Service, which put on a bus in front of and behind theirs and lowered their fares as well. Solleys carried provisions from the local Co-operative shop free; passengers were known to send their provisions via Solleys and travel themselves on the Midland bus, much to the annoyance of the former!. As well as this route, Solleys also continued to conduct hire and day tour work

The business of James Clark of Lockerbie was acquired in in June 1930, together with this Thornycroft, a Bean and a service between Lockerbie and Annan, on which this bus is seen. The use of paper stickers to give points en-route and destinations was commonplace. (Robert Grieves Collection)

Dalbeattie Station in July 1930. Services to Dalbeattie terminated here and services through Dalbeattie passed the Station. Again, this was to become a long established feature, Western continuing to use this point long after the station had closed. Also, a short term arrangement was entered into with the L.M.S. at Wigtown station for the garaging of two buses from August 1930. The vehicles (Leylands) were used on a contract to carry workers to Cairnsmore between Creetown and Newton Stewart where construction of a new water supply to Wigtown was being undertaken. Another form of collaboration with the LMS Railway was the introduction of combined road/rail tickets between Newton Stewart and Whithorn. A further joint service was inaugurated with the large S.M.T. organisation in 1931 between Dumfries and Edinburgh (Chambers Street) via Moffat, Broughton and Penicuick. When the service was inaugurated, Caledonian operated the one departure in each direction on Mondays, Wednesdays and Fridays, with S.M.T. operating on Tuesdays, Thursdays and Sundays. On Saturdays two departures were operated in each direction with both companies providing a return journey allowing the buses to return to their home base. Leyland Lions 53 and 54 (SM6918/9) were initially used on the route.

Accounts up to March 1931 reflected a much improved profit of £7499, allowing an increase in dividend to 5%. In May of that year, the main service of S.Solley and Sons of Castle Douglas was acquired. "Solleys Yellow Buses" as they were called, operated from a garage at the rear of the Imperial Hotel King Street, which they also owned. Their main service operated from Castle Douglas

in the area as well as being an early operator of a tour to Blackpool. After acquisition of the Newton Stewart service and vehicles, Caledonian began to garage vehicles in Solleys garage and continued to do so until March 1943 when the requirement to garage vehicles in the town ceased. When Solleys gave up the remainder of their operations in the mid 'thirties, Midland started to garage their vehicles on the Ayr - Castle Douglas route at Solleys premises.

The following services were operated in October 1931 : Dumfries - Lockerbie (operated daily); Lockerbie - Annan via Ecclefechan, Eaglesfield, Kirtlebridge Station and Brydekirk (operated daily); Lockerbie - Annan via Bankshill, Failford, Waterbeck, Eaglesfield, Brecon Beds and Creca Crossroads (operated Thursday - Saturday); Dumfries - Sanquhar via Kirkton and Thornhill (operated daily); Lockerbie - Carlisle (with all journeys being advertised as travelling via the famous Blacksmith's Shop at Gretna Green). The main service diverted to Eaglesfield from Kirtlebridge Station then returned to Kirtlebridge but a few journeys went direct from Eaglesfield to Wyseby Lodge (operated daily); Dumfries - Stranraer via Castle Douglas, Twynholm, Gatehouse of Fleet, Newton Stewart and Kirkcowan (six through journeys operated on weekdays taking 3 hours and 35 minutes. The service followed the main A75, except when diverting to serve the villages of Tywnholm and Kirkcowan - operated daily); Dumfries - Stranraer operated by the same route except it diverted between Dumfries and Castle Douglas to serve Dalbeattie, adding 30 minutes to the journey time (operated daily); Dumfries - Kirkcudbright via

The last of the former Caledonian fleet was sold in 1963, with the disposal of the four Bristol Ks. DB876 is in its last year of service when seen parked at Whitesands. (Dr. J. Sinclair)

Lockerbie, Penpont and Stranraer received their first new double deckers ever! Carlisle received DB1627-32, Kirkcudbright received DB1643, Lockerbie received DB1634/6, Penpont DB1635 and Stranraer were allocated DB1644-7. In the following year, the last batch of MW6Gs purchased by Western were all allocated to the south (DT1704-10 ; TCS151-7), together with the first two FLF6Gs (DB1711/2 ; TCS159/60), which were allocated to the busy Locharbriggs - Lincluden cross town service in Dumfries. Secondhand arrivals from Greenock were 1955 Lodekkas DB1151-59 (GCS237-245), together with 1956 Lodekkas DB1227-31 (HSD15-19) from Johnstone. DB1151-5/7 were allocated to Carlisle. In 1963, eight of the first batch of 36ft. Leyland Leopards with Alexander DP49F bodies were allocated, taking their place on the Dumfries to Stranraer and Dumfries to Carlisle services. In addition, further secondhand Lodekkas arrived from Johnstone, DB1232-7/41-3 (HSD20-5/9-31) and over 1963/4 further buses of this type were gained, DB1243-5 (HSD31-3) and DB1292-6 (JSD928-32), again from Johnstone. With these arrivals, the last Caledonian vehicles left the fleet with the withdrawal and sale of the four Bristol Ks in 1963. And so, a chapter ended...............

Interestingly, no more new vehicles were received in the region until 1969, when a solitary Leopard coach was allocated to Dumfries. Prior to this, the region again relied on the cascading of used Leopards and, later, Daimler Fleetline double deckers to provide their vehicle intake. Amongst the secondhand Leopards was

a small number of 30ft. L1s built in 1960 which replaced the Guy 'Bombers' on the Carlisle - London service during 1963/4. Admittedly, four Leyland Leopards had been planned for delivery in 1964, but the transfer of the Glasgow Airport service from Scottish Omnibuses Ltd. to Inchinnan garage resulted in a swift change of plan. In that year, the company's vehicles started to carry two digit year codes to identify the age of each vehicle and were soon to be seen on the area's vehicles. The first digit was an alpha character and represented the decade of build, whilst the second digit was a

Exhibited when new at the 1966 Commercial Motor Show at Earls Court, London was 2179, a 38-seat Alexander-bodied Bristol RELH6G coach with onboard toilet built for use on Western's London services.

DL1837 (VCS391), a white & black liveried Leyland Leopard of 1963 vintage with Alexander Y-type multi-windowed coachwork is seen here at Dumfries before leaving on the 05 service to Carlisle. (K.A.Jenkinson Collection)

number representing the year of build. "A" equalled a vehicle built in the 1950's and "B" one built in the sixties. A vehicle carrying A5 was thus built in 1955. Had the scheme been introduced ten years earlier, progress through the alphabet would have been quicker with 1929 vehicles still around! To list all the vehicles which have been used in the Dumfries and Galloway region from the demise of the last of the Caledonian vehicles is impractical although a few deliveries deserve special mention and will be described in the text. Suffice to say a motley collection of Guy UFs, younger LUFs, Leyland Titans, Guy Arabs, Bristol LSs and MWs spent part of their lives or ended their days in the area. Vehicles for the London services were rotated periodically, though the replacements were always secondhand to the area. Many Leyland Leopards and, later, Seddon Pennine VIIs also passed through the region up to the present day, both "second hand" from other garages and also new, though perhaps the best known vehicles in the 'seventies were the batch of Bristol RELHs which were cascaded from the Glasgow - London service and were to feature in the area in various forms for many years until their demise. The Daimler Fleetlines arrived in the 'seventies, mostly second-hand to the area, to operate chiefly on Dumfries local duties as well as school journies from the Stranraer, Whithorn and Wigtown garages.

On the property side, Carlisle Town Council had been proposing that the main operators build a central bus station since 1960 at the "Sands", the overflow parking area used by Western and, previously, Caledonian. All the operators concerned objected and the proposal was dropped in 1962 though, at the Council's request, investigation of the erection of a joint bus station was undertaken which ultimately came to nothing. In contrast, a smooth move was made during 1962 from the Market Square terminus in Annan to the new bus station in Butts Street, just off the High Street. More successful than the long saga at Gretna was the building of a garage at Whithorn on land leased from the Scottish Co-operative Wholesale Society in 1962, near the railway station. Up the road, permission was granted to demolish the existing premises and build a new garage at Wigtown in 1963. The latter two developments are reported to have been as a result of a visit to the area by William Sword and allowed both depots to house double deckers under cover for the first time in their existence.

Of all the developments, perhaps the most intriguing was a proposal which never came to fruition. In 1960, proposals were made split to some of the Scottish Bus Group companies into smaller units to make them more manageable. The idea centred around the dropping of the SMT title in all companies, the split of Alexander into three companies, Midland, Northern and Fife and, particularly interesting, the splitting of Western into Western and Caledonian! This little known proposal would certainly have caused a stir in Dumfries and Galloway! In the event, after further discussion, the names Scottish Buses (Western) Ltd. and Scottish Buses (Southern) Ltd. were proposed, then the proposal was subsequently dropped completely, only the well known Alexander split happening in 1961.

Year codes were introduced in 1964. White and black liveried Alexander-bodied Leyland Leopard DL1901 (XCS922) illustrates the coding applied below its fleet number between the door and front wheel arch.

Having received nine of the first batch of Bristol Lodekkas delivered in 1955 from Greenock in 1962, the region received the remaining eleven in 1964. DB1168 (GCS254) sits in the new Butts Street bus station in Annan, which replaced the Market Square stances in 1962. (E.Shirras)

One of the 1961 batch of Bristol LD6Gs, all of which were allocated to the area, sits outside the nearly new Whithorn garage erected in 1962. (R.F.Mack)

An early delivery for Percivals associated South of Scotland fleet at Dumfries was this dual-entrance Leyland - probably an SG-type. (Robert Grieves Collection)

A number of Albions were also operated by South of Scotland including number 26 which was probably their 1930 PKA26 model, registered SM8565, which carried NCME bodywork and passed to Caledonian in whose fleet it was numbered 113. (Robert Grieves Collection)

South of Scotland was a keen Leyland user like Caledonian, though this Lion PLSC1 did not survive long enough to pass into the fleet. The star within the fleetname garter was common on vehicles in the fleet.

Thornhill and Moniaive had much older origins, being operated together with a route from Stranraer to Drummore by the Glasgow and South Western Railway with Milnes Daimlers during 1906/7. Like the Drummond route, the service was abandoned as unprofitable.

The most important take-over of the year, however, came later in December when Percival's associated South of Scotland Motor Company Ltd. of Dumfries came into Caledonian ownership, the price paid being the very substantial sum of £32,400. Caledonian's efforts to further expand in and around Dumfries had been frustrated by the presence of this company who had introduced local bus

services in Dumfries in 1923 and developed a comprehensive network to cover all portions of the town, as well as running an equally extensive range of "Country" services. Twenty one vehicles, chiefly Leylands, came with South of Scotland Motor Company. The background to this company and its development is an interesting story. Prior to the introduction of buses in Dumfries, there had been talk of operating electric trams between Gasstown on the Annan road east of Dumfries across town to the west, terminating at Maxwelltown on the Dalbeattie road. A William Irving of Dumfries Motor Company brought a saloon from Carlisle and ran it around Dumfries for 2 weeks. It is not known if fares were charged or what

One of the last deliveries to South of Scotland was this Leyland bodied Tiger TS1 (SM 8910) which arrived in 1931. It survived long enough to pass into Western SMT ownership in 1949, albeit with a different (secondhand) body.

the locals reaction was. No further developments appear to have taken place from this trial run until the morning of October 24th 1923, when Richard Percival introduced two Guy single deckers running across town from Brasswell (a little further east along the Annan road than the proposed starting point of the trams) to Dalbeattie road at the junction of Park road (later generally termed Janefield and again near the proposed western terminus of the tram service). The operation was under the control of a Mr.Cook who had served with the Carlisle Tramway company. Though he was officially an inspector his job appeared to be "jack of all trades", his duties not finishing until the last run of 10pm. The service ran on a half hour frequency until 11am, then every fifteen minutes, the Guy single deckers quickly being augmented by further Guys and Leylands to support the service. Initially, vehicles operated with Percivals fleetname, having been drafted in from the main fleet but the company was known as Scottish Southern Motor Services and, apparently, most of the local population had sampled the delights of omnibus travel by the end of the first week of operation. No doubt, many took their first journeys for the novelty value, but support for the new service was sufficiently encouraging for new routes to be operated between the odd sounding suburb of Stoop to the north end of Dumfries and the Crichton Royal Infirmary in the south and between the Cresswell housing scheme and Heathhall, where the car factory of Arrol Johnston generated a considerable amount of traffic. Arrol Johnston had moved to Dumfries in 1911 to be nearer the English markets. Despite its popularity, or perhaps because of it, some people questioned why "locals" had not set up a bus company, rather than allow an "outsider" to reap the rewards. Percival reacted quickly to quell these rumblings by floating a public company called South of Scotland Motor Company Limited (was the original title too close to Scottish Motor Traction for comfort?), which ran in a blue and cream livery. A report in the Dumfries and Galloway Standard in January 1924 stated that the new company's Directors consisted of a majority of Dumfries men with Richard Percival as Managing Director. A total of £15,000 of the capital of £25,000 was issued in £1 shares to the public. The new company acquired ground in Hood's Loaning off English Street and near the centre of Dumfries and built a bus garage with workshops. Surplus ground was sold off in later years to the owners of the Regal Cinema to build a theatre. Late theatre buses were provided for the three flourishing 'Picture Houses' after 10-30pm. With the development of the Locharbriggs housing scheme, the Cresswell to Heathall service was extended and revised to operate via Moffat Road or Edinburgh Road. Also, the building of the St. Michaels Bridge in 1927 allowed new routes to be added in the Maxwelltown area, Maxwelltown being joined to Dumfries in 1929 by Act of Parliament.

Licences for the following Dumfries town services were acquired with the business : Locharbriggs - Queensberry Square : Crichton - Stoop; Troqueer - Cresswell; Janefield - Brasswell; and High Street - Victoria Avenue (this service operated on Saturdays and other days when football matches were being played at the Queen of the South ground at Palmerston Park. The licence allowed the operation of buses every ten minutes to the ground between 1.30pm and the start of the game and then until 5.15pm from the finish). The out of town services were : Dumfries - Castle Douglas (King Street) via Crocketford and Springholm; Dumfries - Castle Douglas (King Street) via Crocketford and Springholm and Kirkpatrick Durham; Dumfries - Moniaive via Newbridge, Dunscore and Crossford; Moniaive - Glencairn Church; Dumfries - Annan via Collin and Carrutherstown; Dumfries - Carlisle via Mouswald, Clarencefield, Cummertrees and Annan; Dumfries - Dalton via Carrutherstown; Annan - Langholm via Kirkpatrick Fleming and Canonbie; and Annan - Dumfries via Cummertrees, Clarencefield and Mouswald.

The garage premises did not pass to Caledonian, however as Eastfield Road was capable of absorbing the increased vehicle requirements.

No new vehicles appeared in 1929 but four Leyland bodied Leyland Lion LT2s (numbered 64-7, SM8315-8) were delivered in 1930 (costing £4753.19.0) followed by a further four in 1931 (70-3, SM8851-4). The delivery of the 1930 signalled a slight simplification of the livery with the abandonment of the deep red waist band. Side destination boards were fitted above the windows, a practice which ceased in the early 'thirties with the movement of vehicles around the area.

The most important (and most contentious) purchase, however, took place on 18th January 1932 when the substantial business of Andrew Harper of Peebles was acquired for £14521. Andrew Harper had been in operation as a "Carrier" in Broxburn, some 10 miles west of Edinburgh, since 1894. He was joined by his sons in the business early in this century and the business developed profitably. Four working horses and their drivers, one two horse lorry, two vans plus a horse and gig for family transport, collected and delivered anything from a small parcel to a bank safe. Furniture removals and emptying ashpits (before the days of refuse collection by the local councils) were typical work, but the major source of business was the contract for delivery of all goods from Holygate Goods Station, owned by the then North British Railway.

After the 1914-18 War, ex War Department lorries were bought and the business expanded further with carrier work from Edinburgh, especially from Leith Docks collecting and delivering basic goods like sugar and flour to merchants in Broxburn, Pumpherston and Bathgate districts. The Broxburn business was probably at its peak around 1920, with the "fleet" including a 4 ton "Sentinal" chain-driven lorry on the Edinburgh/Leith runs and a 2.5 ton Austin Lorry. However, the shale miners and railwaymans strike of 1921 signalled the end of Broxburn as a thriving town, many families moving away and some even emigrating to find work. It also caused Harper's to look around for alternative locations to serve; Andrew Harper's wife suggested that a carrier service should be tried between Leith, Edinburgh, Peebles, Innerleithen and Walkerburn. The Peebles business was started in Spring 1922 with one ex.W.D. 4-ton Dennis solid tyred lorry (SX1469), stabled at Alexander's Garage in Station Road (renamed Dean Park when the former LNER Station was demolished to make way for road developments). Collections were made in the Leith and Edinburgh districts on weekdays (except Wednesdays) with deliveries being made the same evening in Peebles. On Wednesdays and Saturdays deliveries were made in Innerleithen and Walkerburn and "empties" were collected for return to the warehouses on Thursday and Mondays when business was quieter. Some of the carrying was to "accommodation addresses" and could easily have been "poached" salmon but no questions were asked! For the record, charges were around 25/- per ton for sundry goods, with higher rates for carrying spirits and other high-risk goods. The operation expanded, a second Dennis lorry frequently being pulled from Broxburn to pick up complete loads and to help out generally. A reputation for first class service was quickly built up and carefully maintained.

As the Station Road Garage could not accommodate two lorries, to avoid the risk of pilfering, bigger premises were found in what was later Dovecot Road. A corrugated iron shed was rented from Peebles Town Council which had previously been used by them for garaging road rollers, trucks etc. These premises were to continue in use, much enlarged and altered, by both Harper's and, after the take-over, by Caledonian. The Shed is still in use today by Tweeddale District Council (the successor to Peebles Town Council) for a similar purpose as in 1922! By early 1923, three lorries were in use in Peebles and as the Broxburn business was rapidly declining, a decision was made by the family to diversify into the operation of bus services in the Peebles area. Andrew Harper and one of his sons, H.G.Harper set off from Edinburgh by overnight train to London with £700 in their pockets to buy their first bus from a Mr. J.W.Roberts of Shepherds Bush. The bus was a 20-seat Daimler registered XN3932, the chassis being ex.War Department, the body having being built by Roberts. A second hand Dennis was also acquired which had last operated for the War Department but originated with Walter Alexander (MS4054) to start operations. In April 1923, the first service commenced with the newly acquired Daimler, driven by Andrew Harper's other son Joe Harper. The initial route was between Peebles, Innerleithen and Walkerburn. Having obtained permission for picking up and setting down passengers at recognised points, as well as the terminus at Peebles end of the journey from the Peebles and Innerleithen town councils, the terminus at Walkerburn was selected. Walkerburn had no such authority so the terminus was chosen in Hall Street which was not ideal, being a steep hill. The High Street terminus which they would have preferred was foregone, due to objections from the proprietor of the George Hotel, who did not want buses standing outside his premises, sometimes for long periods. Competition on this service became fierce, as other operators worked the same two mile stretch between Innerleithen and Walkerburn. One of these competitors acquired a 14-seat Chevrolet which ran in front of the Harpers bus;

Double deckers were also operated by Murray, including this ex.Plymouth wartime Roe-bodied Guy Arab CDR735. None of the vehicles or the substantial West End garage pictured in the rear passed to Western SMT however. (R.Marshall)

the new parking area. Authorisation was given for the erection of a new garage at Longtown, whilst the long running proposals to build a garage at Gretna being abandoned. The land on which the old dormy shed was sited at Gretna was sold to Dumfries County Council for housing development and the duties of Gretna garage were transferred to the new Longtown garage. In the latter years of its existence, Gretna had been involved in works duties to

Chapelcross, Broom and Mossband, schools work and some duplicates on the Annan to Carlisle services, involving four vehicles.

Early in 1969, Western also gained a share in the Eastern Scottish 095 service from Carlisle to Edinburgh, which had been revised to compensate for the withdrawal of train services on the Waverley line between these two points. A new route was also introduced between Carlisle and Newcastleton numbered 93E, as well as a new Dumfries town route D4H between Dumfries and Twinames estate which provided additional services along the Locharbriggs route and gave connections to both the small residential estate and the Technical College. On the vehicle side, the three-yearly cycle of replacing the "London" fleet saw a few Bristol RELHs arriving from Kilmarnock to replace the Leopards. Of the batch of twenty-one, all but two spent some of their working life at Dumfries and Galloway region garages in various guises, including one retrospectively fitted with bus-type seats and even the two which 'escaped' due to their sale to Highland Omnibuses appeared later, as we shall see. The first new vehicle for six years also arrived in the shape of Leyland Leopard DL2179 (KCS150F), finished in the black and white coach livery.

DL1884 (XCS905) was one of the small batch of Leyland Leopards which formed the Dumfries allocation of the London fleet from 1966 to 1969, before their replacement by the Bristol RELHs.

THE 'SEVENTIES
Passenger losses mount

The year 1970 was to see the first of an increasing number of rural route withdrawals, the first round being in Wigtownshire. The following services ceased or were cut back; 76M Stranraer to New Luce*; 64A Stranraer to Clachanmore*; 66 Stranraer to North Cairn cut back to Ardwell Shop (and chiefly aimed at the carriage of school children); 66C Stranraer - Leswalt - Lochnaw*; 67A Stranraer to Auchenree; 67B Stranraer - Three Mark and 69C Portwilliam - Eldrig. (* inherited from R.Murray and Sons).

Daimler Fleetlines had begun to filter in from the northern garages and one particularly interesting machine was R2117 (GCS170R) which had an experimental cream livery between decks. This lasted for nearly two years before it eventually gained standard colours. The summer of 1970 was also the last season that a separate London - Carlisle service was operated, together with the extension in July and August to Workington. In 1971, the level of losses on many of the rural routes had reached such a point

that drastic action was called for and Western intimated their intention to withdraw a large number of services. Included in the list, surprisingly, were some of the trunk routes; Service 03 Glasgow to Stranraer, 05 Glasgow to Dumfries, 79 Dumfries to Carlisle via Cummertrees and the less frequent 80 which ran via Carrutherstown and Dalton. Other services in the Lockerbie, Annan, Dumfries, Kirkcudbright and Stranraer area were also threatened and a full list is given as follows - Dumfries to Dunscore; Gatehouse; Annan; Castle Douglas; Dalbeattie; Kippford; Stranraer; Moniaive and Glencaple; Castle Douglas to Dalry; Annan to Langholm; Lockerbie; Newington; Moffat and Canonbie; Stranraer to Glenluce; Auchenmaig; Whithorn/Isle of Whithorn; Ardwell; Cairnryan and Drummore; Lockerbie to Gretna, Eaglesfield; Ecclefechan; Hightae; Templand and Carlisle; Newton Stewart to Creetown; Isle of Whithorn and Portwilliam; Carlisle to Langholm; Kirkcudbright to Dalbeattie; Ayr to Castle Douglas; Newcastleton to Canonbie;

Prior to delivery of three new Daimler Fleetlines in 1971, Dumfries had received a steady supply of second hand examples, including DR2117 (GCS170E), one of two painted in an experimental livery with cream between decks.   (P.M.Tulloch)

A further round of cuts resulted in the 86 Annan - Moffat service being withdrawn amongst others. DT1709 (TCS157) is parked in one of the bays at Moffat prior to return to Annan.   (A.J.Douglas)

Penpont to Holm of Drumlanrig and Whithorn to Wigtown. A new operator, Gibson of Mouswald applied to take over the 79 and 80, but withdrew his application when the County Councils offered financial support for some of the workings on this route, whilst the other County Councils responded with limited offers of financial help.

Despite the financial help a further large round of services did cease or were cut back as follows : 76A Dumfries to Stranraer express service ceased, replaced by extending certain of the existing 76 stopping services to Dumfries Railway Station; 86 Annan - Moffat; 83 Lockerbie - Langholm; 94D Carlisle - Longtown via Cliff Inn; 93 Carlisle - Scugg Gate - Nook Gate; 59F Whithorn - Glasgow express; 73 Thornhill Station - Penpont-Moniaive cut back to

operate Thornhill - Penpont only; 84 Lockerbie - Annan via Bankshill and 86 Canonbie - Newcastleton.

On the vehicle front, the first new double deckers in nine years were supplied to Dumfries in 1971, Daimler Fleetlines DR2291-3 (UCS289-91K) appearing, and from 1972 regular allocations of new Leyland Leopards were made to the Dumfries and Galloway region garages. A further round of service reductions resulted in more cut backs and withdrawals in the following year, these being the 74B Penpont - Burnsands; 87C Annan - Kirkpatrick Fleming cut back to Creca and 87D Evertown - Gretna. In 1973, a new local service in Dumfries was introduced between the High Street and the expanding Wimpey housing development at Georgetown. In reverse, the 70J Wigtown - Kirkcowan service, which had previously been cut back from Newton Stewart was withdrawn. In this same year, D15, an AEC Militant recovery vehicle finally entered service having been purchased in October 1970. Its previous body had been scrapped at Kilmarnock after which its chassis had been despatched to Dumfries. The Eastfield Road workshops then spent two years building a new body in between higher priority operational fleet-work. The Matador was then transferred north to Greenock prior to its completion although it made a number of visits south to provide cover until the Militant was ready for use. The Guy tow wagon D30 was also replaced at this same time by a converted Bristol Lodekka (HSD31) which became DW7030. A new service operating in the summer only between Isle of Whithorn and Burrow Head Holiday Camp was tried in 1974 numbered 70G, but was not repeated. The owners of the Caravan Park which had formerly been the wartime Anti-Aircraft Training Camp, subsidised the service, which gave a connection with the 1-15pm Newton Stewart to Isle of Whithorn service and, in practice, ran through. Day tours were also operated from the camp. Rationalisation in the Nith Valley resulted

The three new Daimler Fleetlines delivered in 1971 represented the first new double deckers in the region for nine years. They also started work on the same route as the last new double deckers delivered, namely the Locharbriggs - Lincluden service. DR2291 (UCS289K) manouvres its way through town with a good load, showing the revised route number of 304 (previously D4).

This AEC Militant entered service in 1973 with a body built by the Eastfield Road workshops over a three year period. Renumbered from D15 later to DW7015, the vehicle has recently been retired and is now preserved.
(Garry Ward)

DN1873 (VCS427) was one of the Albion Lowlanders drafted in during 1976 for operation of school journies. They became the first Albions operated in the region for nineteen years since the sale of the four ex.Caledonian vehicles in 1957.

Leaving Carlisle bus station on its way from London to Glasgow is Alexander-bodied Bristol REMH6G NAG114G seen here wearing its original black and white livery.   (K.A.Jenkinson Collection)

Longtown was only being used to store withdrawn vehicles and Carlisle's vehicle requirement was much reduced.

The responsibility for providing subsidies for loss making services passed to the newly formed and geographically large Dumfries and Galloway Regional Council in 1975. One growing trend in the region was the introduction of Post Bus services in the seventies to replace services like those between Annan and Creca as mentioned earlier, and the service from Stranraer to New Luce. Other services supplemented existing services, for example the Annan - Powfoot service. In line with other Western local services, the Dumfries town routes were renumbered. Services D1 Town - Brasswell, Town - Janefield and Town - Troqueer became 301 along with former D3 Town - Stoop. D2 services Town - Larchfield, Town - Hardthorn Road and Town - Maxwelltown Memorial became

in service 72 Dumfries - Kirkton - Auldgirth - Thornhill being withdrawn and covered by diversions of the 47 Dumfries - Ayr service over its route. Some short workings to Auldgirth and Thornhill continued at peak periods. Also in 1973, further economies were investigated with the negotiation with Ribble for the disposal of Longtown and Carlisle depots, but the latter company ultimately advised that they had no interest in the properties. By then,

DL2554 (KRG512F) was one of six Leyland Leopards obtained from Northern Scottish in 1978 in exchange for Albion Lowlanders in an effort to speed up one man operation. Four of the six were operated in the region.
(Garry Ward)

Three new Seddon Pennine VIIs also arrived in 1976, with arguably the most attractive livery treatment on all the Alexander T-type bodies. DS2579 (MSJ385P) was the last of the three and shows both the Seddon and Gardner engine badges carried when new. The gap in the lower grille had been intended for the registration plate, but cooling problems caused them to be moved below. (Garry Ward)

303. D3 Town - Crichton - Kingholm Quay also became 303. D4 Lincluden - Locharbriggs became 304 and D5 Town - Lochside became 305. At the same time, the Stranraer Town services S1 Cross - McMasters Road and S1A Cross - West End Terrace became 680 and 680A, respectively. One growth area, however, was the increase in summer services passing through Stranraer via the ferry to Northern Ireland. The summer 1975 timetable illustrates this with Service 909 Glasgow-Londonderry joint with Ulsterbus, 910 Glasgow - Letterkenny joint with Londonderry and Lough Swilly Railway Company (the latter being purely a bus operator by this date despite its name), 911 Glasgow - Bundoran joint with Ulsterbus and 912 Glasgow - Cardonagh, again joint with Ulsterbus. A further development was a Belfast - Stranraer - London via Birmingham service which was introduced in May 1975. Operated jointly with National Travel (North West) and Ulsterbus, the latter providing the link between Belfast and Larne), the service made use of the Sealink ferry between Larne and Stranraer. Initially, the plan had been to switch to the Townsend Thorenson ferry from Larne to Cairnryan, but this never came to pass. Western had originally intended to operate the Stranraer - London service themselves, but appeals from the National Bus Company right up to Scottish Bus Group board level resulted in National Travel obtaining a share of the traffic.

Increased private hire and express work resulted in Stranraer receiving five new Alexander T-type bodied Seddon Pennine VII coaches in 1978. SS2933-7 are posed inside the garage when new; the unusual placing of the fleet numbers was quickly changed to the standard position due to stone chip damage soon defacing them.

Further pruning came as a result of a survey of the Borders services in 1976; the loss making 095 Carlisle to Edinburgh service had been progressively converted to "One Person Operation" and the number of journeys were reduced. The 79E Annan - Powfoot service also finally ceased, coverage being provided by the Post Bus service already in existence together with the Annan - Creca service which was already covered by Post Buses. Some interesting vehicle movements in that year which were worthy of note was the transfer of Albion Lowlanders for school work to the southern garages, the small Penpont garage inheriting one of the type with a couple going to Stranraer. A sliding window, periscope and reversing lights were fitted into these machines for their new duties. Meanwhile, the Post Bus services were further extended with the introduction of a Kirkcudbright - Borgue route. One man operation progressed rapidly in the year with Dumfries converting to 100% OPO in April, Annan and Kirkcudbright becoming 100% OPO in December and Carlisle and Stranraer in early 1977 and in January 1978 the 03/51/9 services from Glasgow to Stranraer, Castle Douglas and Newton Stewart respectively were converted to OPO. To speed the process, six Albion Lowlanders were exchanged with Northern Scottish for a similar number of 1968 Leyland Leopards during 1976 and four of the batch subsequently appeared at the southern garages. Their stay was comparatively short, however, and they were sold to Central SMT in 1980. In the same year the first new Seddons with Alexander T-type bodies appeared in the form of DS2577-9 (MSJ383-5P).

A further service withdrawal was the route 64B from Stranraer to West Freugh in 1977 as the importance of the base diminished. Worthy of note in that year was the acquisition of four former National Travel (West) Leopards with Alexander bodies and twin speed rear axles dating from 1965 which were allocated to the

Whilst the relationship between the state owned National Bus Company and the Scottish Bus Group allowed surplus NBC vehicles to be sold north of the border, Western had forged a relationship with Essex dealer, Ensign, as well. The latter link resulted in the purchase of two further Leopards originating from North Western Road Car Co. one of which was fourteen year old Alexander-bodied DL2699 (VDB953). *(Garry Ward)*

The infrequent Dumfries - Edinburgh via Moffat service was renumbered from 89 to 99 during 1978. Alexander-bodied Leyland Leopard DL2357 (WSD747K) represents the final livery (cream & red) before the corporate fleet name and adapted paint scheme was introduced. The service passed to McEwans of Dumfries as part of the tendering exercise of 1986. *(Garry Ward Collection)*

region's garages followed by another which had originated from North Western, this time via Ensign (dealer), in the following year, whilst Stranraer received Daimler Fleetlines from the northern garages for school duties, the depots contention being that single deckers were unsuitable for this type of work. The Leopards proved popular with the drivers with their two-speed axles on the longer runs, including Lancashire expresses whilst Bristol Lodekka B1638 (RAG404) was converted to a driver training vehicle (DW7064) and painted in a grey livery. Investigations were carried out in that year by Western and Dumfries and Galloway Regional Council on the feasibility of introducing express journeys between Stranraer and Carlisle (again!) to supplement the British Rail day service via Kilmarnock, though some years were to pass before this got off the ground.

The importance of garages with their own maintenance facilities was recognised with Stranraer garage gaining its own depot code of "S" for the first time; its importance as a base for private hire work through the ferry services as well as express duties compensated for the progressive demise of local routes. Additionally, a number of the famous Bristol REMHs with Greyhound-style windows were drafted into Stranraer to support the London service, some of them arriving from Dumfries. More surprising, however, was the granting of a depot code to Carlisle, code letter "E" being allocated because the more logical letter "C" was already used to identify vehicles operating from Cumnock garage. Carlisle had suffered considerably with the contraction of local routes and the run-down of works transport requirements to 14MU and only three years earlier it had been a candidate for closure.

The new style corporate fleet names were introduced in 1978 to all the Scottish Bus Group's vehicles and the blue Western Scottish "corporate" fleetname complete with saltire was progressively seen as the Dumfries paint shop started to turn them out. This involved some adaption of the red and cream livery and, though a creditable effort, was a poor substitute for the attractive fleet names previously carried.

Further developments which involved Stranraer Garage were the introduction of two new express services; 913 between Stranraer, Cairnryan, Glasgow and Edinburgh, connecting with the Townsend Thorenson ferry which had been introduced from Cairnryan to Larne and 923 between Stranraer, Dumfries, Manchester and Leeds, joint with Ulsterbus and National Travel (West). The garage gained local publicity with the delivery of a batch of Alexander T-type bodied Seddons for its increased express and private hire workload. Two other vehicles of note which arrived in 1978 were the two Bristol RELHs previously operated by Highland Omnibuses (T2701/2 : DSD701/2D), the only two of the batch not having previously seen service in the southern region.

After many years of discussion with the councils on the re-siting of buses to a new bus station Western confirmed in 1979 that the Dumfries Gas Works site at Brooms Road was acceptable. Some consideration was also given to the building of a garage on the site as well, but again the proposal did not come to fruition. A previous site considered in the mid 'seventies was at the front of the Auction Mart on the opposite side of the road from Whitesands. A new Lockerbie local service numbered 82 began operation for the first

DL2660 (DDB161C) was the first of four twelve year old Leyland Leopards with two-speed rear axles which arrived second hand from National Travel (West); they proved popular with drivers for Lancashire express work, but could equally be found on more mundane work like the Newton Stewart - Isle of Whithorn service. *(A.Richardson)*

The Eastfield Road workshops at Dumfries became a recognised centre for the conversion of single deck buses to recovery vehicles, having built bodies on a couple of AEC trucks over the years. SW7065 became Stranraer's tow wagon after conversion from Leyland Leopard L1837 in 1979. The new corporate fleet name, together with the unique mainly red livery treatment is shown here, although it was later repainted into standard cream and red. (Garry Ward)

time during the year from the Main Street to Hill Court four times daily. The two Dumfries - Edinburgh services were renumbered as well; 82 Dumfries - Edinburgh via Thornhill was renumbered service 100, whilst the route via Moffat was renumbered from 89 to 99.

Of the regular allocations of new vehicles received in the area, two were of particular interest being new Seddon dual purpose vehicles in Western's black and white coach livery delivered to Carlisle in 1979 (ES2863/4 ; BSD863/4T), the first new single deckers for the garage for many years. The first of a considerable number of conversions of Leyland Leopards to tow wagons were completed at Dumfries, the first of which was former bus L1837 in 1979 turned out in a unique red livery with single cream band. Such

work was welcomed by the Eastfield Road workshops who also undertook several similar conversions for other Bus Group subsidiaries.

THE 'EIGHTIES - MORE ROUTES GO

In 1980, Carlisle received its first rear engined double deckers, with two being transferred from Paisley. Considerable route alterations were made in conjunction with Cumbria County Council, Borders Regional Council and Dumfries and Galloway Regional Council to the 05 Carlisle - Glasgow, 79 Dumfries - Carlisle, 87 Annan - Langholm, 90 Carlisle - Lockerbie, 91 Carlisle - Langholm and 93 Carlisle - the Crossings - Newcastleton, 94 Carlisle - Gretna, 94C Longtown - Moor Road Scheme, 95 Carlisle - Edinburgh (which reverted to operation by Eastern Scottish only) and 96 Carlisle - Castletown services. The latter service was withdrawn with the diversion of the Carlisle - Lockerbie service to serve Castletown and Rockliffe, though a few operated to Castletown only numbered 90B, actually giving the residents of this area more journeys. A regular hourly service between Longtown and Carlisle was timetabled with extras at peak periods and a journey which gave Longtown residents the opportunity to enjoy an evening in Carlisle. The inhabitants of Penton and Newcastleton gained a Wednesday afternoon shoppers bus. Also, as part of the revisions most journeys timed to arrive in Carlisle at the morning peak were retimed by a few minutes in an effort to avoid late arrival. The most interesting development though was a new route numbered 92 operating three return journeys Monday to Friday between Longtown and Brampton, resurrecting the short lived service operated by Caledonian in the

early 'thirties! In Stranraer, Service 65 Stranraer to Cairnryan was withdrawn, whilst at Dalbeattie the two driver based operation ceased with timetable changes. Some tidying up of service numbers was also initiated; the 76G Dumfries - Shawhead became service 73, the 76M Kirkcudbright - Borgue became service 84, the 76J Kirkcudbright - Castle Douglas via Gelston was re-numbered 83, 76N Castle Douglas - Dalbeattie became service 86 and service 76Y Dumfries - Lochfoot - Haugh of Urr was changed to 89. In Dumfries, service 76G Dumfries to Dalry via Corsock was cut back to Shawhead village and re-numbered service 73.

The year 1980 was also to be important with the allocation of the first new double deckers since three Fleetlines were allocated to Dumfries town services in 1971 (DR2291-3 ; UCS289-91K). A batch of ten Fleetlines with Alexander 75-seat bodies (numbered DR70-9 HSD70-79V) were introduced to the town services, but within a year they had been transferred north with the removal of pick up restrictions within the Glasgow city boundary and the potential of increased passenger loadings. At the same time, a partial closure of Dumfries High Street resulted in the division of some town services and re-routing of the Dumfries to Carlisle service. Mention should be made of one Fleetline - DR2095 (GCS175E) which ran for a year in the Dumfries region in 1981/2 in an all-over red livery. This unrelieved scheme was a result of a quick repaint after its previous

Western made use of broadside adverts to promote their services, including the Belfast - Stranraer - London route. DL54 (GCS54V) carried the advert from new, being one of five Leopards delivered in 1980.   (Garry Ward)

Other cut backs were service 47 which was reduced to operating between Ayr and Cumnock only, connecting with 05 Glasgow - Dumfries which was cut short at Kilmarnock on Sundays; the Dumfries to Carlisle section was operated as the 79 service, whilst the few through passengers to Glasgow changed to the 04 Ayr to Glasgow service. As a result, the reduced number of short workings via Kirkton to Auldgirth and Thornhill were operated under the 05 service. Also, service 89 Dumfries - Haugh of Urr was shortened to Lochfoot, whilst a new single journey on the 073 Dumfries - Shawhead was introduced on Saturdays only to operate via Lochfoot Village, Shawhead village then back to Dumfries via Terreagles as a circular service. The 80 Annan - Dumfries and 87 Annan - Langholm routes lost their Saturday journies. Other changes were mostly related to timing revisions, together with a few additional workings for the 68 Stranraer - Whithorn and 69 Newton Stewart - Portwilliam services. On the vehicle front, the newly introduced coach livery of black, white and grey began to appear in

Alexander-bodied Daimler Fleetline DR2095 (GCS157E) was a candidate for the most drab livery, having had its broadside advert overpainted at the end of its contract in June 1981. Thankfully, its unrelieved red was replaced with the new standard livery a year later. (Garry Ward)

The basic office premises at Port Rodie, Stranraer were vacated at the end of 1981. DL49 (CS2022), one of the Leyland Tiger TS7s rebodied by Alexander in 1950 was still in dual purpose cream and red livery when this photograph was taken, the office being in the background. (Ian Maclean)

Proposals under the SCOTMAP process included the complete withdrawal of Service 68 Stranraer - Whithorn, which Caledonian (and H.Brook before them) had operated. The route ceased in January 1983, Bristol Lodekka DB1295 being seen some years earlier running west along the coast road at Auchenmalg Bay.

broadside advertising contract had expired!

To make more profitable use of Stranraer, tachometer equipment for Stranraer was obtained in 1981, saving "dead" mileage in moving the companies own vehicles and allowing the depot to obtain outside work. At the other end of the region, Carlisle garage was closed in October 1981 and sold during the following year. As a result, the terminal point for services became Lowther Street, Carlisle based vehicles being garaged at Ribble's Willowholme Garage, where space was rented, though the "E" code was surprisingly retained. An office was taken within the Lowther Street bus station to allow bookings, parcels and enquiries work to continue to be handled; this office was lost recently with the reduction and rebuilding of the bus station. Route and service changes continued relentlessly during 1981. Service 51 was diverted between Castle Douglas and Ayr to serve Laurieston and Mossdale (incidentally allowing vehicles to operate through New Galloway High Street without reversing) on Saturdays only, enabling the withdrawal of service 76K between Castle Douglas and Mossdale, which had also partially been covered by a Post Bus service for some years. A large number of service changes were made during the year with the routes withdrawn being numbers 74 Dumfries - Penpont, 81B Dumfries - Lochmaben via Shieldhill, 83 Kirkcudbright - Castle Douglas via Gelston and Annan local 88B Annan - Back of Hill. In Dumfries Sunday frequencies on the town services were reduced, services affected being 301 High Street - Troqueer, 303 High Street - Crichton/Kingholm Quay, 304 Lincluden - Locharbriggs and 305 Queensberry Square - Lochside. Town services withdrawn on Sundays were 301 High Street - Brasswell, Janefield, Broomlands and 303 Queensberry Square - Larchfield.

the region on T-type bodied Seddon coaches whilst as far as the ancillary fleet was concerned, former Lodekka DW7030 (HSD31) was replaced by Dumfries-converted KCS156F, a 1968 Leyland Leopard former coach (L2186) which inherited the Lodekka's 'works number'.

The relentless move towards tailoring services to meet declining demand was given further emphasis with the Bus Group's

Back-ups for the London service were provided by a number of Volvo B58s with the last Alexander M-type bodies supplied to Western in 1975. SV536 (HSD707N) had just returned to Stranraer after repainting into Scottish Citylink colours in August 1983 but was missing the second part of its fleet name.   (Garry Ward)

Sitting in the yard of Ribble's Willowholme depot at Carlisle, at which Western leased space, is red & cream liveried Alexander-bodied Fleetline ER2117 (GCS170E).   (T.W.W.Knowles)

Marketing Analyis Project, christened SCOTMAP. At the heart of the project was the conducting of a series of passenger surveys to establish trips taken by bus and, very importantly, journeys which passengers wanted to take by bus. For this purpose, a double decker bus was suitably converted to carry the SCOTMAP team and made a number of visits to the region. Having started in 1981, the team had reached the Dumfries and Galloway region during the following year. As a result of their comprehensive study further radical changes to the routes operated in the region were proposed and to which Dumfries and Galloway Regional Council objected and whilst consultations took place, a committee was formed to look at the area's public transport and educational needs. The company stated that some £230,000 could be saved with the withdrawal of services 68 Whithorn - Stranraer (one of the routes on which Caledonian started), 84 Kirkcudbright - Borgue (which already had

cover provided by a Post Bus service) and the Dalbeattie - Kippford section of service 78. After further negotiation, the changes were introduced on 5 January 1983. In each district, introduction of the changes was proceeded by delivery of Travel Guide packs which contained "loose-leaf" timetables for that area, an introductory newsletter summarising the changes and a route map. The Stranraer, Machars and Dumfries editions also promoted bargain return fares on the Dumfries - Stranraer service, as well as Tourist Runabout tickets for the summer giving one, three or seven days unlimited travel in the whole region, including Cumbria, in similar style to Caledonian's pre-war tourist ticket promotion.

The services detailed above were all withdrawn whilst service 76 between Dumfries and Stranraer was re-cast to serve Dalbeattie with short workings to Kirkcudbright via three routes; service 76 operated from Dumfries to Stranraer via Dalbeattie, Haugh of Urr and Castle Douglas, though reduced from six to four through journeys (replacing 86 Castle Douglas - Dalbeattie),service 77 operated from Dumfries to Kirkcudbright via Kirkpatrick Durham and Castle Douglas (the old 77 Dumfries - Dalbeattie - Kirkcudbright - via Auchencairn and Dundrennan being withdrawn) and service 78 operated from Dumfries to Kirkcudbright via Dalbeattie, Auchencairn and Dundrennan (the old 78 Dumfries - Dalbeattie - Kippford being withdrawn as mentioned above). At the same time, the 76 service diverted west of Castle Douglas to serve Rhonehouse Village at school times, Kirkpatrick of Castle Douglas having operated to Rhonehouse previously. Disappearing at the same time was the infrequent 76L Kirkcudbright - Castle Douglas via Tongland service and the 76T Stranraer- Glenluce via Limekiln, a short working operating direct on the main road as the 76 instead. The new group of services was marketed under the "Galloway Ranger" name with a neat card timetable carrying the side profile of a Alexander bodied T-type Seddon. Service 84 Kirkcudbright - Borgue circular was replaced by a schools service over the same route under service 76. Providing a partial replacement for the Whithorn - Stranraer route,

LM208 (4672 NT), an ex.Newton of Dingwall Van Hool Alicron integral was the regular vehicle on the Carlisle - Stranraer service maintained in conjunction with British Railways for the summer of 1986. It retained the contract livery in which it was acquired until its sale late in the year. The bus is negotiating the Creetown bypass amongst summer tourist traffic. (Tom MacFarlane)

A wet day in Carlisle bus station is the setting for this view of blue and white-liveried Duple-bodied Volvo B58 V129 (GGE129X) which was on its way from London to Glasgow.   (K.A.Jenkinson)

service 70 was routed daily from Newton Stewart via Portwilliam to Whithorn, operating daily as a circular in either direction. This replaced the old 69 Newton Stewart - Portwilliam and 70 Newton Stewart - Isle of Whithorn service and at the same time provided connections for Stranraer at Newton Stewart (albeit via a more circuitous route). Further consolidation was achieved with the closure of Wigtown garage, its duties being transferred to Whithorn, and closure of the office at Portrodie, Stranraer. Some useful additional revenue had been obtained through the garaging of post office vans overnight from the early 'seventies at Wigtown, but certainly the remaining work did not justify retention of the garage.

In the Dumfries area, developments as a result of SCOTMAP included resurrection of the old service 75 from Dumfries to Thornhill, this time operated via Moniaive, re-introducing Western vehicles over the section between Moniaive and Thornhill. As a result, service 72 between Thornhill and Penpont ceased. Also making a comeback was a separate service to Auldgirth via Kirkton, with extensions to Thornhill, carrying the number 74. To provide more journeys through Kirkton, the 05 service retained some workings by this route and the infrequent Edinburgh via Thornhill was re-routed via Kirkton as well at the same time. In Dumfries, substantial revisions were made to the services; a new bus route to Lochvale to be interworked with the Georgetown service was proposed for mid-1983 numbered 316 (and later introduced), together with a new local service also numbered 316 to Summerhill replacing the previous 303 route to Hardthorn Road. The Lochside routes were split into separate services to Heston Avenue (service 315) and Kenilworth Road (service 305). Another new service was 306, a circular via Laurieknowe, Janefield, Broomlands and

Pleasance Avenue, replacing the previous 310 Janefield service. The Brasswell local virtually disappeared on Mondays to Fridays reducing from 29 to 3 journies, a basically hourly service being provided on Saturdays; on weekdays, the route was covered by the existing 79 Dumfries to Carlisle. Similarly, the 303 High Street - Stoop service was withdrawn and covered by Service 81 Dumfries - Lockerbie. The revisions in Dumfries provided connections to previously unlinked points; 306 High Street - Janefield via Broomlands, 304 Lincluden - Crichton, 313 Crichton - Lochside and also 313 Crichton with Locharbriggs, the journeys to Crichton being geared for both workers and visitors to the Dumfries hospitals. Service 71 Dumfries - Caerlaverock - Glencaple was re-numbered into the local services and given number 323. A new express connection between Dumfries and Glasgow was offered for the first time under the Citilink banner numbered 581, operating via Moffat and the A74., with one journey in either direction daily except Fridays and Saturdays, when two journies operated.

In Stranraer, the 64 Drummore service finally had its terminus changed to Port Rodie from West Pier, an historic "throwback" to when Murrays had operated the service and also had some journeys reduced to School Days only. Service 66 Stranraer to Ardwell Shop was reduced from five workings to one on school days only with three short workings to Kirkcolm. 67 Stranraer to Portpatrick was halved from ten to five journeys with an additional school days and Saturdays only journey. The Stranraer town services were renumbered from 680 to 65 and improved to hourly; a new local circular service to Belmont was also introduced. Although Stranraer received a number of Volvo B58s to bolster its London service, the mainstay of this incredibly popular roure became four Leyland Tigers

Two Leyland Nationals were borrowed from the newly formed Lowland Scottish Omnibuses in October 1985 in exchange for two Dumfries Leyland Leopards. The Nationals worked town services and were fitted with blinds for their stay; Lowland's 161 (BSF771S) leads 162 at the now pedestrianised Queensberry Square.   (Tom MacFarlane)

Certain older vehicles allocated chiefly to school work were fitted with a removable illuminated board at the rear as an additional safety precaution. DL530 (HCS815N) illustrates the fitment.
(Garry Ward)

Dumfries was an early recipient of the new black, white and grey livery introduced for the bus fleet in 1985. DR773 (XSJ654T) was fresh out of the paintshop when photographed at Lincluden terminus in September 1985.   (Garry Ward)

with Duple Goldliner bodywork which maintained the tradition of Greyhound-style windows. A comment made at the time indicated that the number of coaches should have been doubled, such was the demand for seats.

SCOTMAP changes followed in Annan and Cumbria in April of that year. 79F Annan - Newbie was renumbered 80, 80 Dumfries - Annan via Dalton was covered by diversions of service 79, 81 Dumfries - Lockerbie was extended to Hill Court Scheme whilst the Lockerbie local 82 was withdrawn as was service 81B Dumfries - Lochmaben via Shieldhill. 85 Lockerbie - Annan became 83 some journies being cut short at Eaglesfield requiring a change onto the Carlisle - Lockerbie bus, 87 Annan - Langholm was withdrawn, 88 Annan - Newington became 80 with a new route variation. Also carrying number 80 was a new Annan local service to Hallmeadow. The 90 Lockerbie - Carlisle became 82, 91 Carlisle - Langholm was withdrawn as was 92 Longtown - Brampton (for the second time in fifty years), 93 Carlisle - Crossings - Newcastleton was withdrawn and 94 Carlisle - Longtown - Gretna became 84. The old 84 Longtown local to Moor Road housing scheme was replaced by extending the Carlisle - Longtown workings into the scheme while the 82 Lockerbie - Carlisle was withdrawn on Sundays on which day passengers were advised to travel via Dumfries adding one hour (and additional expense) to their journey! Though the Newcastleton service was withdrawn, someone slipped up in the SCOTMAP office; the map carried on the Annandale and Cumbria folder had moved Newcastleton to where Castletown should have been! As a result of these revisions, Longtown garage was closed. Some compensation for the services was offered by Dumfries and Galloway Regional Council with their A2 schools service between Langholm and Evertown; Bowden of Carlisle also operating between Langholm and Canonbie, and although both services were,

essentially, for school children, they were also available to the public. Additionally, Telford of Newcastleton started operating south to Longtown to link with existing Western services.

In the following year, alterations to Whitesands office were authorised to provide a "Bus Shop" and office accommodation to allow the office block at Eastfield Road to be vacated. Dumfries received ex.London Transport vehicles again after almost 30 years when a small number of 1975/6 Daimler Fleetlines were allocated for Dumfries town services. Also of note was the arrival of two shortened Leyland Leopards L390 (YSD350L) and L405 (YSD365L) for Stranraer, both vehicles having been altered after sustaining accident damage and providing useful smaller capacity vehicles. In May, Dumfries Regional Council, British Railways and Western joined together to sponsor a "Galloway Rail Link" aimed at making the most of Dumfries railway station as a road/rail interchange point. The 76-8 group of services were retimed slightly, with journeys being extended to the station. Through booking was offered to selected stations from Western and British Railways booking offices and

plan was deferred. In November 1985 a new "Shoppers Express" service running on Fridays and Saturdays only numbered X79 was introduced between Dumfries and Carlisle. Three return journeys were offered from Dumfries at 10am, 2pm and 5pm, taking fifty minutes with an intermediate stop at Annan, comparing well with the 1 hour 25 minutes of the normal service bus. Bargain day return fares of £2.95 were offered in comparison with the standard £4.70, with the option of reduced fares to Annan as well, but within five months the service had been reduced to running Saturday only and within a year had ceased entirely.

In October, two Leyland Nationals were borrowed from the newly formed Lowland Scottish company (numbers 161/2 BSF771/ 2S) and both were evaluated at Dumfries on town services; in exchange two Leyland Leopards were transferred to Lowland Scottish (DL55/6 GCS55/6V). As scheduled routes to the more rural outposts ceased, Dumfries and Galloway Region's yellow school buses also provided some basic links along with the Post Buses whilst Western's vehicles which were regularly allocated to school journies were fitted at the request of the Region with an extra set of lights and a large removable "SCHOOL BUS" board at their rear.

With the coming of de-regulation scheduled for October 1986, subsidised services required to be put out for tender and, as a result, Western experienced some considerable cut-backs in their operation. Dickson of Dumfries (an operator who was to figure prominently in subsequent events), gained an early morning contract on the Lochside - Queensberry Square service, as well as most journies on the Dumfries - Glencaple/Caerlaverock service, Western being reduced to two school day only journeys which were

entering into the spirit of things Western applied large fablon stickers, suitably lettered "Galloway Rail Link" to three Seddons DS951/2 (DSD951/2V) and DS960 (DSD960V) which were used regularly on the services. Some temporary service changes had to be made in Dumfries in October when the Buccleugh Street river bridge was partially closed. Meanwhile, pleas from Stranraer for more vehicles for the London service must have been heard as two more Leyland Tigers quickly arrived, these being Duple Caribbean-bodied L165/6 (A165/6TGE). In addition came a pair of Plaxton-bodied Tigers for express and private hire duties (L184/5 ; A184/5UGB), both of which sported the new blue and yellow Scottish Citilink livery.

Consideration was given in 1985 to the purchase of ten minibuses for Dumfries Town service, but after consideration the

Annan garage was down to an allocation of two vehicles prior to its closure; buses were moved to open waste ground at the rear of the Bingo Hall and have only recently moved to more secure premises. (Garry Ward Collection)

numbered again as a "Country Service" (71). Peacock of Dumfries obtained tendered journeys on the Dumfries - Shawhead, Sanquhar, Thornhill, Moniaive and Annan services, resulting in service 75 Dumfries - Moniaive - Thornhill ceasing to be operated by the company, as well as the 79 services from Dumfries to Annan via Dalton. Nelson of Thornhill and Leith of Sanquhar also gained journeys up the Nith Valley from Dumfries to Thornhill and Sanquhar.

An attractive leaflet was produced to coincide with the introduction of the minibuses.

The Western journies were reduced to three Monday to Friday from Dumfries to Cumnock via Sanquhar in comparison to six operated in 1984. Some of the journeys in 1984 had actually operated under the Cityliner service numbers as X5, implying an express operation but, in practice, the running time was the same. Service 74 was reduced to one Monday to Saturday return journey from Dumfries to Auldgirth via Kirkton. In Stranraer a new local service numbered 68 to Ochtrelure operating as a circular was introduced in 1985 (the service being renumbered 65 in October 1989). Yet another attempt was made with a Dumfries to Stranraer "Galloway Express" numbered X76, taking two hours and ten minutes and operating once daily via Kirkcudbright. The X76 lasted for less than a year, however, disappearing by October 1986 following little demand for an express service originating from Dumfries in a westerly direction with most traffic coming the opposite way from the ferries. The timing of the service resulted in ordinary passenger traffic being extracted from the 76 service bus between Newton Stewart and Stranraer, the express operation being some ten minutes earlier than the normal service bus. Time constraints resulted in the bus leaving Stranraer fifteen minutes before the arrival of the ferry, further handicapping the chances of success. The day service 921 from Stranraer to London was also advertised as providing a local express service between Stranraer and Dumfries. Both services operated to Stranraer Harbour and connections were advertised at Dumfries with the 581 express service to Glasgow. The 921/4 day/night services had one journey in each direction extended to Cairnryan Harbour on Sundays only.

A new black, white and grey livery was also introduced in 1985, complimenting the revised coach livery launched in 1981, and Daimler Fleetline DR773 (XSJ654T) was an early recipient, operating regularly on town services. Meanwhile the driver training vehicle RAG404 was replaced by a more modern Lodekka, PBL57F which created a stir four years later when it was repainted into the original red and cream livery. On the property side, further efforts were made to reduce costs when in May the company moved offices within Dumfries from Eastfield Road to the offices at the Whitesands. For a short period, the vacated offices were rented out to T.C.Farries, a local bookseller.

In 1986, Lockerbie, Kirkcudbright, Penpont and Annan garages were closed in a further round of cost cuts. At the time of closure, Lockerbie's allocation of vehicles had dwindled to two single deckers from an allocation of three single and six double deckers in June 1958. Kircudbright was down to four single deckers from three single and three double deckers whilst Penpont lost its last vehicles upon its closure having in June 1958 garaged two single and four double deckers. Annan had only two double deckers remaining from eight single and four double deckers! In Annan, its two double deckers were outstationed on waste ground at the rear of the Bingo Hall, to support the local services to Newington and Hallmeadow plus the Annan - Lockerbie workings whilst at Lockerbie, buses were moved to a new outstation at a haulage contractor's yard in the northern part of the town. At Kirkcudbright the depot was sold but arrangements were made to continue to garage vehicles until

Allocated to Dumfries depot for driver training duties, Bristol FLF6G DW1064 which was gained from Alder Valley in the NBC/SBG Bristol FLF/VRT exchange during the early 'seventies, was unique in being repainted in the old Western red & cream livery complete with cream advert panels.   (K.A.Jenkinson)

Kilmarnock. Stranraer received the unique 1985 Volvo B10M with Berkhof Esprite coachwork which featured a demountable toilet thus allowing it to operate as a standard 53-seater or, with its toilet in situ as a 49-seater making it useful for all types of work. Meanwhile, Carlisle had some success in gaining useful tendered work with the winning of five new services in October. The most interesting of these was service 85 Carlisle - Kirkbride - Anthorn which took Western vehicles eastwards from Carlisle for the first time on a stage carriage route. The service had previously been operated by the well known independent Blair and Palmer of Carlisle and was actually started during August, prior to full deregulation of services. An interesting swap appears to have been arranged with Alan Palmer of Carlisle who took over Western's Carlisle to Rockliffe and Castletown service, which extended on certain journeys to Gretna and Longtown. The service actually fitted in with school contracts which he already held to Rockliffe, as well as journeys to 14 MU which had once been the domain of Caledonian and later Western SMT and at the same time, Western also reduced their direct Carlisle - Longtown - Gretna services, which Palmer's service was also partially substituting for.

It is probably worth mentioning at this point that Alan Palmer's brother George also ran a service for a time under the title "Borderbus" during the late 'eighties with a single journey from Gretna to Carlisle in the morning replacing a Western working, but this was abandoned not only due to falling demand but also due to ever increasing congestion in Carlisle, making the service unviable. Borderbus also picked up a school contract connecting Kirkpatrick Fleming, Creca and Chapelcross with three schools and Annan Academy on the demise of Littles of Annan in 1989 and this ran as a public service, though in a very "low key" manner.

To return to tendered services, Western also gained a Saturdays only shoppers service 86 Carlisle - Walton Green, two evening Carlisle city services, 87 Carlisle - Houghton and 88 Carlisle - Lowry Hill and a Carlisle - Dalston service numbered 90. To help to operate these services, a couple of Dodge minibuses were drafted in from Ayr, later to be replaced by Mercedes. In the Annan area school journeys to the Academy from Springfield, Gretna and Eastriggs were numbered 79B. Having tried one shoppers service without success, a second service numbered 72 was launched in October with more success, operating one return journey between Moffat and Dumfries, giving shoppers nearly two hours in Dumfries, in direct competition with Gibson of Moffat for the second time, the first occasion being Caledonian - its predecessor - nearly forty years earlier. The service was inaugurated to make better use of a vehicle which operated on a contract from Dumfries to Moffat in the morning which would otherwise have had to return empty to Dumfries. On the negative side the infrequent former Caledonian/SMT service 99 from Dumfries to Edinburgh via Moffat was taken over by McEwan of Dumfries. The 82 Carlisle - Lockerbie was further pruned at the same time, most journeys starting from or terminating at Gretna causing through passengers to have to change to or from the 79 Carlisle - Dumfries service. The "Galloway Rail Link" initiative was withdrawn in the same year, being partially replaced by a tendered Whitesands - Railway Station linkage, which operated as a circular town service. Gibson of Moffat originally maintained this with a suitably lettered vehicle, later to be replaced by Western and finally operated by McEwan; the service was abandoned in 1991. The 79A Dumfries - Brasswell was further revised with the few journies to the Brasswell Farm terminus being replaced by two return journeys

1989 when the proprietor required the space (vehicles from this date to the present being parked outside), whereas Penpont entailed a complete closure with the loss of previously subsidised workings to competitors. The practice of outstationing a vehicle at Newton Stewart overnight also ceased. Until the 1960s the premises of McKeands had been used for garaging one "sleeper" bus overnight, but on the sale of his premises to the regional council the bus had been moved up to the old Goods Yard site of the railway station. A feature of operation at Newton Stewart has always been the operation of buses into the town schools in the morning, with long layovers for the majority of the vehicles until school closing time. This caused some difficulties over the years with local residents and the council, because a suitable parking area was hard to find; the building of the proposed depot would certainly have solved that problem. In the 'fifties, vehicles were parked up the hill from Dashwood Square in Station Road, moving round the corner into one of the offshoot streets after complaints and later, in the early 'sixties, onto waste ground at the side of Dashwood Square. After closure of the station, vehicles were moved up to the station site, a hut even being used in which the Portwilliam driver could brew a welcome "cuppa". This became the last base as well for the bus which required to be parked overnight.

In June of that year, a new express service between Carlisle railway station and Stranraer Harbour operating one return journey was introduced for a seventeen week period, in conjunction with British Railways, some nine years after the feasibility of providing a similar service had been investigated. The regular vehicle drafted in for the route was an ex.Newton's Van Hool Alicron integral (LM208 ; 4672NT) acquired in December 1985. This was based at Carlisle and operated in the TWA livery which it had carried with Newtons. The service ceased in September and did not resume the next year, being little used and following this, the coach was transferred to

Gibson of Moffat provided partial substitution for the abandoned rail link service to Dumfries station with a tendered circular service starting from Whitesands. Plaxton-bodied Leyland Leopard RMB407V was the regular performer on this service which later passed to Western and ultimately to McEwan before complete withdrawal.   (Garry Ward)

Further competition was experienced over the Annan - Carlisle route in particular, with Annan Minibus Service using an attractive Mercedes minibus D24TSW on a service operated four days per week. The bus is seen in Lowther Street with one of Western's Dodge minibuses, drafted in from Ayr to operate lightly trafficked routes. (Garry Ward)

operated on Monday to Saturdays, from Dumfries to Collin while further trimming resulted in the few diversions off service 77 via Drumslees, service 76 diversions via Rhonehouse and also the diversion via Kirkgunzeon Village all ceasing in October 1986.

Further consideration was given in 1987 to the introduction of minibuses for Dumfries town services. The company believed that considerable advantages could be gained through greater penetration of housing estates, increasing frequencies, presentation to the public of a modern image, plus the dual advantages of saving eight "conventional" size vehicles and, most importantly, detering competition, which was increasing considerably. When the opportunity to purchase one year old minibuses from Kelvin Scottish (a fellow Bus Group company formed in 1985 in preparation for de-regulation of services) came along, a move was made and sixteen Alexander 21-seat Mercedes were taken into stock and painted in a new variation of the new livery, which had become black, white, grey and red in that year. The new arrivals were put to work in November on five of the town services, which had been renumbered at the same time, bringing back the "D" prefix, D1 Town Centre - Troqueer - Janefield, D2 Town Centre - Lincluden, D5 Lochside - Lochvale, D6 Lochside - Georgetown and D7 Summerhill - Larchfield. Marketed as "Buzzers", as they had been when introduced in Ayr a comprehensive marketing drive was undertaken with specially produced leaflets which carried a drawing of one of the Mercedes vehicles on the front cover. The action was prompted after a wrangle with Dickson of Dumfries who successfully initiated a Dumfries - Lochside (Heston Avenue) service in January, operating every 20 minutes. For the first eight weeks, the new service was operated free of charge, with any donations being given to charity. In June of that year, Dickson started another commercial

service between Queensberry Square and Locharbriggs, also operating on a twenty minute frequency. Again, no fares were charged for the first week. Of all the competition these encroachments were the most serious, operating on the two most profitable town routes. "big-bus" routes retained were the 303 to Crichton (Kingholm Quay); 304 to Locharbriggs and 314 to Twinames Estate. Competition was also experienced elsewhere within Dumfries and Galloway Region and Annan Minibus Service expanded with subsidised Annan - Dumfries journeys along with a commercially operated service between Annan and Carlisle running on Tuesdays, Thursdays, Saturdays and Sundays which started in November as well. In the same year, Western found itself paying rent to new owners of Willowholme garage in Carlisle following Stagecoach's acquisition of Cumberland Motor Services in July as part of the sell-off of the National Bus Company empire. Stagecoach were to feature again later in the course of events. A new company, Dumfries and Galloway Minibus Services Ltd. of Dalbeattie began operations on five routes, also in June; Dalbeattie - Kippford - Rockliffe - Sandyhills, Dumfries - Dalbeattie - Castle Douglas - Kirkcudbright, Dalbeattie - Haugh of Urr - Castle Douglas and two Dumfries town service to Troqueer and Locharbriggs, the latter two being short lived, however, ceasing within a year. A more unlikely competitor was Ulsterbus who won school day contracts for Newton Stewart - Glentrool and Newton Stewart - Isle of Whithorn services, vehicles being provided by their Stranraer sub depot. The company advised that they had no plans to expand services in south-west Scotland and that the move was simply to achieve better vehicle utilisation and to provide a more "local" identity, vehicles used on the services were labelled "Macharsbus".

Western withdrew their remaining peak journeys on the Dumfries to Glencaple service in August 1987, with Dickson starting a full day service over the route as a replacement. Further re-tendering resulted in more losses in October 1987 with Dumfries local Sunday morning Lincluden journeys and Sunday all day journeys to Georgetown being taken over by Dickson, whilst the Sunday Dumfries to Biggar journeys of service 100 also passed to that operator. Nelson of Thornhill won tendered journeys on the Dumfries - Kirkton - Thornhill - Sanquhar service while Western

Representing the fleet of Dickson, Dumfries is Plaxton-bodied Leyland Leopard NCY473R which began life with South Wales Transport. Pictured at Butts Street, Annan, it was working the former Western service to Dumfries via Dalton and Carrutherstown. (Garry Ward)

Alexander-bodied Mercedes 608D mini DZ270 (D130NUS), one of eight purchased from Kelvin Scottish in 1987 stands at Whitesands, Dumfries whilst working a local service. (K.A.Jenkinson)

Resting at Whitesands, Dumfries are a pair of Alexander-bodied Leyland Leopards. On the left is DL390 (YSD350L) which had been shortened by Western whilst alongside it is DL929 (BSJ929T) in standard form.
(T.W.W.Knowles)

gained the former Peacock journeys to Shawhead village, but Peacock gained more Dumfries - Moniaive journeys on the constant "merry - go - round" of tenders. Service 303 High Street - Crichton (Kingholm Quay) and 314 High Street - Twinames Estate became minibus services D3 and D4 respectively. More positive was the arrival of the area's first new Dennis Dorchesters with Alexander TC-type coach bodies to both Stranraer and Dumfries carrying the then current wedged black, white and grey coach livery and standard blue and yellow Citilink colours. Secondhand additions to Stranraer came in the shape of ex.West Midlands Fleetlines, though the cost of maintaining them gave considerable local concern, while Dumfries received one of the short Leyland Leopards (YSD350L) from fellow SBG subsidiary, Northern Scottish with whom it had served for a year. Operations in Stranraer were boosted considerably by the 'Purple Warrior' military exercises, some 11,000 additional miles being operated as a result while extended hire work for a number of tour operators to places such as Edinburgh and Llandudno also continued to grow.

January 1988 dawned with the announcement that the companies which made up the Scottish Bus Group were to be privatised. Interesting route developments were a Sundays only service from Carlisle to Gretna market, operated by Cumberland Motor Services and Western. The tendered shuttle service between

Whitesands and Dumfries railway station passed to Western from Gibsons and was numbered D9. At the same time another new service was introduced to give better utilisation of the minibuses, with a service between Dumfries and the small estate at Cargenbridge beyond Janefield, numbered D8. Service D9 survived for a year before passing on to McEwan of Dumfries and ceasing entirely in 1991 as mentioned. The pedestrianisation of portions of Dumfries town centre resulted in the partial return of full size vehicles to the Lochside and Lincluden areas in October 1988; the Kenilworth Road and Heston Avenue services being converted back to "big-bus" operation and numbered 305/6 respectively with the Lincluden service being similarly treated and numbered 302. Additionally service 74 Dumfries to Auldgirth ceased to be operated by Western, although the 100 Edinburgh service continued to serve Kirkton.

In the following month Dumfries and Galloway Minibuses Ltd ceased and their services returned to Western. The company had been in financial difficulties and Western had briefly stepped in when their service had temporarily ceased prior to their final demise. For a second time, Western took over operating the services, with minibuses, chiefly carrying service number 476 on their routes. Ironically, some journeys to Castle Douglas or Kirkcudbright via Kirkpatrick Durham and Lochfoot or Shawhead village had only passed to them from Western in the previous month. Their return to the major operator was short lived, however, as McEwan of Dumfries took over the routes in January 1989. Later in the year,

Pulling out of the Whitesands stance at Dumfries at the start of its journey to Twinames on the 305 service is former London Transport Fleetline DR996 (KUC917P). Wearing Western's white, black & grey livery is still retained its London-style destination indicator, albeit part of which was overpainted.   (T.W.W.Knowles)

Alexander lowbridge-bodied 1961 vintage Leyland PD3A/3 AD1684 (RCS382) pictured here in Carlisle depot carries advertising on its side panels for Western SMT's Glasgow to London coach service, the fare for which was a mere 55/-.

With the Solway Firth as a backdrop, SR805 (NOB325M) sits at Drummore school ready for its next scholars working to Stranraer, the only journies now worked by Western since 1989. Of the ten Fleetlines acquired from West Midlands PTE in 1987, seven were operated from Stranraer and Whithorn garages.

the shoppers service 72 between Moffat and Dumfries was abandoned. By the end of 1988 Dumfries garage had an allocation of 10 minibuses, 8 full size single deckers and one double decker for town services, plus thirteen full size single deckers and one double decker for country services, in comparison with 28 full size single deckers and 28 double deckers in 1957, illustrating the extent of the contraction. As a result of the ongoing reductions, portions of the Eastfield Road premises were now no longer required and the former paint shop was leased to the Skills Training Commission, the paint shop being re-located within the depot. The tendered services operated from Carlisle which had been gained in October 1986 ceased from June 26th 1988 with the exception of the Anthorn and Dalston services, due to a cash crisis in Cumbria County Council and were never resurrected. In the Stranraer area, certain journies on the Stranraer - Drummore and Stranraer - Glenluce routes passed to A. and F. Irvine of Glenluce, whilst some school day only journies on the Stranraer to Ardwell Shop, Stranraer to Portpatrick and Stranraer to Glenluce services passed to J.McCulloch of Stoneykirk, although Western continued to operate as far as Kirkcolm. Irvine also took on the twice-weekly service to New Luce which had been abandoned by Western some years previously while the journies operated by Ulsterbus passed to J.King of Kirkcowan at the same time. In 1989 services within Dalbeattie were diverted to operate clockwise via the High Street and back in via the Dalbeattie bypass, thereby filling a gap left since the abandonment of the Kippford extension. The Carlisle depot code which had been abandoned with the reduction of the operation to a sub-depot of Dumfries was resurrected on the vehicles (although it had always existed "on paper").

In Carlisle, tendered service 90 to Dalston ceased from 1st April leaving the Anthorn route as the only survivor of the original tender gains. Further changes were also made within Dumfries during April as a result of the pedestrianisation of the High Street, some changes being temporary until new bus stances were built at Shakespeare Street and Great King Street. Some further service

A reminder of the pre-1989 operations on the Drummore service, Alexander-bodied Fleetline SR308 (PCS817H) approaches Port Logan along narrow roads typical of this portion of the route. Further south, the owners of a cottage on a sharp bend had to ensure its windows were closed to allow the bus to squeeze through! (Garry Ward)

renumbering involved 302 Town Centre - Lincluden to D12, 304 Town Centre - Locharbriggs to D14, 305/6 Town Centre - Lochside to D15/6 and 307 Town Centre - Lincluden via Lochside to D17, the latter route operating early morning and on some Sunday journies, where demand did not warrant separate services to the two estates. Having moved out of the offices at Eastfield Road in 1985, Western returned to them, albeit using the ground floor only, during October 1989. For a spell, the top floor was rented out to Dumfries and Galloway Enterprise and is presently used by Dumfries and Galloway Regional Council's Commercial Group. Dumfries also started to see the new adapted bus livery of red, white, grey and black appear on vehicles with its application to the ex.London Fleetlines.

A major blow to Western was the loss of a considerable amount of work as a result of local operator Dickson of Dumfries winning thirty of the seventy tenders put out by Dumfries and Galloway Regional Council for renewal in late October. Western lost a lot of school contracts, together with 82 Lockerbie - Carlisle, 83 Lockerbie - Annan and some Dumfries - Kirkcudbright - Stranraer journies. Dickson won Dumfries to Kirkcudbright tenders via three routes, together with the three through journies to Stranraer. Caledonian Express tried their hand at a Dumfries - Stranraer service combined as part of their competitive Stranraer to London via Birmingham service, advertising this for the Dumfries - Carlisle section as well. One link from Midland Bus Service days which disappeared was service 51 which had by then been cut back to operate between Castle Douglas and Dalmellington only, connections to Ayr and Glasgow being afforded at Dalmellington. Western also lost some day and evening journies on the Dumfries - Lockerbie service, whilst long-established operator Gibson of Moffat experienced competition from Creightons Coaches of Moffat on the service from that town into Dumfries. The 581 express service to Glasgow was diverted via Lockerbie, resurrecting the service abandoned by Blue Band Motors, this service having passed to Western control from Citilink in 1988, after operating briefly as service 981 by the latter and, incidentally, being extended by Western to the Scottish Exhibition Centre for the duration of the Glasgow Garden Festival. Another local operator Peacock of Dumfries lost his tendered journies on the former Western route from Dumfries to Annan via Dalton to Dickson, whilst Western gained his other service 72 Dumfries - New Abbey - Southerness - Rockliffe. This service had originally been operated by Carruthers of New Abbey, who had been bought out by Peacock in December 1983, Western thus gaining a service which Caledonian had abandoned more than 62 years earlier! A return was made to the Dumfries - Moniaive - Thornhill route with the winning of a tendered Sunday only service. In Dumfries itself, the Crichton/Kingholm Quay, Troqueer, Cargenbridge/Janefield, Summerhill/Sandside and Larchfield services had their routes revised with some additional journies being introduced. Service 80 Annan - Newbie was

Further west, the company experienced competition from the Stranraer garage of Ulsterbus. Enterpisingly, they labelled vehicles like this Plaxton bodied Leyland Leopard AJD165T with the local identity of "Macharsbus". The vehicle is seen at Newton Stewart, operating the the service to Isle of Whithorn, in the "Machars" district. Despite the local name the side fleetname of "Ulsterbus Tours" must have caused some initial local confusion.   (Tom MacFarlane)

One of a number of Alexander-bodied Renault S56 minibuses transferred to Carlisle from Ayr to satisfy the need for additional small capacity vehicles, DD222 (D222NCS) retains its former depot's 'Buzzer' local identity logos.   (K.A.Jenkinson)

One of Peacock of Dumfries' vehicles, Plaxton Paramount-bodied Bedford C821EUG is seen here operating a private hire duty. (T.W.W.Knowles)

WESTERN

Wearing Western's cream & red livery and standing in the yard of Ribble's Willowholme depot at Carlisle is Alexander-bodied Leyland Leopard DL616 (OSJ616R). (K.A.Jenkinson)

withdrawn, whilst more contraction was suffered with the loss of most journeys on the 70 Newton Stewart - Whithorn service. The 64 Stranraer - Drummore routee was lost, except school journeys whilst the 66 Stranraer - Kirkcolm was lost completely. Lockerbie outstation was abandoned, despite local management objections, after which vehicles were supplied from Dumfries and, with the reduction of vehicle needs, the survival of Dumfries depot's Eastfield Road premises was threatened. Kirkcudbright was reduced to two

vehicles which were parked outside and operated on school runs and some commercial journeys to Dumfries in competition with Dickson, as well as a competing Stranraer return commercial journey. Meanwhile, the Stagecoach empire made its first encroachment into Dumfries and Galloway region with the acquisition of Palmer of Carlisle in 1989. Included in the takeover was the service to Rockliffe and Castletown with extensions to Gretna and Longtown.

INTO THE 'NINETIES
Picking up the pieces

In April 1990, the National Express/Caledonian Express competing day service from Stranraer to London Victoria was withdrawn; the service had offered local connections as far as Carlisle and competition had been intense on this London service. Townsend Thorenson had also introduced a London service from their Cairnryan ferry point in January 1983, terminating at the International Hotel in Cromwell Road, London. In 1986, the service passed to Dodds of Troon and for a period operated in competition with the Citilink service, before the services were amalgamated during 1990. Dodds, Ulsterbus (from its Stranraer base) and Western then joined together to provide the Citilink service, operating from Stranraer; Dodds and Ulsterbus each repainted one of their vehicles into Citilink livery and, unusually, carried bold lettering on the vehicle sides giving the "Ulsterman" marketing name of the service. Western refrained from the practice, choosing simply to carry standard "Citilink" lettering, although they did transfer in a few five year old Volvo B10Ms with Plaxton bodywork which had previously been regular performers on the Glasgow - London service. In practice, over recent years, Kilmarnock has regularly supplied a vehicle which has operated 'light' to and from Stranraer

to assist on the service at busy times. In addition, a useful contract gained by Stranraer garage was that for the transportation of Sealink ferry personnel to Ayr railway station (always an odd operation in some people's eyes in view of a rail service being available from Stranraer Harbour station, but without flexibility in times). Part of the deal was the painting of the regular performer of this duty - Seddon coach SS434 (DSD934V) into Sealink livery.

A listing of services operated in April 1990 illustrates the routes operated by then by 'Western' : Service 03 Ayr and Stranraer; 05 Kilmarnock and Dumfries; 64 Stranraer and Drummore; 65 Stranraer Town Services; 67 Stranraer and Portpatrick; 70 Newton Stewart and Whithorn Circular; 72 Dumfries and Rockliffe; 73 Dumfries and Moffat; 74 Dumfries and Moniaive; 75 Stranraer and Kirkcudbright; 76 Dumfries and Kirkcudbright via Dalbeattie; 77 Dumfries and Kirkcudbright (Direct); 78 Dumfries and Kirkcudbright via Auchencairn; 79 Dumfries and Carlisle; 79A Dumfries and Collin; 79B Annan Academy Services; 80 Annan Town Service; 81 Dumfries and Lockerbie; 82 Lockerbie and Gretna/Carlisle; 83 Lockerbie and Annan; 84 Carlisle and Longtown/Gretna; 85 Carlisle

Looking somewhat shabby and in need of a repaint is white, black & grey-liveried Alexander-bodied Leyland Leopard GCS40V which, after the division of Western became part of the Clydeside Scottish fleet. (K.A.Jenkinson)

The final journey between Kirkcudbright and Stranraer was withdrawn in July 1990, isolating Stranraer Garage from what had been its headquarters at Dumfries. In happier times, Seddon DS687 (RSD990R) wears a broadside advert for Solid Fuel as it stops to drop off a parcel in Kirkcowan village. (Garry Ward)

As part of the contract to transfer Sealink crew to and from Stranraer, the regular vehicle allocated, SS434 (DSD943V), was repainted into Sealink colours, The bus is at Ayr picking up crew from the railway station. (Garry Ward)

Two Leyland Tigers with Duple Caribbean bodywork were received by Stranraer to bolster the Belfast - London service. Numbered L165/6 (A165/6TGE), they are seen here at Kilmarnock prior to entering service from that depot in June 1984.   (Garry Ward)

and Anthorn. Schools and Workers Services - 401 Carlisle Schools; 402 Carlisle Works; 403 Dumfries Schools; 404 Dumfries Works; 405 Stranraer Schools; 406 Stranraer Works. Dumfries Local Services - D1 Troqueer; D2 Larchfield; D3 Kingholm Quay; D4 Twinames; D5 Lochvale; D6 Georgetown D7 Summerhill via Sandside; D8 Cargenbridge via Janefield; D9 Dumfries Station Shuttle; D12 Lincluden; D14 Locharbriggs; D15 Lochside (Kenilworth Road); D16 Lochside (Heston Avenue) and D17 Lochside & Lincluden circular; and Express service 581 Glasgow - Dumfries.

One service which made a return, albeit limited to one non-school days Mondays - Fridays, was that to Newbie which operated under the Annan 'local' number of 80. In July, the last remaining journey between Stranraer and Kirkcudbright was withdrawn, resulting in the section between Tywnholm and Newton

Stewart being abandoned for the first time in sixty three years of Caledonian and Western operation. Thus, Stranraer garage was effectively cut off from the rest of the Dumfries and Galloway region. A minor extension was the routing of the school journeys from Stranraer to Drummore further south to Damnaglaur; "Western" vehicles were travelling further south than Scotland's most southerly village whilst still remaining in Scotland! To support operation of these school services, a couple of Daimler Fleetlines from the absorbed Clydeside Scottish fleet arrived, still in their former owner's red and yellow livery which they retained for a few months. Although a new service (71) from Dumfries brought Western vehicles back to Glencaple and Bankend, the ex.Blair and Palmer service 85 from Carlisle to Anthorn was lost. Two months earlier, the office at Carlisle had been lost with its closure and demolition, as part of the rebuilding of the bus station, and resulting from this, the stance inspector then shared an office with Cumberland Motor Services. North from Dumfries, the last remnants of the 05 were withdrawn in November with Dickson's of Dumfries, Nelson of Thornhill and Leiths of Sanquhar covering the needs, whilst the 581 diversion via Lockerbie ceased.

Tendering featured more on the Dumfries local services and a summary of the competitor's operations on these services as at July 1990 will give an idea how much ground Western had lost.

McEwans Coaches of Dumfries operated on the following routes : Whitesands - Dumfries Railway Station; 3A Town Centre - Crichton; 4 Town Centre - Twinames Estate (evening journeys); 8A Town Centre - Broomlands and 18 Whitesands - Woodlands Estate (one journey).

Dicksons of Dumfries operated the following services all of which were from the town centre : 3 Kingholm Quay (evening and Sunday morning journeys); 3A Crichton (chiefly infrequent afternoon journeys); 4 Twinames Estate (evening journeys); 5 Lochvale (Sunday service); 6 Georgetown (Sunday service); 12 Lincluden (some early morning plus Sunday late evening journeys); 14 Locharbriggs; 15 Kenilworth Road (Sunday late evening journeys);

Dodds of Troon repainted its Van Hool-bodied Scania E760TCS into the two-tone blue & yellow colours of Scottish Citylink complete with 'Ulsterman lettering for use on the Belfast - Stranraer - London service.   (Paul Savage)

Ulsterbus repainted two of its coaches employed on the Belfast - Stranraer - London service into Scottish Citylink colours complete with 'The Ulsterman' promotional lettering on their side panels. 681 (RXI6681), a former London Coaches Duple-bodied DAF is seen here at Stranraer prior to taking up its duty on the 921 service. (Garry Ward)

Western kept their vehicles in standard Citilink livery, using 1985 Volvo B10Ms with Plaxton bodies originally used on the Glasgow - London service; SV191 (VCS391) had been transferred from Kilmarnock and is seen in the new Citilink livery in this 1992 view at Stranraer. (Garry Ward)

Reclining at the rear of Dumfries depot, Alexander T-type bodied Seddon Pennine VII DS453 (DSD953V) looks extremely attractive in its new black, white, grey & red livery. (T.W.W.Knowles)

16 Heston Avenue (Sunday late evening journies); 16A Lochside/ Lincluden; 18 Woodlands Estate; 79 Brasswell (infrequent) and 81 Stoop.

Returning to Western, a pair of Leyland National Is were transferred down to Dumfries chiefly for use on town services (DL566/7 ; BSF766/7S), these being the first buses of this type to be allocated to the area since the experiments with the pair borrowed from Lowland Scottish several years earlier! The AEC Militant recovery vehicle DW7015 was rendered surplus with the arrival of an ERF B-series recovery truck registered RBE312S, taken over with the Kilmarnock portion of SBG Engineering and numbered DW7096, the Militant then passing to a local preservationist in November 1991. On the property side, investigations were made during 1990 into the possibility of obtaining alternative depot premises to Cumberland's Willowholme garage; but after property on an industrial estate in Longtown was viewed, the search were abandoned due to the company's impending privatisation. The biggest bombshell, however, was to drop on Dumfries and Galloway region in 1991, when on Wednesday 8th May, with little warning, Dicksons of Dumfries ceased to trade and receivers were called in. Rumours had been rife for some time that all was not well with that company's finances, but the speed with which the operation ceased threatened to cause major disruption in the region. Children were in the middle of vital "O" Level and Higher Grade exams and first priority was given to transporting them by Dumfries Regional Council. Whilst Dicksons

thirty five vehicle fleet of elderly Leyland Leopards with Duple and Plaxton bodies, along with a couple of Leyland Nationals lay mothballed at their Lockerbie Road premises, other operators and, in particular Western, organized emergency cover. Dicksons blamed their demise on spiralling costs, especially fuel as a result of the Gulf Crisis and efforts had been made to re-negotiate the contracts which still had some eighteen months to run in the case of the Education Authority tenders. However, many people, not least Western, had questioned the commercial viability of the quotes

Ironically, Alexander-bodied Leyland Leopard RAG385M of McEwan, Dumfries began life with Western SMT with whom, under its new ownership, it later competed. (M.Currie)

submitted to win the tendered services; and indeed Dicksons bids had been rumoured to be half a million £'s less than Western's! Whatever the reasons, with a network of services that spread from the border at Gretna in the east, across the border to Carlisle in the south, to Stranraer in the west and Cumnock in the north, swift action was needed if total chaos was to be avoided. The immediate problem was to cover the rural schools services, then the tendered services, then the Dumfries local schools services. Dicksons commercial services were not viewed as requiring coverage as they had competed so closely (and painfully!) with Western. However, the other services needed a considerable number of vehicles if large gaps were to be avoided. A huge effort was made at Eastfield Road with every bus in the garage sent out on the Wednesday morning.

Several of Western's withdrawn Seddon Pennine VIIs were quickly reinstated at Dumfries following the sudden demise of Dicksons in May 1991. Seen behind Eastfield Road depot are DS531, DS534 & DS514 of which the outer pair carry the old white, black & grey livery whilst DS534 in the centre wears the later scheme incorporating a red band. (K.A.Jenkinson)

Although the majority of the fleet were former coaches, Dickson also had a couple of Atlanteans, as well as two of Leyland Nationals, including JTH766P seen here on a Dumfries local. (Garry Ward)

Still wearing the orange, brown & white livery of Greater Manchester Buses, from whom it was acquired, is Atlantean DA807 (UNA772S) seen here resting in the yard of Dumfries depot in April 1992. (K.A.Jenkinson)

The old cream & red livery, the final examples of which had finally disappeared, made a sudden come-back as a result of the Dickson collapse with the swift recertification of a number of withdrawn Seddons and Leyland Leopards stored at Dumfries depot. One such bus was Alexander-bodied Seddon Pennine VII DS517 (YSD817T) seen here passing through Castle Douglas in May 1991. (Jim Paterson)

Emergency services were operated until 13 May when emergency tenders were put into force whilst the Regional Council set about inviting re-tenders for the work.

From the outset, Western, even though they were the major operator, faced a hugh challenge given the amount of pruning in the fleet over recent years. Vehicles were drafted in immediately from the northern garages, including the thirty year old semi-preserved Leyland PD3, bringing back a rear entrance vehicle for the first time

Following their withdrawal from services in the Glasgow area, several of Western's former Clydeside Scottish Routemasters were stored at the Eastfield Road depot at Dumfries awaiting sale. Amongst these were VLT110 and 152CLT seen here in March 1990. (K.A.Jenkinson)

After the Dickson collapse, Western were left with the unenviable task of searching for buses to cover their defunct operation at short notice. Only Fife Scottish remained by then with Western in the Scottish Bus Group and two Duple bodied Leyland Leopards were borrowed and had 1200 added to their existing Fife numbers. Fife's 210 (CFS110S) complete with "On hire to Western" stickers kept its existing number on the bus, but sister bus 214 had a "1" added. (Garry Ward)

A regular feature of Stranraer has been the rotation of double deckers to operate chiefly school services in the area. SR869 (XSJ669T) was transferred from the newly amalgamated Clydeside fleet and operated from the garage in their livery for a few months before repaint. They replaced the ex. West Midlands Fleetlines. (Garry Ward)

Dicksons collapse, a great credit to the effort from Western's engineering staff. Appropriate destination blinds were found for all the vehicles except the two Fife Leopards and all the hired buses were given fleet numbers, the Atlanteans being DA1200-7 (UNA853/63S, WVM884/77S, ANA211T, BNC936T, RJA702R, UNA772S) and the Fife pair having 1000 added to their existing numbers, making them DL1210/24 (CFS110S and GSG124T). Drivers and inspectors also put in an enormous amount of effort to get the vehicles out on the road and some even cancelled their holiday leave. The Dumfries local tendered journies were covered by Western from Friday 10 May with the town school service being covered from Monday 13 May. Also commencing on 13 May were the daytime Stewartry services to Kirkcudbright etc. together with the Dumfries - Glencaple/Bankend; Dumfries - Annan via Dalton and Dumfries - Lockerbie tendered journies, the Leyland PD3 putting in appearances on the latter in addition to some school duties. The strangest development, however, was on the Dumfries - Stranraer route which Western operated from Friday 10 May until Sunday 12 May when McEwan of Dumfries and McCulloch of Stranraer took over! Western had hoped to link back up with

in many years. Indeed, Dumfries may well have received the company's two remaining operational ex.Clydeside Routemasters had it not been for the need to cover the services of a Greenock operator who had also ceased trading. Ironically, it had only been a few months earlier that Dumfries garage had been home to several withdrawn Routemasters awaiting disposal! To provide further assistance, two Leyland Leopards borrowed from fellow Bus Group subsidiary Fife Scottish were received on the Saturday whilst approaches were made to Carlton dealer, Ripley, with a view to hiring back some Leyland National Is which had recently been sold. This proved impossible due to legal difficulties in Ripley obtaining the buses back from the operator to whom he had agreed to sell them. An alternative was offered, however, in the form of ex.Greater Manchester Buses Leyland Atlanteans, and five of these were received in May with a further three travelling northwards in June, a ninth vehicle being returned unused due to engine problems. This allowed the release of Seddon single deckers to more rural duties. While all this activity was taking place, a 'flying squad' of mechanics was sent down to help the Dumfries staff prepare a number of withdrawn Seddon Pennine VIIs and Leyland Leopards resident in the depot yard for Department of Transport examination. Ten of these sixteen vehicles had been recertified within a week of

Stranraer and, with marketing in mind, 'remind' the public of their presence in the area again. However, when the emergency tender was examined, the company discovered the requirements had been altered to the need for a 33-seater, a size of vehicle which Western was unable to provide. A retired driver was re-employed and a castle Douglas outstation for one bus was established again to cover part of the Kirkcudbright workings whilst similarly, Lockerbie duties required two part-time drivers and the stationing of two buses in the station yard overnight for a short time. Services up the Nith Valley to Moniaive and Thornhill were not operated for the first week after which Steele of Dumfies and McEwan took them over.

As a result of re-tendering in August 1991, further changes were made with the 76 Dumfries - Shawhead becoming the 73 operating five return journeys with one less on Sundays and Lochfoot also being operated under the same number. McEwans gained the Stewartry services, Nelson of Thornhill extended his services to New Cumnock and Western retained the Lockerbie, Carlisle and Annan area routes while one notable gain from Irvine of Glenluce was the evening journeys on the Stranraer locals to West End, belmont and McMasters Road. Further changes in October resulted in the Dumfries locals D1 (Troqueer) and D3 (Crichton/

The previous Western coach livery varied in its application and effectiveness. Dennis Dorchester DN421 (D221NCS) wears the arguably uncomplimentary previous style. (Garry Ward)

The attractive coach livery is now appearing on an increasing number of vehicles, including the unique Berkhof bodied Volvo SV198 (now re-registered WLT720 from a London Routmaster). The Western Garter, of a style last used in 1946, has made a comeback on some coaches as well. (Garry Ward)

Kingholm Quay) terminating at the Loreburn Centre whilst the D7 to Summerhill was diverted via the Loreburn Shopping Centre. The D5 service to Lochvale was extended within the estate to Urquahart Crescent and a new 'hospital link' service was introduced at this same time. Numbered D13, this operated from Whitesands via the town centre and the Loreburn Shopping Centre to the Dumfries and Galloway Royal Infirmary and Crichton Royal Hospital.

Having put in so much effort since the Dicksons collapse, staff had the niggling doubt that their efforts may have been for other's

benefit and it was with some relief that they learned in October that Western's management and employees had successfully purchased the company from the Scottish Bus Group. One of the first acts was to buy the previously hired Leyland Atlanteans which have subsequently been repainted into the coach-style livery which is to become standard for the company's bus fleet. In addition, they have been converted from fully automatic to semi automatic transmission. Some of the batch have since been transferred away from Dumfries, although substitutes have subsequently been drafted in to cover for

Wearing their owner's white, black & red livery, Alexander-bodied Seddon Pennine VIIs DS543 (ASD843T) and DS551 (BSD851T) illustrate the old and new-style fleetnames as they stand behind Dumfries depot in April 1992. (K.A.Jenkinson)

potential increases in traffic as a result of the Dumfries and Galloway region offering concessionary fares to senior citizens. Additionally, the disasterous fire in 1992 at Strathclyde Buses' Larkfield garage in Glasgow in which 60 vehicles were lost resulted in the transfer on loan of all the remaining Dumfries area Atlanteans to that operator. In the case of those still retaining Greater Manchester colours, these were repainted in full Strathclyde livery whilst those in Western colours had their front and rear painted in Strathclyde orange.

Ironically, at the turn of the year in 1991, Whitesands bus stance was converted into a basic bus station with 'sawtooth' bays some forty five years after discussions on the building of a proper bus station had been mooted in H.Merchant's report! Vehicles enter from the south side of Whitesands, leaving from the north end and as buses are only allowed a maximum of ten minutes waiting time,

Western's vehicles now have to return 'light' to Eastfield Road between service turns. The option of waiting further down the 'Sands' suggested by Merchant in his 1946 report was no longer viable due to car traffic having taken much of the space previously available.

A more recent 'development' has been rather a sad one. Some sixty five years after Caledonian first entered the city of Carlisle, its successor has all but withdrawn its stage carriage services in the area with the cessation of all except a couple of tendered journeys from Annan and Lockerbie from 10 February 1992. As mentioned above, prior to its privatisation, Western had been looking for alternative premises to Cumberland's Willowholme depot. The Stagecoach-owned company had been applying increased pressure on Western to withdraw from the area, culminating in the application for a service from Carlisle to Dumfries in December 1991 and the threat to spread into Dumfries itself. A compromise was reached with the agreement to cut back the main service 79 from Dumfries to terminate in Annan where connections would be made with a newly-extended Cumberland service. The 84 Carlisle - Longtown service was also transferred to Cumberland, leaving the few incursions listed above, with Annan to Carlisle journies carrying the number 278 to indicate a subsidised operation. Carlisle-based vehicles were transferred to Dumfries and the 'E' depot code passed into the annals of history. One piece of peculiar administrative work which ceased as a result of the closure was the need to register vehicles normally based at Carlisle with the North

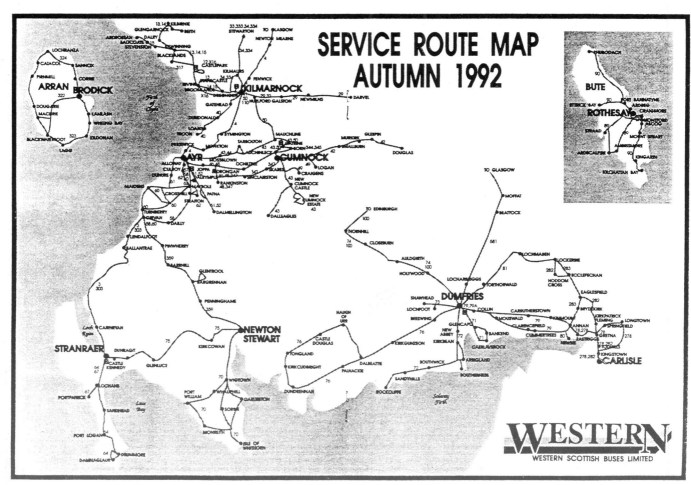

SERVICE ROUTE MAP AUTUMN 1992

WESTERN
WESTERN SCOTTISH BUSES LIMITED

Several of Western's ex.Greater Manchester Atlanteans were hired by Strathclyde Buses following the disasterous fire at its Larkfield garage in 1992. Amongst these was BNC936T which retained its new-style Western livery but gained a Strathclyde orange & black front.   (P.T.Stokes)

Another of Western's ex.Greater Manchester Atlanteans hired to Strathclyde Buses after its Larkfield garage fire was DA807 (UNA772S). With part of its Manchester-style destination display panelled over, it was repainted into full Strathclyde livery of orange & black before taking up its temporary duties in Glasgow.   (Garry Ward)

SCOTTISH CITYLINK

Unusual Plaxton Integral SH108 (J8WSB) is the latest new arrival for Stranraer. Fresh out of the Kilmarnock paintshop, this vehicle was about to head south for its new depot in September 1992. Tom MacFarlane)

Two of Dumfries depot's Dennis Dorchester coaches, Alexander-bodied DN421 (D221NCS) and Plaxton-bodied DN140 (VLT226) show off their attractive new two-tone grey, white, black & red livery in April 1992. (K.A.Jenkinson)

West Area Traffic Commissioner which resulted in these buses carrying a different operators disc. Efforts over the years to have this ruling changed failed despite the argument that the vehicles concerned could regularly end their working day 'north of the border' in Dumfries or Annan!

To cope with an increased work load, the Annan sub-depot of Western was moved from behind the Bingo Hall to a slightly more secure yard to the south of the town, with four vehicles - including normally three double deckers - now being allocated during school terms. The 'deckers are required to work the school journeys from Gretna and Eastriggs to Annan, the Gretna workings now being renumbered from 79B to 78 and in addition, they normally undertake the Annan local services to Newington and Hallmeadow as well as a new local route over older parts of the town to Summervale Avenue introduced in January 1993 and some duties to Lockerbie. A fifth single decker works down on a service from Dumfries to support the schools duties in the afternoon and returns at night. Since the closure of Annan garage, the logistics of operating from the town have been made more complex; vehicles having to return to Dumfries due to the lack of facilities at Annan. The Annan-based single decker returns nightly whilst the double deckers return every three days. In December, the vehicles were re-sited across the yard as a result of the company from which Western originally rented space goping into liquidation. Ironically, this yard was previously occupied by the now defunct coaching concern, Little of Annan who ceased trading largely as a result of the loss of contracts to Dickson of Dumfries who, as has been documented earlier, also is no longer! Such are the ways of deregulation .... A move has also been required in Kirkcudbright within the harbour area due to the

redevelopment of the site, whilst two further moves to record are the closure of the Whitesands office during May 1992 as costs remained under tight scrutiny, and the first signs of the new adaption of the coach livery to appear in the area with Stranraer's Berkhof Esprite-bodied Volvo SV198 (WLT720) and Dumfries garage's Dennis Dorchester DN421 (D221NCS) sporting the new style. Meanwhile, having lost its Sealink contract, Stranraer gained a new one for the transportation of passengers from the rival Sea-Cat hydrofoil service from West Pier to Stranraer town centre. The appearance of SS434, still in Sealink contract livery one morning on the new service was not appreciated and care has since been taken to ensure that this has not been repeated! Actually, since 1991 Stranraer has been under the control of Ayr depot's operations manager rather than maintaining its historic link with Dumfries.

Judging by developments which took place in 1992 it would appear that nothing is new as far as services are concerned, as in November Caledonian's successor gained the tender to operate the route from Lockerbie to Moffat, this having been Caledonian's first service in 1927, gained from Annandale Motor Services but which was later abandoned. Operated by working an additional morning journey on the 581 service as far as Moffat, with a return run to Dumfries at night, a minibus was normally used to work the four Monday to Saturday return journeys. Numbered 384 by Western, vehicles however actually carry route number 111 from the Dumfries and Galloway Regional Council tendered service block of numbers. Western's portion of the contract for the 920/1 Belfast - Stranraer - London service was due for renewal in May, a condition of which was the use of a new vehicle. As a result, an order was placed for a Plaxton 425 integral coach which, after some delay, entered service

Basking in the shadows behind Dumfries depot in April 1992 are ECW-bodied Fleetlines DR834/7 (ASA24/7T), both of which were acquired from Northern Scottish in 1987. As can be seen, DR834 has had its front upper deck windows replaced with fixed glazing while DR837 still retains its push-out ventilators. (K.A.Jenkinson)

Its destination blind already set for its return journey to Annan on a service taken over from Western, Stagecoach subsidiary Cumberland Motor Services Alexander-bodied Leyland Olympian 1028 arrives in Carlisle in November 1992. (K.A.Jenkinson)

The Caledonian fleet name was resurrected by National Express for its Tayside Travel Service subsidiary, formed upon the acquisition of Stagecoach's express services. One of the first vehicles to gain the new Caledonian Express names was former Stagecoach Duple-bodied Volvo B10M, D447FSP seen here at Walnut Grove depot, Perth in 1989. (K.A.Jenkinson)

in September. Numbered SH108 (J8WSB) and painted in Citilink livery, its operation has, however, been somewhat spasmodic due to bodywork problems. On a happier note, the coach-shop and paint-shop facilities at Eastfield Road, Dumfries made a welcome comeback towards the end of 1992 after being 'mothballed' for around two years to take pressure off the busy Nursery Avenue facilities at Kilmarnock. One of its first duties was to prepare for service and repaint former Greater Manchester Atlantean KA810 (UNA824S) and after this, recently-acquired ex.Bluebird Buses Leyland National KL795 (MSO10W) was similarly treated along with several vehicles which underwent standard repaints.

More recently, in the spring of 1993, Dumfries has gained two further ex.Greater Manchester Leyland Atlanteans, one being DA811 (UNA840S) which although having its front destination box rebuilt to Western style retained its side and rear route number blinds, the other, DA801 (UNA863S) having been returned from its long-term hire to Strathclyde Buses on 16 April who repainted it back into Western colours but left its Greater Manchester-style front destination box intact! On the service front, from 19 April in conjunction with Dumfries and Galloway Regional Council, the Lockerbie - Moffat servuice 384 (Dumfries & Galloway route 111) was extended within Moffat to provide a local service from High Street to the Annandale Road and Beechgrove areas (a flat fare of

23p being applied on all the local journies with senior citizens and disabled persons with travel cards carried free of charge) whilst in Dumfries the town centre terminus of the 371 Glencaple service was altered from Shakespeare Street to the Loreburn Centre. Some three weeks later, on 10 May, McEwan began a new commercially-operated Monday - Saturday Kirkcudbright Circular service operating via Merse and Longacres Road and on the same date revised their Dumfries - Kirkcudbright/Gatehouse service.

Whilst tne original Caledonian company disappeared some forty five years ago, its fleet name was revived in August 1989 following the formation by National Express of Tayside Travel Services to acquire the express services of Perth-based Stagecoach operating within or originating in Scotland. Despite the Stagecoach name being retained on Tayside Travel Services vehicles for a given period of time, the coaches also carried the name Caledonian Express which was additionally used on all that company's promotional material etc. Although this led one to believe that the old-established Caledonian title had gained a reprieve, sadly it would appear that this was only to be short lived as recent repaints have been outshopped with standard National Express identities. From this, it would seem that famous names never die, but merely fade away ....

CALEDONIAN FLEET LIST
Buses & Coaches

Fleet No.	Reg.No.	Built	Chassis	Body		Withdrawn	Acquired From	Disposal
1927								
	LS1272	1923	Ford		Ch	1927	H.Brook & Co.	King (dealer) Stranraer
	SH1709	1923	Ford		Ch	1927	H.Brook & Co.	
	OS764	1923	Ford		Ch	1927	H.Brook & Co.	
	OS1047		Ford			by 1943	H.Brook & Co.	
	OS1237	1924	Berliet		B20	by 1930	H.Brook & Co.	King (dealer) Stranraer
	VA2889		Berliet		B20	by 1943	H.Brook & Co.	
	OS1318	1923	Ford		Ch	1927	H.Brook & Co.	
	OS1358	1926	Berliet		B20	1928	H.Brook & Co.	
	OS1510	1926	Daimler		B32	by 1933	H.Brook & Co.	Muir, Dumfries
	V8161	1925	AEC		Ch	1928	H.Brook & Co.	
	AH9205	1924	AEC		Ch	1927	H.Brook & Co.	Reid & Adams
11	IB3235		AEC		B32	by 1943	H.Brook & Co.	
	BN5924	1924	Fiat		Ch	1928	H.Brook & Co.	
	NH7054		Dennis		B19	by 1943	Brooks Motor Co.	
	SW2270	1926	Dennis		B19	1934	Brooks Motor Co.	Unknown owner, London
27	SW2289	1926	Dennis		B19	1935	Brooks Motor Co.	Unknown owner, Lanarkshire
	SW2290	1926	Dennis		B19	1932	Brooks Motor Co.	Fairly, Kelty
	SW2291	1926	Dennis		B19	1932	Brooks Motor Co.	Wallace, Leith
	SW2326	1926	Dennis		B30	1933	Brooks Motor Co.	Bastable (showman), Edinburgh
	SW2327	1926	Dennis		B30	1934	Brooks Motor Co.	Lawler, London (as lorry)
24	SW2396	1926	Dennis		B14F	1934	Brooks Motor Co.	Elliot, London (as lorry)
	SM2725	1924	Leyland 36hp		Ch	1927	J & J Scott	Andersons Motors, Dumfries
	SM2948	1924	Leyland 36hp		Ch	1927	J & J Scott	Andersons Motors, Dumfries
	TC5273	1925	Leyland 36hp		B	1928	J & J Scott	
	TC6411	1925	Leyland 36hp		B	1928	J & J Scott	
	SM4190	1924	Leyland GH7		B26	1927	J & J Scott	Unknown owner, Lanarkshire
	SM4202	1924	Leyland GH7		B29	1927	J & J Scott	Unknown owner, Edinburgh
	SM4630	1924	Leyland A7		Ch	1928	J & J Scott	Unknown owner, Stirlingshire
	SM4681	1924	Leyland C7	Leyland	B30	1929	J & J Scott	Unknown owner, Glasgow
	SM4704	1924	Leyland C7	Leyland	B30	1933	J & J Scott	Scrapped
	SM4731	1924	Albion PE24	Stewart	B21	1928	J & J Scott	Unknown owner, Glasgow
33	HS4008	1925	Albion PH24	NCME	B20	1934	J & J Scott	Milvain, Dumfries (as lorry)
	SM5601	1926	Albion PJ24	Penman	B24F	1934	J & J Scott	J.Dickson, Dumfries
	SM5609	1926	Morris		B14	1933	J & J Scott	Dunlop, Thomas & Wilson, Lockerbie
	SM5802	1926	Albion Viking	Cowieson	Ch18	1932	J & J Scott	Unknown owner, Kirkcudbright
	SM5958	1926	Albion PJ26	NCME	B25F	by 1937	J & J Scott	Caledonian lorry H13
37	SM6230	1927	Albion PJ26	NCME	B25F	by 1938	J & J Scott	Caledonian parcel van P2
38	SM6231	1927	Albion PJ26	NCME	B25F	by 1938	J & J Scott	Caledonian parcel van P3
	SM4799	1925	Vulcan n.c.		B	1928	Annandale Motor Co.	Unknown owner, Glasgow
19	SM6022	1926	Vulcan n.c.		B20	1933	Annandale Motor Co.	Unknown owner, Edinburgh
	SM4943	1924	Gotfredson 21hp		B14	1928	G.P.Bell	Scrapped by Caledonian
	SM5882	1926	Thornycroft A1		B20	by 1934	G.P.Bell	Unknown owner, Perthshire
43	SW2543	1927	ADC 416	Strachan & Brown	B32F	1939	New	Scrapped by Caledonian
44	SW2544	1927	ADC 416	Strachan & Brown	B32F	1936	New	Unknown owner, Glasgow
45	SW2545	1927	ADC 416	Strachan & Brown	B32F	1934	New	Montgomerie (showman), Carlisle
39	SW2546	1927	Dennis n.c.	Strachan & Brown	B28F	1934	New	Harris, London (as lorry)
40	SW2547	1927	Dennis n.c.	Strachan & Brown	B28F	1933	New	Law (showman) Cowdenbeath
41	SW2548	1927	Dennis n.c.	Strachan & Brown	B28F	1934	New	Chambers Wharfe Cold Store, London
42	SW2549	1927	Dennis n.c.	Strachan & Brown	B28F	1933	New	Strand (showman), Edinburgh
47	SW2550	1927	Leyland PLSC3	Leyland	B32F	1947	New	Scrapped by Caledonian
46	SW2551	1927	Leyland PLSC3	Leyland	B32F	1945	New	Scrapped by Caledonian
1928								
48	SW6741	1928	Leyland PLSC3	Leyland	B32F	1949	New	Connor (dealer), Dumfries
49	SW6742	1928	Leyland PLSC3	Leyland	B32F	1942	New	Scrapped by Caledonian
50	SW6743	1928	Leyland PLSC3	Leyland	B32F	1945	New	Unknown owner
51 ?	RM1966	1925	Bean		B14	1932	T.G.Wood	Grange, Barnard Castle
52 ?	RM2987	1926	Morris		B17	1930	T.G.Wood	Witherington, Carlisle (as lorry)
53	SM6918	1928	Leyland PLSC3	Leyland	B32F	1947	New	Scrapped by Caledonian
54	SM6919	1928	Leyland PLSC3	Leyland	B32F	1949	New	Connor (dealer), Dumfries
55	SM6920	1928	Leyland PLSC3	Leyland	B32F	1942	New	Caledonian parcel van P13
56	SM6948	1928	Leyland PLSC3	Leyland	B32F	1949	New	Connor (dealer), Dumfries
57	SM6963	1928	Leyland PLSC3	Leyland	B32F	1949	New	Last licensed 3/49
58	SM6964	1928	Leyland PLSC3	Leyland	B32F	1949	New	Connor (dealer) Dumfries
59	SM6965	1928	Leyland PLSC3	Leyland	B32F	1948	New	Scrapped by Caledonian
60	SM6966	1928	Leyland PLSC3	Leyland	B32F	1947	New	Last licensed 11/47
61	SM6967	1928	Leyland PLSC3	Leyland	B32F	1949	New	Last licenced 3/49
62	SM6950	1928	Albion PK26	Mitchell	B29F	1935	John Robertson	Caledonian parcel van P4
63 ?	SM4387	1924	Guy	Massey	C20	by 1943	John Robertson	J.Dickson, Dumfries
1930								
64	SM8315	1930	Leyland LT2	Leyland	B26F	1949/50	New	WSMT / Scottish Omnibuses Ltd.
65	SM8316	1930	Leyland LT2	Leyland	B26F	1949/50	New	WSMT / Scottish Omnibuses Ltd.

Fleet No.	Reg.No.	Built	Chassis	Body	Withdrawn	Acquired From	Disposal
1930							
66	SM8317	1930	Leyland LT2	Leyland B26F	1949/50	New	WSMT / Scottish Omnibuses Ltd.
67	SM8318	1930	Leyland LT2	Leyland B26F	1946	New	Caledonian parcel van P12
68	SM6233	1927	Thornycroft A2 long	B26F	1936	D.Clark	Adcroft (dealer), Glasgow
69	SM7909	1929	Bean	Willowbrook B20	1935	D.Clark	Gibson, Falkirk (as mobile cafe)
		1928	Albion PK26	NCME B29F	by 1943	D.Clark	?
1931							
70	SM8851	1931	Leyland LT2	ECW B31R (1948)	1949/57	New	WSMT / J.Russell, Dumfries
71	SM8852	1931	Leyland LT2	ECW B31R (1948)	1949/57	New	WSMT / Millburn (dlr), Glasgow
72	SM8853	1931	Leyland LT2	ECW B31R (1948)	1949/57	New	WSMT / Millburn (dlr), Glasgow
73	SM8854	1931	Leyland LT2	ECW B31R (1948)	1949/57	New	WSMT / Millburn (dlr), Glasgow
74	SW2678	1927	Albion PK26	Albion B29F	1935	S.Solley & Sons	Unknown owner, Stirlingshire
75	SW2324	1926	Albion PK26	NCME B29F	1936	S.Solley & Sons	O'Brien (showman), Bonnybridge
76	XV6861	1928	Daimler CF6	Bell B32	1936	Ribble Motor Services	Caravan
77	WK9824	1929	Daimler CF6	Hall Lewis B32	1936	Ribble Motor Services	Fletcher, Maryport
78	HH4802	1929	Daimler CF6	NCME B32	1935	Ribble Motor Services	Last licensed 1935
79	VC1247	1929	Daimler CF6	Willowbrook B32	1936	Ribble Motor Services	Adcroft (dealer), Glasgow
80	HH5412	1930	Daimler CF6	NCME B32R	1936	Ribble Motor Services	Kelly (dealer), Glasgow
81	HH5413	1930	Daimler CF6	NCME B32R	1937	Ribble Motor Services	Kelly (dealer), Glasgow
93 ?	SM4285	1924	Fiat	B14	1933	Farrar & Faulder	Scrapped by Caledonian
82 ?	HH2839	1925	Maudslay ML4	B26	1939	Farrer & Faulder	Last licensed 10/39
83 ?	HH3345	1926	Maudslay ML2	B20F	1938	Farrer & Faulder	Last licensed 6/38
	VA4675	1926	Dennis n.c.	B18	by 1943	Farrer & Faulder	?
84 ?	HH4040	1927	Maudslay ML4B	B26	1938	Farrer & Faulder	?
92 ?	HH4109	1928	Dennis n.c.		c1938	Farrer & Faulder	Caledonian parcel van P7
	XV5034	1928	Dennis n.c.	B18	by 1943	Farrer & Faulder	?
94 ?	GE2263	1928	Laffley	C20	by 1943	Farrer & Faulder	?
85	HH4400	1928	Maudslay ML4B	B26	by 1942	Farrer & Faulder	Showman
86	HH4888	1929	Maudslay ML4B	B26	1938	Farrer & Faulder	Last licensed 10/38
87	HH5180	1930	Maudslay ML3BC	B32	by 1941	Farrer & Faulder	Scrapped by Caledonian
88	HH5596	1931	Maudslay ML3E	Barnaby B32	1947	Farrer & Faulder	Fagan, Coatbridge (as lorry)
89	HH5595	1931	Commer Invader	B20	1937	Farrer & Faulder	Last licensed 11/37
95 ?	SM5361	1925	Leyland 30hp		1932	South of Scotland Motor Co.	Unknown owner, Edinburgh
96 ?	SM5859	1926	Leyland A13	Leyland B20F	1932	South of Scotland Motor Co.	Unknown owner, Carlisle
97 ?	SM5878	1926	Leyland A13	Leyland B20F	1934	South of Scotland Motor Co.	Unknown owner, Kent
98	SM6975	1928	Leyland PLSC3	Leyland B35F	1949	South of Scotland Motor Co.	WSMT - not used
99	SM7208	1928	Leyland PLSC3	Leyland B35F	1948	South of Scotland Motor Co.	Connor (dealer), Dumfries
100	SM7682	1929	Leyland PLSC3	Leyland B35F	1946	South of Scotland Motor Co.	Slater (showman), Dumfries
101	SM7012	1928	Leyland PLSC1	Leyland B31R	1949	South of Scotland Motor Co.	Scrapped by Caledonian
102	SM8910	1931	Leyland TS1	ECOC B32R (1932)	1949/50	South of Scotland Motor Co.	WSMT / Scottish Omnibuses Ltd.
103	SM8861	1931	AEC Regal		1942	South of Scotland Motor Co.	War Department 1942
104	SM7018	1928	Leyland PLC1	Leyland B26F	1947	South of Scotland Motor Co.	Bow (showman), Edinburgh
105	SM6527	1927	Leyland PLC1	Leyland B26F	1936	South of Scotland Motor Co.	Robinson & Davidson, Lockerbie
106	SM6107	1927	Leyland PLC1	Leyland B26F	1940	South of Scotland Motor Co.	Scrapped by Caledonian
107	SM6221	1927	Leyland PLC1	Leyland B26F	1939	South of Scotland Motor Co.	Scrapped by Caledonian
108	SM6371	1927	Leyland PLC1	Leyland B26F	1938	South of Scotland Motor Co.	Testo (showman), Glasgow
109	SM8673	1931	Albion PK49	NCME B20F	1940	South of Scotland Motor Co.	J.Carruthers, New Abbey
110	SM8808	1931	Albion PKA26	NCME B29R	1938	South of Scotland Motor Co.	Scrapped by Caledonian
111	SM8920	1931	Albion PKA26	B29F	1938	South of Scotland Motor Co.	Scrapped by Caledonian
112	SM8304	1930	Albion PKA26	NCME B29F	1940	South of Scotland Motor Co.	Caledonian parcel van P11
113	SM8565	1930	Albion PKA26	NCME B29R	1940	South of Scotland Motor Co.	Scrapped by Caledonian
114	SM6993	1928	Albion PK26	Cowieson B29R	1936	South of Scotland Motor Co.	Robinson & Davidson, Lockerbie
115	SM6994	1928	Albion PK26	Cowieson B29R	1937	South of Scotland Motor Co.	Kelly (dealer), Glasgow
147 ?	HH2776	1925	Guy BA	B20	1932	Huntington Bros.	Last licensed 1932
148	FR8209	1927	Lancia	C20	1933	Huntington Bros.	Robe, Caerlaverock (as lorry)
1932							
116	DS1209	1926	Thornycroft A1	NCME B24F	1937	A.Harper	Kelly (dealer), Glasgow
117	DS1302	1927	Thornycroft A2 long	Beadle B24F	1934	A.Harper	Clark, Glencaple
118	DS1304	1927	Albion PM28	Porteous B32R	1938	A.Harper	Kelly (dealer), Glasgow
119	DS1342	1927	Thornycroft A2 long	United B20F	1936	A.Harper	J.L.Thom, Kelty
120	DS1356	1927	Thornycroft LB	Grant, Cameron & Curle B30F	1938	A.Harper	Kelly (dealer), Glasgow
121	DS1362	1927	Albion PM28	NCME B32R	1938	A.Harper	Testo (showman), Glasgow
122	DS1403	1928	Albion PNA26	Cowieson C26F	1936	A.Harper	Caledonian parcel van P6
123	DS1404	1928	Thornycroft A6	Strachan & Brown C20F	1936	A.Harper	Adcroft (dealer), Glasgow
124	DS1406	1928	Thornycroft A6	Strachan & Brown B24F	1936	A.Harper	Caledonian parcel van P5
125	DS1421	1928	Thornycroft A6	Hall Lewis B20F	1936	A.Harper	Adcroft (dealer), Glasgow
126	DS1438	1928	Thornycroft A6	NCME B24F	1936	A.Harper	Pinder (shownam), Carlisle
127	DS1474	1929	Thornycroft BC	Grant, Cameron & Curle B31R	1938	A.Harper	Kelly (dealer), Glasgow
128	DS1475	1929	Thornycroft BC	Grant, Cameron & Curle B31R	1938	A.Harper	Kelly (dealer), Glasgow
129	DS1476	1929	Albion PM28	Grant, Cameron & Curle B31R	1936	A.Harper	Robinson & Davidson, Lockerbie
130	DS1477	1929	Leyland LT1	Leyland B26F (1931)	1949/50	A.Harper	WSMT / Scottish Omnibuses Ltd.
131	OU8821	1931	Thornycroft BC	C26F	by 1939	A.Harper	Broughton, Edinburgh
132	DS1521	1929	Thornycroft BC	Cowieson B30R	1936	A.Harper	Adcroft (dealer), Glasgow
133	DS1593	1930	Thornycroft LC	B31R	1938	A.Harper	McFadden (dealer), Rutherglen
134	DS1594	1930	Leyland LT1	Stewart B32R	1940	A.Harper	War Department 1940
135	DS1595	1930	Thornycroft LC	B31R	1938	A.Harper	Kelly (dealer), Glasgow
136	DS1596	1930	Thornycroft LC	B31R	1938	A.Harper	Kelly (dealer), Glasgow
137	DS1617	1930	AEC Regal	Stewart C32F	1943	A.Harper	Royal Navy

Fleet No.	Reg.No.	Built	Chassis	Body	Withdrawn	Acquired From	Disposal
1932							
138	DS1618	1930	Thornycroft LC	C30F	1937	A.Harper	Leonard (dealer), Glasgow
139	DS1690	1931	Leyland LT2	Grant, Cameron & Curle B32R	1940	A.Harper	War Department 1940
140	DS1691	1931	Albion PW65	Porteous B32R	1947	A.Harper	J & J Leith, Sanquhar
141	DS1698	1931	Commer Invader	Willowbrook C20F	1938	A.Harper	M.Forbes, Dundee
142 ?	SM6451	1927	Morris	C20	1934	J.Bell	Milvain, Dumfries (as lorry)
149	SM9335	1932	Thornycroft Cygnet	Harrington C30F	1946	A.Harper	Scrapped by Caledonian
150	SM9484	1932	Thornycroft Cygnet	Harrington B31F	1947	A.Harper	Hicks (dealer), Glasgow
151	SM9501	1932	Leyland LT5	ECW B33R (1949)	1949/57	New	WSMT / Millburn (dealer), Glasgow
152	SM9502	1932	Leyland LT5	ECW B33R (1949)	1949/57	New	WSMT / Millburn (dealer), Glasgow
153	SM9503	1932	Leyland LT5	ECW B32R (1943)	1949/55	New	WSMT / Millburn (dealer), Glasgow
154	SM9504	1932	Leyland LT5	ECW B32R (1943)	1949/54	New	WSMT / Millburn (dealer), Glasgow
155 ?	SM7229	1928	Bean 14hp	B	1934	Williamson & Proudfoot	Unknown owner, Kirkcudbright
1933							
157	SM9971	1933	Dennis Lancet I	ECOC B32F	1949/53	New	WSMT / Hunter (dealer), Leith
158	SM9972	1933	Dennis Lancet I	ECOC B32F	1949/50	New	WSMT / Millburn (dealer), Glasgow
159	SM9973	1933	Dennis Lancet I	ECOC B32F	1949/50	New	WSMT / Millburn (dealer), Glasgow
160	SM9974	1933	Dennis Lancet I	ECOC B32F	1949/53	New	WSMT / Hunter (dealer), Leith
161	SM9975	1933	Dennis Lancet I	ECOC B32F	1949/53	New	WSMT / Hunter (dealer), Leith
162	SM9976	1933	Dennis Lancet I	ECOC B32F	1949/50	New	WSMT / Millburn (dealer), Glasgow
163	SM9977	1933	AEC Regal	ECOC C28F	1949/53	New	WSMT / Chassis scrapped
164	SM9978	1933	AEC Regal	ECOC C28F	1949/53	New	WSMT / Windriff (bkr), Mouswald
165	SM9979	1933	AEC Regal	ECOC C28F	1949/53	New	WSMT / McNaughton (bkr), Airdrie
166	SM9980	1933	Thornycroft Cygnet	ECOC C28F	1949	New	Hicks (dealer), Glasgow
167	SM9981	1933	Thornycroft Cygnet	ECOC C28F	1949	New	Hicks (dealer), Glasgow
168	SM9982	1933	Thornycroft Cygnet	ECOC C28F	1949	New	Hicks (dealer), Glasgow
1934							
169	SM8332	1930	Morris Viceroy	C20F	1938	F.Bisset & Son	Dumfries Motor Salvage Co.
1935							
170	BSM170	1935	Leyland TS7	ECW B33R (1943)	1949/55	New	WSMT / Millburn (dealer), Glasgow
171	BSM171	1935	Leyland TS7	ECW B33R (1943)	1949/55	New	WSMT / Millburn (dealer), Glasgow
172	BSM172	1935	Leyland TS7	ECW B33R (1943)	1949/55	New	WSMT / Millburn (dealer), Glasgow
173	BSM173	1935	Leyland TS7	ECW B33R (1943)	1949/54	New	WSMT / Carruthers (bkr), Dumfries
1936							
174	BSM820	1936	Dennis Lancet II	Weymann B32F	1949/57	New	WSMT / Millburn (dealer), Glasgow
175	BSM821	1936	Dennis Lancet II	Weymann B32F	1949/55	New	WSMT / Millburn (dealer), Glasgow
176	BSM822	1936	Dennis Lancet II	Weymann B32F	1949/55	New	WSMT / Millburn (dealer), Glasgow
177	BSM823	1936	Dennis Lancet II	Weymann B32F	1949/55	New	WSMT / Millburn (dealer), Glasgow
178	BSM824	1936	Dennis Lancet II	Weymann B32F	1949/55	New	WSMT / Millburn (dealer), Glasgow
179	BSM825	1936	Dennis Lancet II	Weymann B32F	1949/57	New	WSMT / Millburn (dealer), Glasgow
180	BSM826	1936	Dennis Lancet II	ECW B35R (1948)	1949/57	New	WSMT / Millburn (dealer), Glasgow
181	BSM827	1936	Dennis Lancet II	Weymann C32F	1949/55	New	WSMT / Millburn (dealer), Glasgow
182	BSM828	1936	Dennis Lancet II	Weymann C32F	1939	New	Burnt out in Annan garage fire
183	BSM829	1936	Dennis Lancet II	Weymann C32F	1939	New	Burnt out in Annan garage fire
184	BSM830	1936	Dennis Lancet II	Weymann C32F	1940	New	War Department (1940)
185	BSM831	1936	Dennis Lancet II	Weymann C32F	1949/56	New	WSMT / Millburn (dealer), Glasgow
186	BSM832	1936	Dennis Lancet II	Weymann C32F	1940	New	War Department (1940)
187	BSM833	1936	Dennis Lancet II	Weymann C32F	1949/57	New	WSMT / Millburn (dealer), Glasgow
188	BSM834	1936	Thornycroft Handy AE	Brush C20F	1946	New	Dawson & Gordon, Crieff
189	BSM835	1936	Thornycroft Handy AE	Brush C20F	1946	New	Dawson & Gordon, Crieff
190 ?	DB5111	1927	TSM B9A	Tilling B39R	by 1938	North Western	?
191 ?	DB5113	1927	TSM B9A	Tilling B39R	by 1938	North Western	?
192	DB5119	1927	TSM B9A	Tilling B39R	by 1938	North Western	?
193	DB5117	1927	TSM B9A	Tilling B39R	by 1938	North Western	?
194	DB5116	1927	TSM B9A	Tilling B39R	by 1938	North Western	?
1937							
195	CSM602	1937	Thornycroft Dainty CF	Brush C20F	1939	New	Burnt out in Annan garage fire
196	CSM603	1937	Thornycroft Dainty CF	Brush C20F	by 1947	New	Dawson & Gordon, Crieff
197	CSM604	1937	Thornycroft Dainty CF	Brush C20F	by 1947	New	Dawson & Gordon, Crieff
198	CSM766	1937	Dennis Lancet II	ECW B32F	1949/57	New	WSMT / Millburn (dealer), Glasgow
199	CSM767	1937	Dennis Lancet II	ECW B32F	1949/57	New	WSMT / Millburn (dealer), Glasgow
200	CSM768	1937	Dennis Lancet II	ECW B32F	1949/54	New	WSMT / Millburn (dealer), Glasgow
201	CSM769	1937	Dennis Lancet II	ECW B32F	1949/55	New	WSMT / Millburn (dealer), Glasgow
202	CSM770	1937	Dennis Lancet II	ECW B32F	1949/55	New	WSMT / Millburn (dealer), Glasgow
203	CSM771	1937	Dennis Lancet II	ECW B32F	1949/55	New	WSMT / Millburn (dealer), Glasgow
204	CSM772	1937	Dennis Lancet II	ECW B32F	1949/54	New	WSMT / Millburn (dealer), Glasgow
205	CSM773	1937	Dennis Lancet II	ECW B32F	1949/57	New	WSMT / Millburn (dealer), Glasgow
206	CSM774	1937	Dennis Lancet II	ECW B32F	1949/54	New	WSMT / Millburn (dealer), Glasgow
1938							
207	DSM450	1938	Thornycroft Dainty CF	Brush B20F	1949	New	Millburn (dealer), Glasgow

Fleet No.	Reg.No.	Built	Chassis	Body	Withdrawn	Acquired From	Disposal
1938							
208	DSM451	1938	Thornycroft Dainty CF	Brush B20F	1949	New	Millburn (dealer), Glasgow
209	DSM452	1938	Leyland SKPZ2	Harrington C20F	1949	New	WSMT / Badger (contractor)
210	DSM453	1938	Dennis Lancet II	ECW B35R (1948)	1949/57	New	WSMT / Millburn (dealer), Glasgow
211	DSM454	1938	Dennis Lancet II	Brush C32F	1949/54	New	WSMT / Millburn (dealer), Glasgow
212	DSM455	1938	Dennis Lancet II	Brush C32F	1949/54	New	WSMT / Millburn (dealer), Glasgow
213	DSM456	1938	Dennis Lancet II	Brush C32F	1949/56	New	WSMT / Millburn (dealer), Glasgow
214	WH2601	1930	Leyland TD1	Roberts L27/24RO	1940	Bolton Corporation	Scrapped by Caledonian
215	WH2602	1930	Leyland TD1	Roberts L27/24RO	1939	Bolton Corporation	Burnt out in Annan garage fire
216	WH2603	1931	Leyland TD1	Roberts L27/24R	1940	Bolton Corporation	Donnelly (dealer), Dumfries
217	WH2605	1931	Leyland TD1	Croft L27/24R (1944)	1949/54	Bolton Corporation	WSMT / Carruthers (breaker), Dumfries
218	TR5944	1928	Leyland PLSC3	Leyland B35F	1949	Hants & Dorset	WSMT / Scrapped by WSMT
219	TR5946	1928	Leyland PLSC3	Leyland B35F	1949	Hants & Dorset	WSMT / Scrapped by WSMT
220	RU8055	1928	Leyland PLSC3	Leyland B35F	1949	Hants & Dorset	McConner
221	RU8056	1928	Leyland PLSC3	Leyland B35F	1949	Hants & Dorset	?
222	RU8103	1928	Leyland PLSC3	Leyland B35F	1939	Hants & Dorset	Burnt out in Annan garage fire
223	RU8452	1928	Leyland PLSC3	Leyland B35F	1939	Hants & Dorset	Burnt out in Annan garage fire
224	RU8057	1928	Leyland PLSC3	Leyland B35F	1949	Hants & Dorset	?
225	RU8518	1928	Leyland PLSC3	Leyland B35F	1949	Hants & Dorset	?
226	RU7556	1928	Leyland PLSC3	Leyland B35F	1949	Hants & Dorset	?
227	RU8451	1928	Leyland PLSC3	Leyland B35F	1949	Hants & Dorset	?
228	RU8679	1929	Leyland PLSC3	Leyland B30F	1939	Hants & Dorset	Burnt out in Annan garage fire
229	RU5395	1927	Leyland PLSC3	Beadle B32F (1932)	1944	Hants & Dorset	Scrapped by Caledonian
230	TR6170	1929	Leyland PLSC3	Leyland B35F	1949	Hants & Dorset	WSMT / Scrapped by WSMT
231	RU8054	1928	Leyland PLSC3	Leyland B35F	1949	Hants & Dorset	?
232	XJ827	1932	Leyland LT5	ECW B32R (1943)	1949/54	North Western	WSMT / Carruthers (breaker), Dumfries
233	XJ828	1932	Leyland LT5	ECW B32R (1943)	1949/54	North Western	WSMT / MacPherson (breaker), Dumfries
1939							
234	TM3744	1928	Leyland TD1	Leyland L27/24RO	1940	Eastern National	Scrapped by Caledonian
235	TM3824	1928	Leyland TD1	Croft L27/26R (1947)	1949/54	Eastern National	WSMT / Chassis scrapped by WSMT
236	TM3843	1928	Leyland TD1	Croft L27/26R (1947)	1949/54	Eastern National	WSMT / Chassis scrapped by WSMT
237	TM3846	1928	Leyland TD1	Croft L27/26R (1947)	1949/54	Eastern National	WSMT / Chassis scrapped by WSMT
238	TM3735	1928	Leyland TD1	Roe L27/26R (1942)	1949/54	Eastern National	WSMT / Chassis scrapped by WSMT
239	VX4902	1931	AEC Regent	Short L26/24R	1949/62	Eastern National	WSMT / Skelton (breaker), Kilmarnock
240	TM6307	1930	AEC Regent	W'brk L27/26R (1945)	1949/53	Eastern National	WSMT / Motherwell Engineering Co.
241	ESM484	1939	Bedford WTB	Duple B20F	1949/49	New	WSMT / Millburn (dealer), Glasgow
242	ESM537	1939	Bristol L5G	ECW B35R (1949)	1949/60	New	WSMT / Millburn (dealer), Glasgow
243	ESM538	1939	Bristol L5G	ECW B35R (1949)	1949/60	New	WSMT / Millburn (dealer), Glasgow
244	WW7861	1928	Leyland TD1	Croft L27/24R (1945)	1949/53	Keighley West Yorkshire	WSMT / Marine Engineering, Bridlington
245	WW7862	1928	Leyland TD1	Croft L27/24R (1945)	1949/53	Keighley West Yorkshire	WSMT / McNaughton (breaker), Airdrie
246	WW7863	1928	Leyland TD1	Leyland L27/24RO	1949/55	Keighley West Yorkshire	WSMT / Millburn (dealer), Glasgow
247	WW8358	1929	Leyland TD1	Croft L27/24R (1947)	1949/54	Keighley West Yorkshire	WSMT / Chassis scrapped by WSMT
248	WW8360	1929	Leyland TD1	Leyland L27/24RO	1949/55	Keighley West Yorkshire	WSMT / Millburn (dealer), Glasgow
249	GG8190	1932	Albion PMB28	Stewart B32F	1941	Lochinvar Motor Service	Scrapped by Caledonian
250	US5897	1934	Albion PV70	NCME B32F	1949	Lochinvar Motor Service	?
251	WG2385	1934	Albion PK115	Alexander B31R	1949	Lochinvar Motor Service	?
252	VD988	1931	Albion PW65	Midland B32	1949	Lochinvar Motor Service	?
253	BTB520	1936	Leyland LT7	Leyland B32	1949	Lochinvar Motor Service	?
254	EPD594	1936	Dennis Lancet II	Roe B32F (1941)	1949/54	Lochinvar Motor Service	WSMT / Millburn (dealer), Glasgow
255	KR1729	1930	Leyland TD1	Croft L27/24R (1944)	1949/52	Wilts & Dorset	WSMT / McGrath, Stobo Castle (as caravan)
256	KR1731	1930	Leyland TD1	Leyland H24/24R	1949/52	Wilts & Dorset	WSMT / Chassis scrapped by WSMT
257	KR1733	1930	Leyland TD1	Croft L27/26R (1947)	1949/54	Wilts & Dorset	WSMT / Chassis scrapped by WSMT
258	KR6531	1930	Leyland TD1	Leyland H24/24R	1949/52	Wilts & Dorset	WSMT / Fraser (farmer), Dumfries
1940							
259	WW8605	1929	Leyland TD1	Leyland L27/24R	1949/52	Yorkshire W.D.	WSMT / Chassis scrapped by WSMT
260	HD4360	1930	Leyland TD1	Leyland L27/24R	1949/53	Yorkshire W.D.	WSMT / McNaughton (breaker), Airdrie
261	WW8606	1929	Leyland TD1	Leyland L27/24R	1949/52	Yorkshire W.D.	WSMT / McNaughton (breaker), Airdrie
262	HD3698	1928	Leyland TD1	W'brk L27/28R (1942)	1949/52	Yorkshire W.D.	WSMT / Fraser (farmer), Dumfries
263	HD3700	1928	Leyland TD1	Leyland L27/24R	1949/52	Yorkshire W.D.	WSMT / McNaughton (breaker), Airdrie
264	HD3701	1928	Leyland TD1	W'brk L27/28R (1942)	1949/52	Yorkshire W.D.	WSMT / McCall (breaker), Kilmarnock
265	HD4361	1931	Leyland TD1	Croft L27/26R (1947)	1949/54	Yorkshire W.D.	WSMT / Chassis scrapped by WSMT
266	HD4362	1931	Leyland TD1	Leyland L27/24R	1949/51	Yorkshire W.D.	WSMT / Scrapped by WSMT
267	HD4363	1931	Leyland TD1	W'brk L27/28R (1942)	1949/55	Yorkshire W.D.	WSMT / Millburn (dealer), Glasgow
268	GE2454	1928	Leyland TD1	Leyland L27/24R	1949/55	Glasgow Corporation	WSMT / Millburn (dealer), Glasgow
269	GE2488	1928	Leyland TD1	Croft L27/24R (1944)	1949/55	Glasgow Corporation	WSMT / McNaughton (breaker), Airdrie
270	GE2494	1929	Leyland TD1	Leyland L27/24R	1949/55	Glasgow Corporation	WSMT / Millburn (dealer), Glasgow
271	GE2484	1928	Leyland TD1	Leyland L27/24R	1949/55	Glasgow Corporation	WSMT / Millburn (dealer), Glasgow
272	GE2487	1929	Leyland TD1	Croft L27/24R (1944)	1949/55	Glasgow Corporation	WSMT / Millburn (dealer), Glasgow
273	GE2458	1928	Leyland TD1	Leyland L27/24R	1949/55	Glasgow Corporation	WSMT / Millburn (dealer), Glasgow
274	TE4563	1928	Leyland PLSC3	Leyland B31F	1944	Ribble Motor Services	Scrapped by Caledonian
1942							
275	FSM380	1942	Bristol L5G	ECW B35R (1949)	1949/60	New	WSMT / Millburn (dealer), Glasgow
276	FSM381	1942	Bristol L5G	ECW B35R (1949)	1949/60	New	WSMT / Millburn (dealer), Glasgow
277	FSM435	1942	Dennis Lancet II	Strachan B35F	1949/57	New	WSMT / Millburn (dealer), Glasgow
278	FSM449	1942	Bedford OWB	SMT B32F	1949/50	New	WSMT / Scottish Omnibuses Ltd.
279	FSM450	1942	Bedford OWB	SMT B32F	1949/50	New	WSMT / Scottish Omnibuses Ltd.
280	FSM451	1942	Bedford OWB	SMT B32F	1949/50	New	WSMT / Scottish Omnibuses Ltd.

Fleet No.	Reg.No.	Built	Chassis	Body	Withdrawn	Acquired From	Disposal
1942							
281	FSM452	1942	Bedford OWB	SMT B32F	1949/50	New	WSMT / Scottish Omnibuses Ltd.
282	FSM453	1942	Bedford OWB	SMT B32F	1949/50	New	WSMT / Millburn (dealer), Glasgow
283	FSM454	1942	Bedford OWB	SMT B32F	1949/50	New	WSMT / Scottish Omnibuses Ltd.
284	FSM506	1942	Bedford OWB	SMT B32F	1949/50	New	WSMT / Millburn (dealer), Glasgow
285	FSM507	1942	Bedford OWB	SMT B32F	1949/50	New	WSMT / Millburn (dealer), Glasgow
286	FSM514	1942	Bedford OWB	SMT B32F	1949/50	New	WSMT / Millburn (dealer), Glasgow
287	FSM515	1942	Bedford OWB	SMT B32F	1949/50	New	WSMT / Millburn (dealer), Glasgow
288	FSM516	1942	Bedford OWB	SMT B32F	1949/50	New	WSMT / Scottish Omnibuses Ltd.
289	FSM517	1942	Bedford OWB	SMT B32F	1949/50	New	WSMT / Scottish Omnibuses Ltd.
1943							
290	NV1361	1932	Dennis Lancet I	UCOC B32R	1949/50	United Counties	WSMT / Millburn (dealer), Glasgow
291	FSM623	1943	Bedford OWB	Duple B32F	1949/50	New	WSMT / Millburn (dealer), Glasgow
292	FSM624	1943	Bedford OWB	Duple B32F	1949/50	New	WSMT / Millburn (dealer), Glasgow
293	FSM625	1943	Bedford OWB	Duple B32F	1949/50	New	WSMT / Millburn (dealer), Glasgow
294	FSM626	1943	Bedford OWB	Duple B32F	1949/50	New	WSMT / Millburn (dealer), Glasgow
295	YG3043	1933	Dennis Lancet I	ECOC B34F	1949/50	West Yorkshire	WSMT / Millburn (dealer), Glasgow
296	YG4700	1933	Dennis Lancet I	ECOC B34F	1949/50	West Yorkshire	WSMT / Millburn (dealer), Glasgow
297	YG4701	1933	Dennis Lancet I	ECOC B34F	1949/50	West Yorkshire	WSMT / Millburn (dealer), Glasgow
298	YG5723	1934	Dennis Lancet I	ECOC B34F	1949/50	West Yorkshire	WSMT / Millburn (daeler), Glasgow
1944							
299	TM8807	1931	AEC Regal	Weym'n B32F (1935)	1949/50	Blake, Dunstable	WSMT / Chassis scrapped by WSMT
300	GF481	1930	AEC Regal	Weym'n B32F (1935)	1949/50	Loch Katrine Steamboat Co.	WSMT / Chassis scrapped by WSMT
301	JJ8823	1933	Leyland TS4	Leyland B36F	1949/54	Grey Green, London	WSMT / Lundie (breaker), Kilmarnock
302	ELY529	1938	AEC Regal	Weym'n B32F (1935)	1949/50	Tilling Transport, London	WSMT / Scottish Omnibuses Ltd.
303	YS2003	1935	Albion SP81	Croft L27/26R (1947)	1949/57	Glasgow Corporation	WSMT / Lundie (breaker), Kilmarnock
304	YS2007	1935	Albion SP81	Croft L27/26R (1947)	1949/57	Glasgow Corporation	WSMT / Lundie (breaker), Kilmarnock
305	YS2095	1936	Albion M81	Croft L27/26R (1947)	1949/57	Glasgow Corporation	WSMT / Millburn (dealer), Glasgow
306	YS2100	1936	Albion M81	Croft L27/26R (1947)	1949/56	Glasgow Corporation	WSMT / Millburn (dealer), Glasgow
307	GE7235	1930	Leyland TD1	Cowieson H27/24R	1949/55	Glasgow Corporation	WSMT / Millburn (dealer), Glasgow
308	GG907	1930	Leyland TD1	Cowieson H27/24R	1949/55	Glasgow Corporation	WSMT / Carruthers (breaker), Dumfries
1945							
309	DR9843	1932	Leyland TD2	Weymann L27/26R	1949/55	Plymouth Corporation	WSMT / Millburn (dealer), Glasgow
310	DR9844	1932	Leyland TD2	Weymann L27/26R	1949/54	Plymouth Corporation	WSMT / Millburn (dealer), Glasgow
311	DR9852	1932	Leyland TD2	Mumford L27/24R	1949/55	Plymouth Corporation	WSMT / Millburn (dealer), Glasgow
312	DR9848	1932	Leyland TD2	Croft L27/26R (1947)	1949/54	Plymouth Corporation	WSMT / Chassis scrapped by WSMT
1946							
313	GSM120	1946	Bristol L5G	ECW B35R	1949/60	New	WSMT / Millburn (dealer), Glasgow
1947							
314	GSM121	1947	Bristol L5G	ECW B35R	1949/60	New	WSMT / Millburn (dealer), Glasgow
315	GSM122	1947	Bristol L5G	ECW B35R	1949/60	New	WSMT / Millburn (dealer), Glasgow
316	GSM123	1947	Bristol L5G	ECW B35R	1949/60	New	WSMT / Millburn (dealer), Glasgow
317	GSM124	1947	Bristol L5G	ECW B35R	1949/60	New	WSMT / Millburn (dealer), Glasgow
318	GSM125	1947	Bristol L5G	ECW B35R	1949/60	New	WSMT / Millburn (dealer), Glasgow
319	GSM126	1947	Bristol L5G	ECW B35R	1949/60	New	WSMT / Millburn (dealer), Glasgow
320	GSM127	1947	Bristol L5G	ECW B35R	1949/60	New	WSMT / Millburn (dealer), Glasgow
321	GSM128	1947	Bristol L5G	ECW B35R	1949/60	New	WSMT / Millburn (dealer), Glasgow
322	GSM129	1947	Bristol L5G	ECW B35R	1949/60	New	WSMT / Millburn (dealer), Glasgow
1948							
323	HSM642	1948	Bristol K6B	ECW L27/28R	1949/63	New	WSMT / Millburn (dealer), Glasgow
324	HSM643	1948	Bristol K6B	ECW L27/28R	1949/63	New	WSMT / Millburn (dealer), Glasgow
1949							
325	HSM644	1949	Bristol K5G	ECW L27/28R	1949/63	New	WSMT / Millburn (dealer), Glasgow
326	HSM645	1949	Bristol K5G	ECW L27/28R	1949/63	New	WSMT / Millburn (dealer), Glasgow

NOTES.

157-62 (SM9971-6) are given in PSV Circle records as having been re-engined with Gardner 5LW engines at an unknown date. However, a Caledonian ledger used from 1943 to 1949 and a Passenger Vehicle Schedule produced at the time of the takeover by Western SMT show these vehicles as having Dennis petrol engines. Conversion would have required major surgery to the engine compartment due to the greater dimensions of the Gardner 5LW unit.

256/9/61/3/6 are shown in a depreciation ledger as being rebodied by Willowbrook rather than being rebuilt by that coachbuilder, although other records show them as rebuilds. The confusion is not surprising given that the work must have been extremely comprehensive costing an average of £1,000 per vehicle compared with the price of £1,125 for those which were definately rebodied by Willowbrook.

299/300 were obtained from the Ministry of Supply.

301/2. Speculation exists around whether these vehicles may have received the bodies from Caledonian 170/2. However, a vehicle depreciation ledger indicates the *possibility* that both were secondhand bodies obtained from the Ministry of Supply.

325/6 when new were loaned directly to London Transport (325 from 1.4.49, 326 from 11.3.49) and never operated for Caledonian, arriving at Dumfries on 26.2.50, some weeks after the takeover by Western SMT.

Haulage Vehicles

Fleet No.	Reg.No.	Chassis	Body	Withdrawn	Notes
H1 ?	CC1743	Thornycroft J		by 1938	Ex.Llandudno Coaching Services. Converted to lorry from chara.
H2 ?	CC3164	Thornycroft J		1936	Ex.Llandudno Coaching Services. Converted to lorry from chara.
H3	?	?			
H4	OS3219	Morris		by 1943	Chiefly used for carrying milk.
H5	?				
H6	OS3613	Morris		by 1943	Chiefly used for carrying milk.
H7	OS3614	Morris		by 1943	Chiefly used for carrying milk.
H8	VS2498	Albion ML55	Mitchell	1949	6-ton. Ex.J.Bell, Dunragit.
H9	OS3638	Bedford		by 1943	Chiefly used for carrying milk.
H10	OS3639	Bedford		by 1943	Chiefly used for carrying milk.
H11	OS3733	Morris 3-ton		1943	3-ton. Chiefly used for carrying milk. Scrapped in 1943.
H12	VS2580	Albion K53	Mitchell	1949	4-ton. Ex.J.Bell, Dunragit.
H13	SM5958	Albion PJ26	NCME	by 1943	Originally a bus ex.Scott. Converted to haulage vehicle by 3/37.
H14	OS3890	Albion SPRL59	Rogerson	1949	12-ton 6-wheeler. New to Caledonian.
H15	?	?			
H16	OS3895	Albion SPRL59	Albion	1949	12-ton 6-wheeler. New to Caledonian.
H17	OS4069	Albion SPM550	Albion	1949	4.5-ton. New to Caledonian. Rebodied by Croft 3/49.
H18	?	?			
H19	GD2607	Albion PJ24		1944	Chiefly used for carrying milk.
H20	VS2367	Albion LHB473	Albion	1949	3-ton. Chiefly used for carrying milk.
H21	OS4300	Albion JL127	Albion	1949	2.5-ton. New to Caledonian.
H22	OS4301	Albion JL127	Albion	1949	2.5-ton. New to Caledonian.
H23	?	?			
H24	GD8461	AEC		by 1943	Chiefly used for carrying milk.
H25	MP2562	Albion LK134		1943	Scrapped 1943.
H26	YS9146	Albion ML550	Lawrie	1949	7.5-ton. New to Caledonian.
H27	HH4109	Dennis n.c.		by 1943	Conv'd to haulage vehicle from bus 92 by 3/37 & later to parcel van.
H28	ASM83	Albion LPA37	Mitchell	1949	6-ton. Ex.Learmonts Transport, Dumfries.
H29	ASM836	Albion SPRL59	Albion	1949	6.25-ton. Ex.Learmonts Transport, Dumfries.
H30	BSM36	Albion SPML556	Albion	1949	4.75-ton. Ex.Learmonts Transport, Dumfries.
H31	?	?			
H32	DLG796	Foden DG5/7 1/2	Foden	1949	4-ton.
H33	BGA723	Albion SPM550	Rogerson	1949	4-ton. New to Caledonian.
H34	BGB165	Albion		1945	Destroyed by fire 1/10/45.
H35	CSM994	Morris		1944	3-ton. Scrapped 3/44.
H36	FT2755	Bedford WL		1943	Scrapped 1943.
H37	YS9972	Dodge		1943	
H38	OS5023	Albion KL127	Albion	1949	3-ton. New to Caledonian. Fitted with Gardner 4LK engine in 1946.
H39	DSM971	Albion KL127	Albion	1949	2.5-ton. New to Caledonian.
H40	UJ499	Foden R6	Foden	1946	7-ton. Ex.J.&J.Scott, Dumfries. Converted to breakdown truck 1946.
H41	CSM780	Albion SPPL557	Albion	1949	4.5-ton. Ex.J.&J.Scott, Dumfries.
H42	CSM952	Leyland		1940	4-ton. Ex.J.&J.Scott, Dumfries. Sold to unknown owner, Middlesex.
H43	DSM44	Ford 5cwt	Caledonian	1949	10-cwt. Ex.J.&J.Scott, Dumfries.
H44	DSM71	Albion KL127	Albion	1949	2.5-ton. Ex.J.&J.Scott, Dumfries.
H45	ESM739	AEC Matador 0346	AEC	1949	4.5-ton. Ex.J.&J.Scott, Dumfries.
H46	ESM773	Albion CX1N	Albion	1949	4-ton. New to Caledonian.
H47	ESM774	Albion CX5N	Albion	1949	6.25-ton 6-wheeler. New to Caledonian.
H48	ESM947	Morris CVF13/5	Morris	1949	2.5-ton.
H49	FYT815	Bedford OWL	Bedford	1949	2.5-ton.
H50	FYT816	Bedford OWL	Bedford	1949	2.5-ton.
H51	FYT817	Bedford OWL	Bedford	1949	2.5-ton.
H52	FYT818	Bedford OWL	Bedford	1949	2.5-ton.
H53	FSM686	Bedford OWL	Bedford	1949	2.5-ton.
H54	FSM835	Atkinson L1586	Atkinson	1949	7-ton.
H55	GSM95	Foden DG6/15	Foden	1949	7.25-ton.
H56	JSM578	Foden FG5/7 1/2	Foden	1949	4.5-ton
H57	JSM835	Foden FG5/7 1/2	Foden	1949	4.5-ton.

ANCILLARY VEHICLES

B/L1	UJ499	Foden R6	Foden	1949	Ex.Haulage fleet H40.

WORKS VEHICLES

W1	SC2588	Austin		1946	Works vehicle.
W2	SM8938	Morris Minor 8	Caledonian	1948	Works vehicle.
W3	ESG161	Fordson 10-cwt	Fordson	1949	Ex.Croall, Bryson & Co. (dealer) 12/48. Works vehicle.

CALEDONIAN

Parcel Vans

Fleet No.	Reg.No.	Chassis	Body	Withdrawn	Notes
P1	?	?	?	?	
P2	SM6230	Albion PJ26	NCME	by 1943	Converted from bus 37 by 1938.
P3	SM6231	Albion PJ26	NCME	by 1943	Converted from bus 38 by 1938.
P4	SM6950	Albion PK26	Mitchell	1939	Converted from bus 62 in 1935. To Stewart (Dealer) 9/40
P5	DS1406	Thornycroft A6	Strachan & Brown	1936	Converted from bus 124 in 1936. To Adcroft (dealer) 9/36
P6	DS1403	Albion PNA26	Cowieson	1943	Converted from bus 122 in 1936. Scrapped 4/43.
P7	HH4109	Dennis n.c.		1943	Ex.Haulage vehicle H27 c1938. Scrapped 11/43.
P8	DSM603	Albion SPCL123	Albion	1949	New to Caledonian.
P9	DSM604	Albion SPCL123	Albion	1949	New to Caledonian.
P10	DSM624	Albion SPCL123	Albion	1949	New to Caledonian.
P11	SM8304	Albion PKA26	NCME	1943	Converted from bus 112 in 1941. Scrapped 8/46.
P12	SM8318	Leyland LT2	Leyland	1949	Converted from bus 67 in 11/40. To Road Haulage Exec.1949
P13	SM6920	Leyland PLSC3	Leyland	1949	Converted from bus 55 in 2/42. Scrapped 12/49.
P14	RP5191	Leyland PLSC3	Leyland	1949	Converted from an ex.United Counties bus.
P15	FSM637	Bedford OWLD	Bedford	1949	New to Caledonian.
P16	GSM47	Commer Q25	Commer	1949	New to Caledonian.

TIMETABLES

Early official timetables were very basic with a thin red card cover and dimensions of 5.30in x 4in. In 1932, a more sophisticated version was produced sporting a blue cover incorporating a side view of one of the company's recently delivered Leyland LT1s enclosed within a red block. The size increased to 6.25in. x 4.25in. and contained within its pages regulations, fares, parcel rates (parcels having by then become an important source of revenue), and, in addition to the timetables, an index of routes and a list of agents. In the June 1932 timetable, the attributes of Portpatrick were also advertised, making mention of the fact that the village was once the nearest seaport to Ireland. The layout split the booklet into two sections; a western area covering Wigtownshire and as far east as the town of Gatehouse of Fleet, a northern section covering the Edinburgh routes and additionally the eastern area. A folding map of the company's routes somewhat crudely drawn was incorporated inside the back cover. From 1933, the colour of the front cover changed to fawn and from 1934 some points of interest along the company's routes were listed, as Caledonian promoted tourist traffic, expanding on the limited promotion of 1932.

From 1935, a simplified smaller timetable was produced measuring 3.5in. x 4.5in., the colour of the cover being changed each year and on which a view of Melrose Castle was displayed, despite, ironically, no Caledonian services operating near to this monument. Although the timetables continued to be split into regions, the foldaway map was replaced by maps within the book for each regions operations. Interestingly, from the early days commercial adverts were carried for local businesses, these even being continued during the war years. The most imaginative of these was undoubtedly that for the Steam Packet Inn, Kirkcudbright, which reminded passengers that the Stranraer bus stopped for two minutes, giving passengers time to try Youngers Scotch Ales and the best of spirits!

In the early war years, little change was evident except that the maps disappeared for security reasons, but by 1942 the cost of the timetable had doubled from 1d to 2d. In 1944, despite the wartime shortages of paper etc., a new style timetable was introduced with a green based tartan cover onto which a map of the company's routes was displayed, security concerns having been considerably reduced by this date. From this issue, routes and route numbers began to be carried in a table at the front of the book as well as on the relevant timetable page. This continued with the first timetable produced in June 1950 following the acquisition of Caledonian by Western SMT, as mentioned in the main text, the 'Western' name simply being substituted on the front cover. The route map, however, had been re-drawn to show services extending northwards from Stranraer,

Newton Stewart, Castle Douglas and Dumfries to Glasgow.

In 1951, Caledonian routes were incorporated as the Dumfries and Galloway section within the standard Scottish Bus Group-style timetable. The Caley route numbers continued to be quoted, Western not showing route numbers on their services until 1956

(although they used them for internal administration). They disappeared in the June 1951 timetable only to reappear again in the October 1951 issue before finally disappearing again in 1952.

The standard Bus Group timetable measuring 4.75in. x 6.5in. with a crimson cover to represent the company livery was replaced in the summer of 1965 by an extremely bulky edition of 5.25in. x 8.5in size, running to over 400 pages in Western's case. The timetable was further expanded by 1967 with the addition of United Automobile Services and Ribble Carlisle area routes as well as those of Blue Band Motors of Lockerbie, Gibson of Moffat and Carruthers of New Abbey. Originally carrying a drawing of an Alexander Y-type bodied Leopard, the cover changed in the summer of 1973 to white and black incorporating an 8-bay Alexander-bodied service bus.

From winter 1975, the contents had been rearranged in service number order before being replaced by a series of area booklets from summer 1977. One of the latter was dedicated to Dumfries and Galloway area services, having an orange and yellow cover depicting a Volvo B58 at Stranraer Pier. The last booklets appeared in 1981, the normal twice-yearly issue being replaced by one which simply quoted 'until further notice'. The reason for this was the impending SCOTMAP exercise and passengers had then to make do with separate leaflets until SCOTMAP was introduced to the area in 1983. A full information pack with folder and leaflets was introduced, together with a subscription scheme to allow the public to keep up to date with developments. These leaflets were replaced for a time with the reintroduction of area booklets from 1984 to 1987 (including an edition to coincide with the deregulation of bus services in October 1986), after which leaflets (and a subscription service) made a return, this scheme being continued until the present day.

TICKETS

Caledonian originally used the Bell Punch system with pre-printed tickets which were punched appropriately at the relevant fare and fare stage. However, a 'trade' had developed in the early 'thirties in some of the used tickets which had been dropped on the floor of the buses, these then being 'resold' by a small number of crews to other passengers for re-use, thus causing the company to incur considerable losses. As a result, a change was made to the more secure Willebrew system around 1933 in which long tickets were inserted into the punch and cut to the value of the fare charged. Passengers thus received a ticket which was cut to the appropriate value whilst the portion removed by the punch dropped into its long box for emptying at the end of the day. This enabled the retained part of the tickets to be totalled against the conductor's takings. The pre-printed Willebrew tickets carried the company's name and varied in colour according to their type : Single - green; Return - salmon pink; Dog/Child/Workman 10/12 journey tickets - light green; Dog Singles - light blue or blue; Exchange Ticket - cream; Parcel Ticket - grey-green; Special Ticket - cream with pink stripe and some Workman tickets - orange.

Later in the 'thirties, the Bellgraphic machine was introduced. A concertina of titled tickets and thin counterfoils was enclosed within the machine, the fare details being written on the top copy, visible in a window at the top of the machine, by the conductor using an indelible pencil. This copy was then punched from the machine and given to the passenger, the copy remaining inside the machine for audit purposes at the end of the day. The tickets used were a lighr red/pink colour.

For a three month trial period after the war, the Bell Punch Ultimate machine was tried on the busy Dumfries town services. Rolls of pre-printed tickets of different values were loaded into the machine and dispensed through a series of slots and where a ticket of the appropriate value was not available, multiple issuing was undertaken - i.e. for a 6d fare 2 x 3d tickets could be issued or a 5d fare could, for example, be made up of a 2d and 3d ticket.

As an aside, it is interesting to note that through a bus ticket, Caledonian was on one occasion able to solve a mystery for the police. A woman was found dead at the roadside and although she carried no identification, she was found to be in posssssion of a Caledonian bus ticket. This was taken to the company's offices and after its examination by Chief Clerk John Reid, it was possible to ascertain the area from which her journey had originated. As a result of this, the police were soon able to identify her.

When Caledonian was absorbed by Western SMT, the Bellgraphic and Willebrew machines were replaced by Western's standard Setright Insert machines. The principal of these involved the insertion of a pre-printed ticket, the colour of which varied according to its use in a similar fashion to the Willebrew tickets. The conductor then selected the correct value and fare stage on a dial (having set the date details before starting out on his/her day's duty) and turned the machine's handle to reproduce details of the fare onto the inserted ticket. In the late 'fifties, this system was replaced by the Setright Speed machine in which a titled, but otherwise blank, ticket roll was held. This was printed by the selection of the fare value and other details via a series of dials prior to the issuing of the ticket by the turning of a handle. In the 'eighties, the Setright Speed system succumbed to the more sophisticated Almex machine which used keys to select the fare value etc. and ultimately this was superceded by the Wayfarer machine mounted alongside the driver, this producing much greater detail for traffic analysis purposes and continuing in use to the present day.

CALEDONIAN GENERAL MANAGERS

J.H.Martin	1928 - 1945
J.S.Gavin	1945 - 1946
H.H.Merchant	1946 - 1950

CALEDONIAN
SURVIVORS

BSM822, a 1936 Weymann-bodied Dennis Lancet, ended its life in use as a caravan by Johnston, a Rugby contractor, to whom it was sold in 1955.

SM8851, a 1931 Leyland LT2 which had been given a new ECW body in 1948 did not stray far after its withdrawal by Western SMT in 1957, becoming a mobile shop in Dumfries where it is seen here in September 1962. (A.J.Douglas)